Northern Ireland and the crisis of anti-racism

MANCHESTER
1824

Manchester University Press

Northern Ireland and the crisis of anti-racism

Rethinking racism and sectarianism

CHRIS GILLIGAN

Manchester University Press

Published by Manchester University Press
Altrincham Street, Manchester M1 7JA
www.manchesteruniversitypress.co.uk

British Library Cataloguing-in-Publication Data
A catalogue record for this book is available from the British Library

Library of Congress Cataloging-in-Publication Data applied for

ISBN 978 0 7190 8652 6 hardback

ISBN 978 0 7190 8653 3 paperback

First published 2017

The publisher has no responsibility for the persistence or accuracy of URLs for any external or third-party internet websites referred to in this book, and does not guarantee that any content on such websites is, or will remain, accurate or appropriate.

All author royalties from this book will go to two charities that take a human-centred approach to immigrants: Scottish Detainee Visitors (SCIO: SC033781), and Massive Outpouring of Love (MOOL) Dumfries and Galloway Refugee Action (SCIO: SC046366)

Typeset in 10.5/12.5 Adobe Garamond by
Servis Filmsetting Ltd, Stockport, Cheshire
Printed in Great Britain by
CPI Group (UK) Ltd, CR0 4YY

This book is dedicated to the memory of Marty Gilligan (1969–2011). He judged people by the content of their character, not by the colour of their skin, their religious denomination or their country of origin.

Contents

Preface

This book has had a long period of gestation. Initially I conceived it as a means to stitch together a few different articles that I had written (on peace and conflict in Northern Ireland, on racism and on immigration) in order to create a book-length study that would involve relatively little effort from me. Very early on, however, it became clear that I was guilty of the same flaw that I discerned in the bulk of writing on Northern Ireland; namely, the tendency to intellectually partition the study of sectarianism from the study of racism. I realised that I would have to engage more seriously with the literature on sectarianism and other racisms and to rethink this material in ways that had not been done previously. I am indebted to a number of different authors for helping me to rethink sectarianism and other racisms in Northern Ireland.

Steve Garner's book, *Racisms*, is not the first to present the idea that there are many different forms of racism, but he presents the idea so clearly in the book that it made the conceptual leap of seeing sectarianism as a form of racism so much easier. Making this link was also helped by two veteran writers on Northern Ireland, Robbie McVeigh and Bill Rolston, who have written perceptively about both racism and sectarianism. Alistair Bonnett's book, *Anti-racism*, was invaluable for clearly spelling out many of the ways in which the term covers a whole range of different, often mutually incompatible, ways of conceiving the problem of racisms.

In thinking through the issue of 'race' I have found the concept of racialisation to be invaluable. The concept draws attention to the fact that, contrary to the 'common-sense' view, 'race' is not natural but is actively constructed, reshaped and even occasionally un-made. The concept draws attention to the social processes, the dynamics, rather than to the end products. The work of several authors – but particularly Kenan Malik, Robert Miles and Rogers Brubaker – has been useful in helping me to think in terms of the making of 'race' as a social process. Kenan Malik's approach of examining the changing meanings of 'race' as arising from recurring attempts to reconcile the contradiction between the ideal of equality and the reality of inequality has been particularly fruitful. I have extended this further to draw attention also to racisms as arising from attempts to reconcile the contradictions between the ideals of liberty and fraternity and the inability of capitalism as a social system to realise these ideals. Robert Miles's challenge to conspiratorial ideas regarding racism as a tool that is used to divide the working class was also useful. His argument that the racisms expressed by sections of the working class arise spontaneously in response to ways in which 'race' *appears* to be a real phenomenon proved very fruitful. Rogers Brubaker's challenge to groupism – the tendency to reify groups (such as ethnic or racial ones) – helped me to think past the tendency to treat Irish/Catholic/Nationalists as a bloc that exist in mutual opposition with Ulster/Protestant/Unionists.

I realised at an early stage that if I wanted to rethink racism and sectarianism in Northern Ireland I would have to place the region in a wider context. A number of scholars of the history of 'race' were very useful in this regard. Elazar Barkan's study of the intellectual discrediting of racial science, Frank Furedi's parallel study in relation to the politics of 'race', Alastair Bonnett's critical examinations of the tension between Whiteness and social class, Gerald Horne's critical work on 'race' and empire, Paul Gordon Lauren's work on the issue of racial equality in international politics, Suke Wolton's work on the role of the 'race' issue in the transition from the United Kingdom being the dominant global power to the United States of America becoming the dominant global power, and Matthew Pratt Guterl's work on the relationship between the Black struggle against oppression in the USA and the Irish struggle for self-determination in the Victorian era – all were excellent examples of scholarship that provides insights into understanding the importance of 'race' in the nineteenth and twentieth centuries.

The writing of the book, however, has not just been influenced by the work of scholars. It has also been influenced by developments in the real world and by my engagement in them. I have had the privilege of working, far too superficially and sporadically, with the Refugee Action Group (RAG) in Belfast. Since returning to Scotland I have been humbled by the dedication of the volunteers who I have worked alongside in Scottish Detainee Visitors (SDV) and Massive Outpouring of Love (MOOL). Organisations such as these show that not only is it possible to imagine a different kind of society, a human-centred one, but also that there are people trying to take a human-centred approach to the world already. I have also enjoyed the privilege of being involved in the Glasgow Refugee and Migrant Network (GRAMNet), which is a rare example of an attempt to develop mutually beneficial collaboration between academics and organisations working on migration-related issues. The success of GRAMNet is a testament to the dedication, energy and vision of Alison Phipps, Becka Kay and Sarah Craig. Over the course of the past six years or so that I have been involved with SDV and GRAMNet the world has been shifting in ways that have influenced the writing of this book. The world is undergoing momentous changes. The impact of the recession of 2008 is being felt around the world, and people are resisting the social consequences. The rise of the Indignatos in Spain, Syriza in Greece and the Arab Spring are all testament to the human desire for self-determination – for taking control in a social system that is currently outside human control. The reverberations of the repressive response to the Arab Spring are now being felt in Europe, through the so-called 'migrant crisis'. The response, in Europe, to the migrant crisis shows both the worst aspects of humanity and the best. From the perspective of European institutions, including nation-states, the crisis is the difficulty of how to deal with the problem of migration. From the perspective of humanity, the crisis is the inability of the social system to treat migrants as human beings. Part of the motivation for writing this book has been to challenge the dehumanisation of humanity and to help to promote thinking about how to create a human-centred world.

Throughout the rest of this book I write in the first person plural 'we'. I do so in acknowledgement of the fact that, at an important level, this book is a collaborative effort. It would have taken a very different form if it had not been for the insights of various people. Timofei Agarin, Ravi Bali, Steve Garner, Rachel Gibson, Paul Hainsworth, Pauline Hadaway, Katy Hayward, Ima Jackson, Andrew Kliman, Karim Murji, Ellie Odhiambo and Andrew O'Halloran all read one or more of the chapters in draft form and provided critical comments on them. I am indebted to the team at Manchester University Press for having confidence in the project from the beginning and for helping to steer it from initial ideas to the finished product that you hold in your hands now. The book has also benefited from discussions that I have had with other people, primarily Gerry Boucher and Shane O'Curry, who were unable to provide comments on earlier drafts but helped to shape the ideas nevertheless. The writing of the book also benefited from some opportunities to engage in critical debate. The Liverpool Salon discussions that Pauline Hadaway invited me to speak at provided an opportunity to test out the ideas on a wider audience. The convivial atmosphere for discussion and debate on all things related to Ireland provided by my friends (amigas y amigos) in the *Asociación Española de Estudios Irlandeses* have always helped to recharge my batteries and reinvigorate my writing. One person in the world of academia has stood out from everyone else for the extent of his encouragement and his level of (sometimes critical) enthusiasm for the book – so I would like to reserve a special thank you for Bryan Fanning, who has been immensely helpful and supportive at every stage. All of this input helped to sharpen my argument and make the writing clearer. Any errors, omissions or other flaws are my responsibility – they have happened despite the help of others, not because of it.

This book was a labour of love, written mostly during weekends, evenings and holidays. At many points it felt like an extra burden on top of the often dehumanising experience of wage-labour. My loving thanks go to the people who helped me to feel more human, even (or especially) during the most difficult moments.

Thank you Aisling, Joe, Zoe, Angela, mum, Grandad, Mo, Andrew, Pola, Ania, Bogdan, Kirsty, Frank, the 'Crystal Palace crew' and the 'Wednesdays'. The world is a more human-centred place because of people like you!

Abbreviations

AIA	Anglo-Irish Agreement
APNI	Alliance Party of Northern Ireland
BIA	Border and Immigration Agency (United Kingdom)
CAJ	Committee for the Administration of Justice (Northern Ireland)
CRE	Commission for Racial Equality (England, Scotland and Wales)
DUP	Democratic Unionist Party
ECNI	Equality Commission Northern Ireland
FEA	Fair Employment Agency (Northern Ireland)
ICERD	International Convention on the Elimination of All Forms of Racial Discrimination
INLA	Irish National Liberation Army
IRA	Irish Republican Army
NIAC	Northern Ireland Affairs Committee
NICEM	Northern Ireland Council for Ethnic Minorities
NICRA	Northern Ireland Civil Rights Association
NICRC	Northern Ireland Community Relations Commission
NICS	Northern Ireland Civil Service
NIHRC	Northern Ireland Human Rights Commission
OFMDFM	Office of the First Minister and Deputy First Minister (Northern Ireland)
PSNI	Police Service of Northern Ireland
RUC	Royal Ulster Constabulary
SDLP	Social Democratic and Labour Party
UDR	Ulster Defence Regiment
UNESCO	United Nations Educational, Scientific and Cultural Organization
UUP	Ulster Unionist Party
UVF	Ulster Volunteer Force

1

Introduction

Anti-racist theory and practice has been in crisis for more than a quarter of a century. By the end of the 1980s the emancipatory anti-racism of the 1960s and 1970s had been contained. The anti-racist movement had become fragmented and some elements had become incorporated into helping their respective states to more effectively regulate society. For others, the struggle for human freedom became displaced by identity politics. This crisis of anti-racism was linked to, and in part was an expression of, setbacks for wider projects of human emancipation.

To many people involved in officially endorsed anti-racism the reality appears to be far from one of crisis. It appears as if the period since the end of the 1980s has been one of continuing success for anti-racism. Crucial aspects of White supremacy – most notably, official racial segregation policies in the USA and the colonial domination of people of colour by White Western powers – had been consigned to the history books. Anti-racism, not racism, is now part of the ideological outlook of Western states. This historic shift can be seen in anti-discrimination laws and in the self-description of Western societies as multicultural. The election of Barack Obama, an African-American, to the most powerful position in global politics – president of the USA – appeared to demonstrate the success, not the crisis, of anti-racism. Some scholars and commentators have argued that the election of Obama is a manifestation of broader shifts in attitudes. Some argue that we are at the dawn of a post-racial world.[1]

The success of official anti-racism, however, has been at the expense of the emancipatory dynamic of the anti-racist movement. It has also often been at the expense of racialised minorities. In the USA Black males are six times more likely than White males to be incarcerated in prison. There are, as Michelle Alexander, the Black civil liberties lawyer, points out, 'more African Americans under correctional control today – in prison or jail, on probation or parole – than were enslaved in 1850, a decade before the Civil War began'.[2] It is shocking that, 150 years after the abolition of slavery in the USA, there are more Black people deprived of their liberty than was the case under slavery. It is shocking that under the presidency of Barack Obama the job security and housing security of the average African-American has deteriorated. It is shocking that under the Obama presidency the Immigration and Customs Enforcement Agency has removed more immigrants than were removed under his predecessor, George W. Bush.[3] In Europe too, states have shown little regard for human life when the human beings in question have come from Africa, Asia and the Middle East. In 2015 and 2016 thousands of migrants died in the Mediterranean as a consequence of Fortress Europe immigration controls.[4] In the UK tens of thousands of migrants are interned in immigration detention and removal centres every year (in 2015 alone there were more than 30,000 human souls incarcerated), these detainees are almost exclusively from Africa, Asia and the Middle East.[5] This disjuncture – between the institutionalising of anti-racist policies and the continuing oppression of racialised minorities – is a crucial dimension of the crisis of anti-racism.

The issues that confront anti-racists have also changed in the decades since the 1970s. In the 1960s and 1970s the issue appeared to be relatively straightforward; racism involved the oppression of people of colour. In the twenty-first century things look different. In Europe today, most people of colour are no longer foreign-born immigrants; they are born and socialised in European countries. They are part of the fabric of their societies and have a public profile in national football teams, as television celebrities, as novelists, commentators, journalists and musicians.[6] In many European countries today, and especially in the United Kingdom, concerns about immigration are as likely to be directed at White East Europeans as they are at people of colour. Since the 1990s, and particularly since the terrorist attacks on 9/11 and the Western military interventions into Afghanistan and Iraq, much anti-racist activity has been focused on the issue of Islamophobia.[7] All of these complications – the blurring of colour as a marker of racial discrimination, hostility towards White foreigners, the adding of religion into the mix – have contributed to the crisis of anti-racism.

The wider social context that informed emancipatory anti-racism has also changed. In the 1960s and 1970s 'Third World' anti-colonial movements fought for the freedom of colonised peoples to govern themselves. These movements influenced, and were influenced by, emancipatory anti-racist movements in Europe and the USA. Today, after the end of the Cold War, those who fight against Western imperialism are more likely to be nihilistic anti-Western Islamists (such as Boko Haram in West Africa or Daesh in the Middle East) than they are to be traditional national liberation movements (such as the Kurdistan Workers Party in the Middle East or the Liberation Tigers of Tamil Eelam in South Asia). In the 1960s and 1970s Western governments often characterised anti-colonial struggles as terrorist campaigns (remember that Nelson Mandela, the leader of the African National Congress, was once derided as a terrorist).[8] In the 1960s and 1970s anti-racists often opposed the characterisation of anti-colonial movements as terrorism. They argued that these were liberation movements. It is not possible to make the same argument in the twenty-first century. Daesh, and many other anti-Western organisations, lack any emancipatory impulse.

They are terrorist organisations, not freedom fighters. This wider context compounds the crisis of anti-racism.

The anti-racist struggle has not been helped by the muddled nature of a lot of anti-racist theory. There is a lot of confusion that afflicts anti-racist thinking. The distinction between 'race' and 'ethnicity' is one that has troubled the study of racism since the 1970s.[9] There is, for example, still no consensus on whether they are different words for the same thing, or different, but related, phenomena.[10] Some activists and theorists champion multicultural policies as a welcome recognition of the value of cultural diversity and a bulwark against White supremacy.[11] Others view state multiculturalism as a collection of inherently conservative policies that racialise public life.[12] There is now a widespread recognition among radical anti-racist scholars of a need to rethink anti-racism.[13] This book is an attempt to contribute to the rethinking of emancipatory anti-racism.

Northern Ireland and rethinking anti-racism

There are a number of reasons why Northern Ireland is an important location for rethinking anti-racism. From the perspective of Northern Ireland there have been a number of changes in recent years that have created a need to develop emancipatory anti-racist theory and practice. The peace process of the 1990s led to a transformation of the governance of the region. The 1998 Peace Agreement, which formally brought an end to more than a quarter of a century of violent conflict, created the architecture for this new system of governance.[14] A new, devolved, power-sharing government was established. New legislation on equality and human rights was passed and new quangos to monitor the implementation of this legislation – such as the Northern Ireland Human Rights Commission (NIHRC) – were created. The issue of tackling ethnic diversity and inequality was placed at the centre of government, with the most important ministry, the Office of the First Minister and Deputy First Minister (OFMDFM), being charged with responsibility for this policy area. The new government has been active in developing policy and practice aimed at tackling racism and sectarianism. This activity has been given an impetus by the rapid growth of a 'foreign-born' section of the population (from less than 2 per cent in 2001 to more than 4 per cent in 2011).[15] The development of anti-racist policy, however, has gone alongside a rise in reported incidents of racially motivated crime. The problem of sectarianism also continues to plague the region. The fact that sectarianism persists – after a peace process that has been heralded around the world as a success – suggests that there is a need to critically examine the issue. The fact that some have described Belfast as the 'race hate capital of Europe' suggests that there is a need to critically examine this issue as well.[16]

Robbie McVeigh, a long-standing anti-racist and anti-sectarian activist, draws attention to the need to rethink anti-racism in Northern Ireland. He notes that there has been a convergence between the issue of sectarianism in Northern Ireland and racism in the rest of the UK. This convergence can be seen in 'the rise in and focus on Islamophobia and "institutional religious intolerance" ... recognition of anti-Irish racism, particularly in England and Scotland, the focus on the overlap between anti-Irish racism and anti-Catholicism in sectarianism in Scotland'.[17] He argues that the further development of anti-racism in Northern Ireland is held back by 'the exclusion of sectarianism "from the mix"'.[18]

The corollary of McVeigh's argument is that there is a need to include sectarianism in the mix when thinking about anti-racism in the rest of the UK. The need for anti-racists in England, Scotland and Wales to consider Northern Ireland – with its 'religious conflict' – is more obvious today than it was in the past. The lack of engagement with Northern Ireland on the part of anti-racists is a problem, but it is a deeper problem than simply the need to consider the 'religious dimension'. Northern Ireland has rarely featured in discussions about racism and anti-racism in the rest of the UK, the Republic of Ireland or elsewhere in Europe. With very few exceptions – McVeigh being a notable one – the conflict in Northern Ireland was not considered to be relevant to the issue of racism.

There have been thousands of academic books and journal articles written about the conflict in Northern Ireland. One scholar has even suggested that, 'in proportion to size, Northern Ireland is the most heavily researched area on earth'.[19] The majority of these books and articles, however, tend to 'consider Northern Ireland in isolation' from the rest of the world.[20] Even when the region is included in comparative studies it is almost invariably compared with other situations of violent conflict – such as South Africa, the Middle East, the Balkans or the Basque Country – rather than with other parts of the UK.[21] It is not just that there are very few attempts to compare the region with other parts of the world; Northern Ireland is often not even considered to inhabit the same intellectual universe as the rest of the world. As one scholar has complained, 'the academic study of the conflict in Northern Ireland has been, to a great degree, insulated – intellectually interned, to coin a phrase – from influences and debates at work in the wider academic world'.[22] Despite the fact that Northern Ireland is part of the UK, it is rarely included in academic studies of the UK.[23]

There is a strong tendency to treat Northern Ireland as 'a place apart', as a part of the world that is so peculiarly unique as to defy conventional analysis. Commentators and academics talk about Northern Ireland as a colonial situation in the heart of Western Europe. Others characterise it as a region of ethnic conflict, and for others it is the religious dimension to conflict that makes the place so strange. There is some truth in these views. These perceptions are, however, prejudiced in the sense that they present Northern Ireland as an aberration. They present the region as if it is not like a normal Western democracy. This view conveniently obscures the fact that Northern Ireland is not an independent country; it is a region of the UK. Since its founding in 1921 it has been governed, directly or indirectly, from Westminster. If Northern Ireland is a strange place, unlike other Western democracies, then the UK cannot be considered normal. If Northern Ireland was a movie character it would be the mother in the movie *Psycho*, and the UK would be Norman Bates. We are led to believe that the mother is a deranged and violent threat who needs to be locked away, isolated from normal society. In reality she is Norman's bad conscience which is repressed in order to maintain the façade of normality.

Scholars, journalists, politicians and others are not wrong when they say that Northern Ireland is unique. It *is* different. But this is no excuse for studying it in isolation. There is nothing unique about being unique. Everywhere is unique. Everywhere has its own unique configuration of different elements. Northern Ireland is different from the rest of the UK, and from the Republic of Ireland. The UK is different from the Ukraine, the United States and Uganda. No two places are exactly the same. This is true of places within Northern Ireland, and between places in Northern Ireland and other parts of the world. Ballymena is different to Belfast, and both are different to Brighton, Belgrade, Baltimore, Brisbane and Bangkok. West Belfast is different to east Belfast. The Lower Falls in west Belfast is different to the Upper Falls (which is also in west Belfast). Everywhere is unique, but if everywhere was completely unique it would be impossible to make any generalisations about human society. Any particular society can only be truly unique if it is cut off from the rest of human society. Studying a place as if it were unique is too one-sided. Belfast, Belgrade, Baltimore and Bangkok are all different from each other, but they also have much in common. They are all urban areas. They are all linked, in different ways and to different extents, to a global capitalist economy. They are all places where people work, shop, have families, meet friends, use social media, listen to music, read books and newspapers, and do other things that a very many people all over the world do every day.

The idea that Northern Ireland is a place apart is not an innocent one. It is a place apart, not because it is unique, but because it suits a lot of different interests to treat it that way. Since the mid-nineteenth century the Irish Question has been an irritant for the UK state. At the beginning of the twentieth century it contributed to the breakdown of the Liberal Party, a split in the ruling elite and dangerous political instability in UK politics.[24] Since its creation in 1921 Northern Ireland has been deliberately treated as a place apart by successive UK governments. Academics and the media have, for the most part, colluded in this distancing. Successive UK governments have sought to keep the region at arm's length from the rest of the UK. The UK government did not put any pressure on the government of Northern Ireland to end discrimination against Catholics in the 1920s, 1930s, 1940s or 1950s.[25] As long as Northern Ireland did not threaten to infect the rest of the UK it could be ignored. It was only in the late 1960s, when civil rights protests and the government of Northern Ireland's repression of those protests threatened to destabilise the region, that the UK government began to push for reforms. When protest and repression escalated into rioting and the creation of 'no-go' areas for the Royal Ulster Constabulary, the local police force, the UK government intervened by sending the British Army on to the streets. These soldiers were deployed *before* the Provisional Irish Republican Army (the Provos, or the IRA) came into existence.[26]

The response of successive UK governments, Labour and Conservative, from the late 1960s up to the 1990s was informed by a desire to insulate the rest of the UK from Northern Ireland. The conflict has consistently been presented as one that is driven by factors internal to Northern Ireland – as a religious conflict between Catholics and Protestants, or a terrorist plot. Political debate on the conflict was stifled through a cross-party agreement to prevent Northern Ireland becoming an issue of contention between the parties.[27] The idea that Northern Ireland was a place apart was further promoted through the presentation of the UK government's role as one of neutral arbiter between two warring factions.[28] Anyone who questioned UK policy could expect to be vilified for giving support to terrorists. Attempts to make sense of the conflict were discouraged by sections of the London-based print media, which carried racialised representations of the Irish as 'uncivilised', 'stupid, drunken and backward', 'violent and irrational', ape-like psychopaths.[29] The state television network, the British Broadcasting Corporation, and the commercial television channels placed significant restrictions on coverage of political violence in Northern Ireland. Attempts to try to understand, or even to represent, the point of view of 'terrorists', particularly Irish Republican groups such as the IRA and the Irish National Liberation Army (INLA), were censored or severely curtailed.[30] The government in the Republic of Ireland also viewed the conflict in Northern Ireland as a threat to its own stability, and successive governments put even more restrictive censorship regulations in place and sought to work with the UK government to contain the political dimensions of the conflict.[31]

Since the early 1970s the main driver behind the presentation of Northern Ireland as a place apart, at least in Britain and the Republic of Ireland, was fear of the threat that Irish Republican violence posed to UK rule in the region. This fear has now been tamed. The IRA and INLA have renounced the armed struggle in favour of a purely political path, and the dissident Irish Republican groups that continue to use violence are occasionally lethal, but politically marginal.[32] It is probably no coincidence that the Scottish classical composer James MacMillan compared Scotland to Northern Ireland, and sparked off a major debate about sectarianism in Scotland, in 1999, more than a year after the Northern Ireland Peace Agreement.[33] Before 1998 Northern Ireland was treated as a place apart, and when anyone cared to mention Scotland and Northern Ireland in the same sentence in public it was usually in order to emphasise how different Scotland was to its UK neighbour across the Irish Sea. In England, Scotland and Wales it is now possible to be critical of UK policy towards Irish Republicanism without fear of suspicion that you might be a supporter of terrorism. The apparent success of the peace process has generated interest in Northern Ireland as a place from which lessons could be drawn. Scholars have, for example, explored comparisons between the UK state's treatment of the Irish in Britain as a suspect community from the 1970s to the 1990s and its treatment of Muslims in the twenty-first century.[34] Northern Ireland is also referenced in the policy literature on segregation and community cohesion in Britain.[35] The long-running academic neglect of Northern Ireland as a part of the UK, however, means that the default setting for most scholars seems to be to think in terms of Britain as the UK minus Northern Ireland. This default needs to be reset.

Northern Ireland: a hotbed of hatred?

Northern Ireland *is* a violent place. In the twelve-month period from 1 April 2011 to 31 March 2012, the Police Service of Northern Ireland (PSNI) recorded 1,344 'incidents with a [sectarian] hate motivation'.[36] This report from the *Belfast Telegraph* in early 2012 provides a gruesome example of one of these sectarian incidents.

> A Catholic teenager was left for dead after he was beaten by sectarian thugs as he left a film set in Belfast. James Turley, 18, was working as an extra for the movie when he was attacked and dumped semi-conscious into a wheelie bin as he heard one of the attackers declare: 'That's enough. I think he's dead.' The teenager was confronted by a mob in the loyalist Village area of the city where a production team had just finished filming a scene for a movie, *The Good Man*, starring *The Wire*'s Aidan Gillen … At one stage he tried to hide in a nearby house, calling on the family: 'Please help me. They're going to kill me' … He said. 'They stamped on my head and everywhere. The woman (the householder) said: "Get him out of my garden" and they dragged me out into the alley.'[37]

The 1998 Peace Agreement, which formally brought an end to the violent political conflict which racked the region from the late 1960s to the 1990s, might have been expected to make sectarian crimes a thing of the past. This incident, and the many others reported to the PSNI every year, tells a different story.

Few anticipated that after the signing of the Agreement racist crime would become increasingly common. In 1998–99 the PSNI recorded 93 racial incidents; by 2000–01 this number had risen to 260, and by 2003–04 to 453.[38] This rising number of racist incidents led the London-based *Guardian* newspaper to claim that the region was 'fast becoming the race-hate capital of Europe'.[39] A few years later the *Belfast Telegraph* claimed that 'Northern Ireland is the hate capital of the western world … Not only does Northern Ireland have the highest proportion of bigots [in the West] … but the bigots are on average more bigoted than those in other countries'.[40] The issue of racism in Northern Ireland gained an international profile in 2009 when youths from the Village area of Belfast attacked the homes of a number of Roma families. More than 100 Roma were subjected to several nights of intense harassment and violence. The youths threw rocks and stones through the windows of the families' houses, broke into one of them and threatened the occupants. One of the victims of the attacks told reporters:

> It is not safe. They made signs like they wanted to cut my brother's baby's throat. They said they wanted to kill us. We are very scared. We have young children … Possibly we could go back to Romania but we have no money … I don't know what we will do now. We will stay here for a couple more days but I don't know after that.[41]

After a few days of taking refuge in a local church hall the families were repatriated to Romania.

Racist crimes continue to be a problem in Northern Ireland. In the twelve-month period from 1 April 2011 to 31 March 2012 the PSNI recorded 696 'incidents with a [racial] hate motivation'.[42] And these figures are likely to be an underestimate.[43] In the same month as the sectarian attack on James Turley, the local media reported a racist attack on a family who had come to the region from Africa. The BBC Northern Ireland website reported the incident in the following terms:

> eight-year-old … Promise Awoyelu was asleep at about 05:30 GMT on Saturday when she was hit on the head by a brick thrown through her bedroom window … Two other windows in the house were broken. It is the second attack on the house within a week … The child's father, Charles Awoyelu, who has been living in Northern Ireland for seven years, described the attack as 'shocking'. He said police told him it was racially motivated. 'I don't know what would motivate somebody to target us,' he said. 'We are here to make a living and we are a peace-loving family. I have five children who are terrified in the house, my wife is scared and I'm scared of going to work and coming back because I don't know what will happen when I come back.'[44]

When we read of the cases of Promise Awoyelu and James Turley we can imagine the terror which they experienced. Their cases hint at some of the wider dimensions of racism and sectarianism. The fact that no-one attempted to intervene to help Turley suggests some level of endorsement for the actions of his attackers. Promise's father's comment that he is afraid to leave the house to go to work, because he does not know if the attackers will strike again, indicates that the fear infects life well beyond the site of the incident itself. These news reports, however, are of limited use in attempting to understand racism or sectarianism.

One of the problems with media coverage for any attempt to understand racism and sectarianism is that news coverage tends to have a bias towards the dramatic, to prefer bad news over good news, to present material unambiguously (when the reality is often messier) and to be related to the news agendas of the publisher.[45] Media stories are useful source material, but we need to go beyond the particular instances reported in the media and ask some broader questions. Another problem with media coverage is that it focuses attention on the attitudes of ordinary people, on everyday interactions between people from different backgrounds, and on street-level violence. In doing so it obscures structural dimensions of racism and sectarianism. That is one of the reasons why it is misleading, superficial and dangerous.

Northern Ireland is a violent place. The violent nature of the region, however, can easily be overstated. Often the perception of Northern Ireland as a violent place is a stereotype. It is a prejudice *about* Northern Ireland. Many of the more than a million people who visit the region annually will testify that this part of the island of Ireland is a very friendly place. Every year thousands of tourists visit landmarks such as the Giant's Causeway, visit museums such as the Ulster-American Folk Park or go on one of the city tours around 'trouble-spots' in Belfast. The vast majority of them never encounter any kind of violence. The region is not just a tourist destination. Every year thousands of people move to this part of the UK to settle. It is also a region that provides limited opportunities to thousands of others, who leave each year. Northern Ireland, like every other society in the world, is complex, contradictory and constantly changing. There is violence and bigotry in Northern Ireland, but there are no societies in the world that are free from violence and bigotry. Analyses that treat Northern Ireland as a place apart provide us not just with a shallow understanding of the region, but also a shallower understanding of the rest of the UK and the Republic of Ireland, to which it is intimately linked.

Confusions and the crisis of anti-racism

The crisis of anti-racism is both caused by, and manifested in, theoretical confusion. This confusion is not a major problem for official anti-racism. The power of official anti-racism comes from its endorsement and institutionalisation by states – in domestic and international law and in institutional practice. Theoretical confusion is, however, a major barrier to building an emancipatory anti-racist movement. One of the aims of this book is to interrogate some of the confusions that plague anti-racism in order to suggest some ways to start to resolve the crisis of anti-racism.

In the next chapter we do this through examining what Paul Connolly refers to as a 'debate concerning whether discrimination against Catholics or Protestants – more commonly referred to as sectarianism – should also be defined as racism'.[46] On one side of this debate are those who treat racism and sectarianism as distinct '-isms'. In their conception, racism is similar to sectarianism, but there are also differences between the two, and these differences are significant enough to treat racism and sectarianism as distinct.[47] On the other side are those who treat sectarianism as racism. The debate regarding whether sectarianism is racism may appear to be a specifically Northern Irish concern. We argue, however, that it is symptomatic of a broader problem within the whole academic field that is referred to as ethnic and racial studies – the ambiguous concurrent use of the terms 'ethnic' and 'racial'. The use is ambiguous because sometimes the two terms are employed as if they are distinct and sometimes as if they are synonyms. This ambiguous concurrent usage underlies the debate about whether racism ('racial') is distinct from sectarianism ('ethnic'), or whether sectarianism is racism ('ethnic' as a synonym for 'racial'). In this regard the debate about racism and sectarianism is a useful case study for this thorny problem that afflicts the study of racism, and anti-racist campaigning, in the UK more broadly.

Another basic source of confusion in discussions of racism and sectarianism is the problem that there is no agreement on what the key terms 'racism' and 'sectarianism' mean, or what they refer to. The Northern Ireland government's *Racial Equality Strategy*, for example, defines racism as 'Any theory which involves the claim that racial or ethnic groups are inherently superior or inferior.'[48] In this definition, racism is a way of understanding the social world – it is a *theory*, a way of understanding some aspect of the world. More specifically, racism is a way of understanding the world that involves the assumption that humanity is divided into different racial or ethnic groups and further assumes that some of these groups are inherently superior to other groups. Paul Connolly, in his influential summary of the literature on racism in Northern Ireland, defines racism in a different way, as

> a collective term that refers to all of those ideas, beliefs, actions, customs, practices and policies that have the effect of disadvantaging and/or discriminating against members of particular ethnic groups. The defining feature of racism is therefore the outcomes of particular activities rather than whether those responsible for such activities intentionally wish to disadvantage or discriminate against others.[49]

In Connolly's definition, racism is an umbrella term that refers to a broad range of things – ideas, beliefs, actions, customs, practices and policies. The view that some ethnic or racial groups are superior to others is not crucial to racism. The key to understanding racism, he suggests, is not the worldview or understanding that informs people's actions. Racism, rather, is defined by the *outcome* of actions. In the *Racial Equality Strategy,* racist beliefs are central to racism. In Connolly's definition, racist beliefs are not central; it is disadvantage and/or discrimination that is central, regardless of the beliefs that lead to these outcomes. In Chapter 3 we explore the issue of defining racism in more detail and argue that, despite the variety found within and between scholars and policy-makers, there is a discernible official approach to tackling racism. We characterise this as a Race Relations approach.[50]

Anti-racism is not a unified body of thought and practice. Anti-racists are united in their opposition to racism. This unity is, however, deceptive, because there is no universal agreement on what racism is, what causes it and how it is best challenged. As Alastair Bonnett notes:

> Anti-racism appears to have a double life. If one were foolish enough to believe everything that was said on the topic, one would be forced to conclude that it is both extraordinarily rare and all-pervasive, simultaneously integral to capitalist modernisation and a harbinger of Marxist revolution. Adding to the sense of confusion that surrounds the subject, debate on anti-racism is often confined to the level of polemic. I have heard anti-racism being celebrated as 'essential' and 'necessary', as well as being attacked as 'politically correct nonsense' … from people who prefaced their remarks by claiming to oppose, even to 'hate' racism.[51]

Among anti-racists there are a variety of different motivations for opposing racism. One of the dominant motivations of states, for example, is concern over the disruptive effects of racisms. This motivation gives rise to a form of anti-racism that is concerned with social cohesion and social stability, rather than human liberation. We briefly outline a number of different, sometimes mutually antagonistic, forms of anti-racism in Chapter 4.

The role of the state in relation to racism is one of the most confusing issues underpinning the crisis of anti-racism. The sectarian attack on James Turley and the racist attack on the Awoyelu family are obvious examples of racisms. The assailants appear to have chosen their targets based on their victims' racial or ethnic identity. The actions of the assailants were very likely designed to provoke fear, not just in the individuals that they attacked, but the wider ethnic 'group' that their victims were presumed to represent. Bob Stoker, a local (Ulster Unionist Party) councillor, condemned the attack on Turley, saying that: 'I think it is nothing short of wanton thuggery and these people have to be dealt with by the community, by the police and by the court system.'[52] Stoker's presentation of the problem is probably the most widely expressed understanding of sectarianism and other racisms, namely that the problem lies in the pathological mindsets and behaviours of some ignorant and aggressive individuals and that the state – in this case represented by the police and the court system – is key to tackling racisms.

Some anti-racist and anti-sectarian activists and writers disagree with this common-sense view of the role of the state regarding racisms. Ronit Lentin and Robbie McVeigh, for example, 'insist that the key responsibility for racism lies with the state'.[53] They point to state policies, such as the imprisonment of asylum seekers without trial and the denial of employment rights to migrant workers, which disproportionately disadvantage ethnic minorities. Regarding street-level violence and intimidation, such as was directed at James Turley and the Awoyelu family, they argue that part of the problem is 'the sustained collusion between [loyalist paramilitary] organisations involved in racist violence and political parties and government'.[54]

Instead of locating pathology in the minds of individuals, they argue that state policy is the *source* of the ideas that racists act upon. They argue, for example, that

> the *British* racial state … defines certain categories of people in the north [of Ireland] in ways that deny them equality and human rights – as 'illegal immigrants' or 'asylum seekers' or 'refugees' or 'migrant workers' … It is hardly surprising that the most pro-state, pro-British communities in the north of Ireland begin to manifest their 'loyalty' to that state by mimicking British state racism and 'defending' communities in the same brutal, racist, way. Since the state spends much time and resources dedicated to keeping 'them' out of the country, it is not at all surprising when others turn their energies to keeping 'them' out of the community.[55]

In Lentin and McVeigh's view, Bob Stoker's condemnation of prejudice and thuggery is duplicitous. Politicians like Stoker candidly condemn street-level manifestations of ideas and behaviours. These street-level ideas and behaviours, however, mirror ideas and practices of the state and representatives of the state. Stoker, and other representatives of the UK state, however, rarely criticise racist ideas and practices perpetuated by that state.

The role of the state in relation to racism and anti-racism is a genuinely puzzling. States all over the world have, since the 1960s, introduced anti-racist measures into their own domestic legislation. These anti-racist laws and policies exist alongside racist practices – such as the use of racial profiling by immigration officials at airports, or by the police in using their powers to stop and search. The approach of states towards racism and anti-racism appears to be arbitrary, rather than intentionally racist. As Bryan Fanning notes of the Republic of Ireland:

> the state comes to orchestrate categories for migrants that racialise some (the asylum seekers unwanted by the state), exploit others (immigrant workers on permit systems that foster their economic exploitation as bonded labour) yet privilege some (high-skilled and professionals from some countries of origin).[56]

Fanning draws attention to the fact that racist policies are contingent on a number of factors, rather than based on any consistent approaches by the state towards 'racial' and 'ethnic' minorities. People arriving in Ireland from the same country – India, for example – could be racialised (if they seek asylum), exploited (if they arrive as workers with a fixed-term contract and limited rights) or privileged (if they, for example, have been employed to work as a surgeon in a hospital). It is something other than the 'race' of the immigrant that explains the approach of the state.

The UK state, like most nation-states in the world today, is avowedly anti-racist. It is a signatory to many international anti-racist agreements and it has enacted legislation and policies aimed at tackling racisms. Yet the same state is also perpetrating racist acts. In Chapter 4 we examine the development of what we call the Race Relations approach, the dominant approach of official state anti-racism in the UK and around the world. We outline the contradiction between avowed anti-racism and disavowed racism as a consistent feature of the Race Relations approach from its origins in the USA at the end of the First World War and during its internationalisation after the Second World War.

The paradox that liberal democratic states are both racist and anti-racist, we argue, is a product of the fact that capitalism as a social system generates both racism and anti-racism. We argue that official anti-racism is not the antithesis of racism, but rather that they are two sides of the same coin. Both racism and anti-racism are integral to capitalism. Capitalism, for example, upholds the principle of equality and enshrines this in equal opportunities law. This commitment to equality is not rhetorical, or a mask covering some ulterior motive, it is integral to capitalism as a social system. Exchange in the market involves exchanges of equivalents. In capitalist exchange someone's commodities are not worth more, or less, because of the qualities of the person who owns them, but because of the value embodied in them. Capitalism also, however, creates inequality. In a capitalist society the vast majority of people need to earn wages in order to survive. The small minority who employ wage labourers do so in order to extract surplus wealth from the labour of the workers. This surplus wealth, and the relationship of exploitation that it is based on, generates huge inequalities. This inequality does not inevitably map on to 'race', but it is inevitable in a capitalist system. Nation-states play a key role in mediating between the inequality that is an inherent feature of capitalism and the outcome of racial inequality – both domestically (within nation-states) and internationally (between nation-states). We outline and develop this argument most explicitly in Chapter 5.

Rethinking anti-racism

Clearing up some of the confusions that have arisen in anti-racist theory and practice is necessary to the task of rethinking racism. The task will not be easy, because contemporary anti-racism encompasses a range of competing viewpoints and interests. Robert Miles and Malcolm Brown warn anti-racists that the concept of racism is

> heavily negatively loaded, morally and politically … racism has become a term of political abuse. This presents special difficulties for the social scientist who defends the use of the concept. Whatever definition is offered has significance for not only academic work, but also political and moral debate.[57]

The morally and politically loaded nature of the concept of racism is a consequence not just of the fact that there are various different interpretations and vested interests involved in anti-racism. It is also a consequence of the fact that at the heart of racism and anti-racism are fundamental issues about what it means to be human, and how society should be organised.

The conventional social science approach of Race Relations theory views the morally and politically loaded nature of racism and anti-racism as a major difficulty for attempts to understand racisms. In the conventional social science conception of research, the subjective outlook of the researcher is something that should be minimised, in order to gain an objective understanding of society. Social scientists, in this view, should aim to position themselves as observers who look at society from the outside in a dispassionate manner. They should attempt to penetrate beyond the surface appearance of social phenomena and discern underlying patterns and causal mechanisms. These patterns and mechanisms are not evident to the ordinary member of society because the ordinary member of society interprets the social world from their own individual subjective perspective. The social scientist is a specialist who has been trained in use of the tools of their trade; the lay person is an untrained observer who draws naive conclusions from their experience of the world.

We argue that the approach of conventional social science is part of the problem. Its approach is inherently elitist and sets up one section of society (social scientists) as superior to society. The method of approach to understanding society that is embedded in Race Relations theory reproduces the distinction between mental and manual labour. It artificially separates out thinking and doing. This artificial separation is one that needs to be overcome in both theory and practice. We argue that the Marxism of Marx – not the spins and interpretations on it that have been given by various post-Marx Marxists – provides a good starting point for the development of a human-centred, emancipatory anti-racism.[58] We develop this argument in Chapter 5.

Race Relations theory and policy treats society as an object to be manipulated. It treats Race Relations theorists and practitioners as the active element – as people who are actively trying to understand society (theorists) and actively trying to change it (practitioners). It treats human interactions as something that need to be managed. All of the perspectives on the integration of racialised minorities into society – whether this integration is viewed as assimilation (eradication of difference), a two-way process (adaptation by both minorities and the majority) or multiculturalism (the maintaining of difference) – view these as processes that need to be managed. The state and civil society actors are viewed as the active elements that need to educate the public in anti-racist values, or to chastise or prosecute those who sin against these anti-racist values. This Race Relations approach, either because its proponents do not acknowledge racism as something that is spontaneously generated by capitalism, or because they think that humans are flawed, treats racism as something to be managed rather than eradicated. In the process, the freedom of some members of society is curtailed in the name of giving freedom to others.

Race Relations theory and practice suffers from, at best, a limited conception of humanity, or at worst, an elitist view of humanity. It is true that humans are objects that are acted on. Many of our individual choices and decisions are shaped by forces outside our control. Humans, however, are also active subjects. We do make choices and we do, sometimes, combine collectively in attempts to transform our own conditions of existence. The course of history is replete with examples of ways in which humans have struggled against the constraints that nature and society places on us. Events like the American, French and Russian revolutions, the Chartist movement, the struggle to abolish slavery in the USA, anti-colonial movements for independence, the American civil rights movement, the revolts against Stalinist and Maoist 'communism' in East Germany, Hungary, Czechoslovakia, Poland, China and Tibet – all of these events demonstrate the enduring desire of human beings for emancipation. Emancipatory anti-racism needs to engage with this desire for human emancipation, and it needs to acknowledge that ordinary working people, racialised minorities and other people who are exploited and oppressed are not passive objects to be managed or pitied, but active subjects who need to be an integral part of the project of human emancipation.

Emancipatory anti-racism and authoritarian anti-racism

In Chapters 6 and 7 we explore racism and anti-racism through specific examples. In Chapter 6, we examine the way that anti-racist ideas were central to the civil rights movement that emerged and developed in Northern Ireland in the late 1960s in opposition to institutionalised sectarian practices. We sketch out the social context that facilitated the emergence of the civil rights movement, and how sectarian state repression and radical resistance helped to bring about popular mobilisation to demand equal rights and an end to state anti-Catholic repression. We note, however, that within the civil rights movement there were different conceptions of why racisms are a problem and these different conceptions contributed to splits within, and the decline of, the civil rights movement. We argue that the decline of the movement created the conditions in which a racialised multicultural anti-racism was able to develop and become institutionalised. This multicultural anti-sectarianism has advanced through the defeat of the movement for equality and liberty. The crowning achievement of this multicultural anti-sectarianism was the Peace Agreement of 1998. The Agreement incorporated former opponents of the British state in the running of the British state in Northern Ireland, and institutionalised a multicultural form of governance in the region in the process.

In Chapter 7 we examine the argument, made by advocates of Race Relations, that their critics tend to ignore or downplay the everyday racisms that people like the Awoyelu family or James Turley experience. Advocates of Race Relations (community relations or good relations) argue that official state approaches to anti-racism have been effective at stigmatising racisms and provide the most realistic means of tackling racisms, because they are focused on everyday racisms. We examine this defence of Race Relations by looking at hate crime policy, which is the most recent innovation in state anti-racism. We argue that hate crime policy is built on, and extends in new directions, the official multicultural approach that underpins the peace agreement and the political institutions that have been built on the Agreement. Hate crime policy has both been made possible by, and reveals the extent of, the ever-widening gulf between ordinary people and the power elites in Northern Irish society. The policy is also worrying from the perspective of emancipatory anti-racism, because of the way that it erodes the principle of equality in law and demonstrates little regard for human freedom.

The case of hate crime indicates the dangers when the forces for human emancipation are weak. When the sense of humans as agents for change is weak, humans are treated as objects to be manipulated. The weak belief that humanity can be the active subject in history, the limited sense that we can transform the conditions for our existence, is itself the product of objective conditions. The long series of defeats suffered by various emancipatory movements around the world since the 1970s, the existence of the Soviet Union as a perversion of Marx's idea of a communist society, and the betrayals by 'leaders' of emancipatory movements all combined to discredit the struggle for human emancipation in the minds of many people. The collapse of the Soviet Union, as a self-proclaimed alternative to capitalism, served to further enhance the idea that no alternative to capitalism is possible. The recession of 2008, however, has begun to undermine the idea, which once seemed unshakable, that capitalism is the best way to organise human society. The emergence of grassroots struggles against capitalist austerity – from the Indignatos to the Arab Spring – demonstrates that the human desire for emancipation can suffer defeats, but can never be defeated. Once again people are beginning to view capitalism as a limited and dehumanising system. Once again people are beginning to say that another world is possible. The conditions for the re-emergence and further development of emancipatory anti-racism are ripening.

Notes

1 Tatishe M. Nteta and Jill S. Greenlee, 'A change is gonna come: generational membership and white racial attitudes in the 21st century', *Political Psychology* 34.6 (2013): 877–897.
2 Michelle Alexander, 'The war on drugs and the new Jim Crow', *Race, Poverty & the Environment* 17 (2010): 75–77.
3 Nora Caplan-Bricker, 'Who's the real Deporter-In-Chief: Bush or Obama?', *New Republic*, 18 April 2014; Tim Rogers, 'Obama has deported more immigrants than any other president. Now he's running up the score', *Fusion*, 7 January 2016.
4 *Missing Migrants Project*, http://missingmigrants.iom.int/

5 *Detention*, Office of National Statistics, www.gov.uk/government/publications/immigration-statistics-april-to-june-2015/detention

6 Nissa Finney and Ludi Simpson, *'Sleepwalking to segregation'? Challenging myths about race and migration* (Bristol: Policy Press, 2009).

7 See, for example, Commission on British Muslims and Islamophobia, *Islamophobia: issues, challenges and action* (Stoke-on-Trent: Trentham Books, 2004); EUMC, Christopher Allen and Jorgen S. Nielsen, *Summary report on Islamophobia in the EU after 11 September 2001* (Vienna: European Monitoring Centre on Racism and Xenophobia, 2002); Liz Fekete, 'Anti-Muslim racism and the European security state', *Race & Class* 46.1 (2004): 3–29; Nasar Meer, 'Racialization and religion: race, culture and difference in the study of antisemitism and Islamophobia', *Ethnic and Racial Studies* 36.3 (2013): 385–398.

8 Frank Furedi, *Colonial wars and the politics of Third World nationalism* (London: I.B. Tauris, 1994).

9 In this book we place the term 'race' inside inverted commas in order to remind the reader that 'race' is a way of thinking, not something which is real. For the same reason terms such as White, Black, and Whiteness are capitalised in order to draw attention to the fact that these are particular (and problematic) ways of thinking about humanity.

10 Chris Gilligan, 'Race and ethnicity', in *Routledge handbook of ethnic conflict*, ed. Karl Cordell and Stefan Wolff (London: Routledge, 2011), 79–88.

11 Les Back et al., 'New Labour's white heart: politics, multiculturalism and the return of assimilation', *Political Quarterly* 73 (2002): 445–454; Peter Geoghegan, 'Multiculturalism and sectarianism in post-Agreement Northern Ireland', *Scottish Geographical Journal* 124.2–3 (2008): 185–191.

12 Kenan Malik, 'Making a difference: culture, race and social policy', *Patterns of Prejudice* 39.4 (2005): 361–378; Brian Barry, *Culture and equality: an egalitarian critique of multiculturalism* (Cambridge: Polity Press, 2001).

13 See, for example, Floya Anthias and Cathie Lloyd (eds), *Rethinking anti-racisms* (London: Routledge, 2002); Jenny Bourne, 'The life and times of institutional racism', *Race & Class* 43.2 (2001): 7–222; Alana Lentin, *Racism and anti-racism in Europe* (London: Pluto Press, 2004); Yin Paradies (ed.), *Ethnic and Racial Studies* 39.1 (2016), special issue, *Whither anti-racism?*; Ben Pitcher, *The politics of multiculturalism: race and racism in contemporary Britain* (Basingstoke: Palgrave Macmillan, 2009).

14 The official title is *The Agreement: Agreement reached in the multi-party negotiations*. However, it is more commonly referred to as the Good Friday Agreement (usually by Irish Nationalists), the Belfast Agreement (usually by Ulster Unionists) or the British-Irish Agreement (by some academics who highlight the fact that although all the main political parties in Northern Ireland were involved in the negotiations leading to the Agreement, it is an official intergovernmental agreement, signed into law by the UK government and the government of the Republic of Ireland). For more on the Agreement see, for example, *Aspects of the Belfast Agreement*, ed. Rick Wilford (Oxford: Oxford University Press, 2001).

15 Given the contested nature of Northern Ireland, we are not including those born in the Republic of Ireland, which is formally a sovereign nation-state independent from

the UK, as 'foreign-born'. Data on the demography of Northern Ireland is available at www.nisra.gov.uk

16 Colin Knox, 'Tackling racism in Northern Ireland: "the race hate capital of Europe"', *Journal of Social Policy* 40.2 (2010): 387–412.

17 Robbie McVeigh, *Sectarianism in Northern Ireland: towards a definition in law* (Belfast: Equality Coalition, 2014), 4–5.

18 Ibid., 5.

19 John Henry Whyte, *Interpreting Northern Ireland* (Oxford: Clarendon Press, 1990).

20 John McGarry and Brendan O'Leary, *Explaining Northern Ireland: broken images* (Oxford: Blackwell, 1995).

21 See, for example, Rogelio Alonso, 'Pathways out of terrorism in Northern Ireland and the Basque Country: the misrepresentation of the Irish model', *Terrorism and Political Violence* 16.4 (2004): 695–713; Sean Byrne, 'Israel, Northern Ireland, and South Africa at a crossroads: understanding intergroup conflict, peace-building, and conflict resolution', *International Journal of Group Tensions* 28.3–4 (1999): 231–253; Greg M. Maney, 'The past's promise: lessons from peace processes in Northern Ireland and the Middle East', *Journal of Peace Research* 43.2 (2006): 181–200; John Darby, Nicholas Dodge and A. C. Hepburn, *Political violence: Ireland in a comparative perspective* (Belfast: Appletree, 1990); John McGarry (ed.), *Northern Ireland and the divided world: post-Agreement Northern Ireland in comparative perspective* (Oxford: Oxford University Press, 2001); Sammy Smooha, 'Control of minorities in Israel and Northern Ireland', *Comparative Studies in Society and History* 22.2 (1980): 256–280.

22 M. L. R. Smith, 'The intellectual internment of a conflict: the forgotten war in Northern Ireland', *International Affairs* 75.1 (1999): 77–97.

23 Chris Gilligan, 'The place of Northern Ireland in ethnic and racial studies in Britain: what place?', *C-SAP: teaching race and ethnicity in Higher Education* (2008), www.teachingrace.bham.ac.uk/media/document/Place-of-NI-in-ERS.pdf (accessed 10 January 2017).

24 David George Boyce, *The Irish Question and British politics, 1868–1996* (Basingstoke: Macmillan, 2nd edn, 1996); George Dangerfield, *The strange death of Liberal England* (London: Granada Publishing, 1972).

25 Michael Farrell, *Northern Ireland: the Orange state* (London: Pluto Press, 2nd edn, 1980); John Whyte, 'How much discrimination was there under the Unionist regime, 1921–1968?', in *Contemporary Irish Studies*, ed. Tom Gallagher and James O'Connell (Manchester: Manchester University Press, 1983), 1–35.

26 Chris Gilligan, 'The Irish Question and the concept "identity" in the 1980s', *Nations and Nationalism* 13.4 (2007): 599–617; Greg Martin and Graham Ellison, 'Policing, collective action and social movement theory: the case of the Northern Ireland civil rights campaign', *British Journal of Sociology* 51.4 (2000): 681–699; Bob Purdie, *Politics in the streets: the origins of the civil rights movement in Northern Ireland* (Belfast: Blackstaff Press, 1990); Niall O'Dochartaigh, *From civil rights to Armalites: Derry and the birth of the Irish Troubles* (Cork: Cork University Press, 1997).

27 Michael J. Cunningham, *British government policy in Northern Ireland, 1969–2000* (Manchester: Manchester University Press, 2001).

28 Kevin Boyle, Tom Hadden and Paddy Hillyard, *Ten years on in Northern Ireland: the*

legal control of political violence (London: Cobden Trust, 1980); Desmond Hamill, *Pig in the middle: the army in Northern Ireland 1969–1985* (London: Methuen, 1986).

29 Liz Curtis, *Nothing but the same old story: the roots of anti-Irish racism* (London: Information on Ireland, 1985).

30 Bill Rolston and David Miller, *War and words: the Northern Ireland media reader* (Belfast: Beyond the Pale, 1996).

31 John Bowman, *De Valera and the Ulster Question, 1917–1973* (Oxford: Clarendon Press, 1982); Gilligan, 'The Irish Question and the concept "identity" in the 1980s'; Betty Purcell, 'The silence in Irish broadcasting', in Rolston and Miller (eds), *War and words*, 253–64; Bill Rolston, 'Political Censorship', in Rolston and Miller (eds), *War and words*, 237–243.

32 Kevin Bean, '"New dissidents are but old Provisionals writ large"? The dynamics of dissident Republicanism in the new Northern Ireland', *The Political Quarterly* 83.2 (2012): 210–218; Jonathan Tonge, '"No-one likes us; we don't care": "dissident" Irish Republicans and mandates', *The Political Quarterly* 83.2 (2012): 219–226.

33 Tom Devine (ed.), *Scotland's shame? Bigotry and sectarianism in modern Scotland* (Edinburgh: Mainstream, 2000).

34 Mary Hickman et al., *'Suspect communities'? Counter-terrorism policy, the press, and the impact on Irish and Muslim communities in Britain* (London: London Metropolitan University, 2011); Henri C. Nickels et al., *A comparative study of the representations of 'suspect' communities in multi-ethnic Britain and of their impact on Irish communities and Muslim communities: mapping newspaper content* (London: Centre for Irish Studies Working Papers, 2009); Mark McGovern, *Countering terror or counter-productive? Comparing Irish and British Muslim experiences of law and policy* (Ormskirk: Edge Hill University, 2010).

35 Ted Cantle, *Community cohesion: a report of the Independent Review Team* (London: Home Office, 2001); Commission on Integration and Cohesion, *Our shared future* (Wetherby: Commission on Integration and Cohesion, 2007).

36 PSNI, *Trends in hate motivated incidents and crimes recorded by the police in Northern Ireland, 2004/05 to 2011/12* (Belfast: PSNI, 2012).

37 Matthew Symington, 'Beaten Catholic teenager left for dead after sectarian attack', *Belfast Telegraph*, 10 January 2012.

38 Northern Ireland Affairs Committee (NIAC), *The challenge of diversity: hate crime in Northern Ireland, volume 1: Report, together with formal minutes* (London: House of Commons, 2005).

39 Angelique Chrisafis, 'Racist war of the Loyalist street gangs', *The Guardian*, 10 January 2004.

40 Kathryn Torney, 'Northern Ireland: hate capital of Western world', *Belfast Telegraph*, 7 February 2007.

41 Henry McDonald, '"They said they wanted to kill us": Romanians holed up in Belfast speak of ordeal', *The Guardian*, 17 June 2009.

42 PSNI, *Trends in hate motivated incidents, 2004/05 to 2011/12*.

43 Robbie McVeigh, *The next Stephen Lawrence: racist violence and criminal justice in Northern Ireland* (Belfast: Northern Ireland Council for Ethnic Minorities, 2006).

44 'Child, 8, hurt in racist brick attack in Dundonald', BBC News, 21 January 2012.

45 Tony Harcup and Deirdre O'Neill, 'What is news? Galtung and Ruge revisited', *Journalism Studies* 2.2 (2001): 261–280; Johan Galtung and Mari Holmboe Ruge, 'The structure of foreign news', *Journal of Peace Research* 2.1 (1965): 64–91.

46 Paul Connolly, *'Race' and racism in Northern Ireland: a review of the research evidence* (Belfast: OFMDFM, 2002), 7. See also Coreen Walsh, '"These things are simply very difficult": an exploration of the existence of and the relationship between sectarianism and racism in present-day Northern Ireland', *Independent Study Project Collection* 785 (2009), http://digitalcollections.sit.edu/isp_collection/785/ (accessed 10 January 2017).

47 John D. Brewer, 'Sectarianism and racism, their parallels and differences', *Ethnic and Racial Studies* 15.3 (1992): 352–364; Peter Geoghegan, *A difficult difference: race, religion and the new Northern Ireland* (Dublin: Irish Academic Press, 2010).

48 OFMDFM, *A racial equality strategy for Northern Ireland: 2005–2010* (Belfast: OFMDFM, 2005), 82.

49 Connolly, *'Race' and racism in Northern Ireland*, 7.

50 In this book the term Race Relations is capitalised when referring to Race Relations theory and to Race Relations practice; lower case is used when discussing Race Relations theorists talking about relations between 'races'.

51 Alistair Bonnett, *Anti-racism* (London: Routledge, 2000), 1

52 Symington, 'Beaten Catholic teenager left for dead after sectarian attack'.

53 Ronit Lentin and Robbie McVeigh, *After optimism? Ireland, racism and globalisation* (Dublin: Metro Eireann, 2006), 162.

54 Ibid.

55 Ibid., 162–163.

56 Bryan Fanning, *Racism and social change in the Republic of Ireland* (Manchester: Manchester University Press, 2nd edn, 2012), 198.

57 Robert Miles and Malcolm Brown, *Racism* (London: Routledge, 2nd edn, 2003), 3.

58 The concept 'post-Marx Marxism' is taken from the work of Raya Dunayevskaya. See, in particular, *Rosa Luxemburg, women's liberation and Marx's philosophy of revolution* (Chicago: University of Illinois Press, 2nd edn, 1991).

2

Differentiating racism and sectarianism

The issue regarding whether sectarianism is racism or whether the two are distinct phenomena might initially appear to be a pedantic one. Duncan Morrow, a politics lecturer at Ulster University and former chief executive of the Community Relations Council, implies this when he says that both racism and sectarianism play a part in dividing Northern Irish society, and argues for a good relations strategy as 'an approach that will enable racism and sectarianism to be addressed equally and together'.[1] Morrow focuses on a social problem – divisions in society – that everyone can agree is a problem. This kind of problem-solving focus is characteristic of much anti-racist activity in Europe today. Morrow evades the issue of whether sectarianism is a form of racism by focusing on the problem, rather than defining racism and sectarianism. The policy area that deals with racism and sectarianism in Northern Ireland is commonly referred to as good relations policy. Robbie McVeigh argues that 'the synthesis of racism and sectarianism within the "good relations" paradigm', the dominant approach within official anti-racism in Northern Ireland, is far from innocent. The effect of this good relations policy approach, McVeigh argues, has been to move 'anti-racism as well as anti-sectarianism away from a focus on international standards and human rights compliant approaches', and in the process has perpetuated the idea of Northern Irish exceptionalism.[2] In McVeigh's view, defining racism and sectarianism is important because these definitions determine what legislation and legal precedent is available to anti-racist campaigners.

There are a number of different ways of differentiating racism and sectarianism. Probably the clearest, and the closest to ordinary common-sense understandings, is the one provided by Peter Geoghegan when he says that

> sectarianism and racism are not the same thing, despite their continual conflation. Sectarianism denotes the complex interaction between religion and politics … through which ideas about religious difference are used to infer political identities … Racism, on the other hand, refers to the assumption that people can be divided according to physical and biological criteria.[3]

In this view, racism and sectarianism are distinct. They both involve prejudice, discrimination against distinct groupings of human beings, but the basis on which humanity is viewed as divided into distinct groups differs. Racism involves prejudice and discrimination against people on the basis of racial origins and relies on visible markers of racial difference, such as skin colour. Sectarianism involves prejudice and discrimination against people on the basis of religious markers of difference, such as surname or denominational affiliation.

As John Brewer puts it, the 'chief distinction between the two concepts … lies in the nature of the social marker used'; religion or 'race'.[4] In the context of Northern Ireland the term racism is routinely applied to incidents where there is conflict between the 'indigenous' population and immigrants, and the term sectarianism to cases of conflict between 'indigenous' Northern Irish Catholics and Northern Irish Protestants. So the distinction is clear and obvious. Except that it isn't clear or obvious at all.

A few paragraphs after his brief definitions, Geoghegan refers to racist incidents in which 'eastern Europeans were intimidated out of their homes and relations between migrants and the so-called indigenous population suffered badly'.[5] Either Geoghegan thinks that the (predominantly White) east Europeans have, in the incidents he refers to, been identified on the basis of their physical appearance or some 'biological criteria', which seems unlikely, or his definitions are not very helpful when it comes to trying to understand racism and sectarianism in Northern Ireland. Geoghegan's criticism of the continual conflation of racism and sectarianism is also problematic. The clear distinction between racism and sectarianism does not always hold up in practice. We can see this through looking at an example of an attack on a Polish family in Northern Ireland's second city (Derry/Londonderry) in May 2006.

In the very early hours of a Saturday morning, men armed with a hatchet burst into a house in the Waterside area of the city. Inside the house a young couple from Poland, their two-year-old son and four other Polish male adults were asleep in their beds. The intruders smashed up the living room, the bathroom and the stairs, and were believed to have tried to use the hatchet to break into the bedroom where the terrified occupants of the house had barricaded themselves for protection. The incident was reported as 'a horror race attack' by the local (Irish Nationalist) newspaper, the *Derry Journal*, and as a 'racist attack' by the Belfast-based (Ulster Unionist) newspaper, the *News Letter*. The same newspapers, however, also pointed to a sectarian dimension to the attack. The *Derry Journal* noted that 'there were reports from some locals that a non-national was seen in the area wearing a Celtic football top' and the *News Letter* that the attack was 'believed to have been started because a Polish immigrant couple were wearing Glasgow Celtic shirts in a Protestant area'.[6] In Northern Ireland the Celtic football top is commonly used to proclaim the wearer's political identity as Irish Nationalist and/or their religion as Catholic. So the attack on the Polish family is an example of people being targeted through, as Geoghegan puts it, a process in 'which ideas about religious difference are used to infer political identities'. Yet Geoghegan writes about attacks on Poles as racist, the newspapers reported the attack on the Poles in Derry/Londonderry as a racist incident and the police investigated it as an attack with a racist motive. The incident indicates some of the difficulties involved in mechanically separating racism and sectarianism when attempting to understand them. The Poles were attacked, the evidence suggests, because they were foreigners (non-nationals, as the bureaucratic newspeak puts it) *and* because they were identified as aligned with the Nationalist/Catholic enemy.

Robbie McVeigh argues that the distinction between racism and sectarianism in Northern Ireland has not been clear or straightforward. The question 'is sectarianism racism?', he argues, 'has been central to those who have compared racism and sectarianism'.[7] In this chapter, we explore the question 'is sectarianism racism?' In the first part, we examine three different arguments in favour of treating racism and sectarianism as distinct phenomena. In the second part, we outline and elaborate on the case for treating sectarianism as racism. Central to the debate about whether to treat sectarianism as racism lies a difficulty that bedevils ethnic and racial studies more broadly, the distinction between 'race', 'nation' and 'ethnic group'. We draw on this wider discussion in examining the case for treating sectarianism as racism. In the third part we argue that the question 'is sectarianism racism?' is misleading. We draw on Steve Garner's use of the concept of *racisms* to argue that, rather than thinking of racism in the singular, it is more useful to think of racism as taking many different forms, and we suggest that it is useful to think of sectarianism as being a form of racism. In the fourth section we relate the debate on racism and sectarianism to the broader issue of Northern Irish exceptionalism.

The case for treating racism and sectarianism as distinct

In this section we examine the attempts to provide a rationale for treating racism and sectarianism as distinct. We do so through an examination of three key authors, Peter Geoghegan, John Brewer and Paul Connolly. Most scholars of Northern Ireland have ignored the scholarly work on racism and many of them have avoided the concept of sectarianism – or only used it in a loose sense. So anyone who attempts to understand racism and sectarianism in Northern Ireland will find that they almost inevitably have to rely on Brewer, Connolly and Geoghegan as reference points. Brewer and Geoghegan, to their credit, have examined both racism and sectarianism and attempted to differentiate between them conceptually. Connolly has also examined racism and sectarianism, but not together in the same analysis. He provides a pragmatic rationale for treating them as two distinct phenomena.

Racism and physical and biological criteria

Geoghegan's claim that racism 'refers to the assumption that people can be divided according to physical and biological criteria' provides a useful starting point for an examination of racism. His claim contains two common misconceptions: that humanity is composed of different 'races', and that we can tell 'races' apart because of outward appearances, such as skin colour, or genetically inherited characteristics which aren't necessarily outwardly obvious but do provide genetic markers of 'racial' difference.

The idea that 'races' exist is deeply engrained in societies all over the world. This idea seems to be everyday common sense to many people. If we know anything about history, we know that Black Africans were forced, by White Europeans, to work as slave labourers in the plantations of the southern states of the USA. We might be aware that ideas about racial difference were used as a justification for slavery in the Americas and for the Atlantic slave trade.[8] It is also fairly common knowledge that after the abolition of slavery in the United States, ideas about the racial inferiority of Black Africans and their descendants still informed American society and were used to justify 'Jim Crow' laws that enforced segregation and underwrote the second-class status of Black Americans. It was not until after the Civil Rights campaigning of the 1950s and 1960s that Jim Crow laws were abolished.[9] Most people will also know that in South Africa for much of the twentieth century apartheid laws, similar in many respects to Jim Crow laws, distinguished between three categories of 'races': White, Black and Coloured. These categories were central to the South African state's apartheid policy and were drawn on to enforce segregation of different 'races' and enact a hierarchical ordering of society, with Whites at the top and Blacks at the bottom.[10]

It is not just people of African descent who have been subject to racism. Skin colour and eye shape differentiated Chinese immigrants from the descendants of White Europeans. And Chinese immigrants were subject to racist treatment in the United States and Australia in the late nineteenth and much of the twentieth centuries.[11] The colonial domination of people of colour in Africa, Asia and Latin America was also justified, in part, through ideas about the racial superiority of the White 'race' (and the inferiority of colonised people).[12] When, after the Second World War, people of colour from European colonies (and former colonies) started to emigrate to Europe in significant numbers, they were subject to racial discrimination and explicitly racist immigration laws which were used to restrict immigration from the former colonial world.[13]

Forced enslavement of Black Africans by White Europeans, apartheid, 'Jim Crow' laws, colonial domination and immigration controls targeted at people from former colonies are all examples of racist practice. They all involved discriminating against people on the basis of 'racial' difference. But the idea that humanity 'can be divided according to physical and biological criteria' does not have to involve racial discrimination. In contemporary Anglo-American culture, and in globalised culture more broadly, there are a whole range of ways in which 'race' is made to appear to be a self-evident fact of life. We have Black music and Asian cooking. We have Black History Week and Chinese New Year. In the cinema we have famous actors – such as Chris Rock, Whoopi Goldberg and Eddie Murphy – who are routinely employed to play stereotypically 'Black' characters.[14] New media platforms, such as YouTube, have not been free from old-style stereotyped representations of 'race', which can be found not just in the outputs of media corporations, but also predominate in user-generated content.[15] It is not just in popular culture that we are routinely encouraged to think in terms of racial categories. People in Northern Ireland (and the rest of the United Kingdom) are familiar with ethnic monitoring forms and ethnic questions which are asked on the census, on attitude surveys and on other kinds of public surveys. These often ask people to categorise themselves as 'Black' or 'White' or 'Asian' or 'Chinese'. So the idea that 'races' exist has a long history; it is something that is perpetuated through contemporary popular culture and that people in the UK are encouraged to think in terms of, through official 'race' (or ethnic) monitoring.[16]

The association between physical appearance and 'race' is most explicit in scientific racism (or racial science), which was based on the assumption that humanity is composed of biologically distinct 'races'. Racial science was very influential during the Victorian era, and was central to a range of state policies in Nazi Germany. Racial science included a hodgepodge of competing theories, disciplinary specialisms and methodological approaches. What they all had in common was the starting assumption that humanity was composed of different races and that through the application of scientific techniques it was possible to identify the biological basis for these differences and classify humanity into different racial groups based on the criteria that science identified. Physical appearance was often taken as an outward sign of something biologically inherent. This can be seen in craniology, one of the sub-disciplines in racial science, which was devoted to the study of skull shape and size. Craniologists argued that Anglo-Saxons or Aryans or Nordics (the use of different terms indicates the hodgepodge of different views on what races existed) had larger skulls (to accommodate their larger brains). In addition, they also had proportionately larger frontal lobes (the area of the brain where the frontal cortex is located; the frontal cortex is considered to be the part of the brain devoted to higher order thinking, such as logical reasoning).[17]

The idea of racial difference was often conjoined with ideas about evolution to provide a hierarchical classification of 'racial' groups based on their stages of evolution. The phrase 'survival of the fittest' was applied by Social Darwinists to justify this hierarchical ordering of humanity. In this view those of African origin were the least evolved and Anglo-Saxons (or Aryans or Nordics) the most evolved

branches of the human species.[18] The Irish were often portrayed as racially inferior in racial science. John Beddoe's influential book *The Races of Man* (published
in 1885), for example, argued that 'scientific' analysis of skull shape showed that
the Irish were closer to prehistoric man than modern Europeans 'and hence must
have had links with the "Africinoid" races'.[19] Skull size and shape was not the
only criteria used to classify humanity by 'race'. Blood-line descent was used by
the Nazis to categorise the Jews and other 'racial groups'. The relative unimpor-
tance of skin colour in racial thinking can perhaps be most clearly seen in the
case of Nazi racial thinking. One of the consistently central ideas proclaimed by
a range of different Nazi racial thinkers was that the Aryans were a master race
and that Slavs, Gypsies and Jews were inferior 'races'. This is not a colour-coded
ordering. The Aryan 'race' included 'Brown' people from the Middle East and
India. The 'inferior' Slavic-speaking people were White. Nazi racial thinkers
thought of 'race' in terms of descent, and in this view colour was only one outward sign of 'race', and a relatively unimportant one at that.[20] Nazi laws pre-
scribed which marriage partners were suitable and unsuitable. They prohibited
'persons of German or related blood' from marrying or having sexual relations
with Jews, 'Gypsies, negroes or their bastards'. Couples who wanted to marry
had to have a 'certificate of fitness to marry', which they could only obtain after
subjecting themselves to examination by a public health authority. These laws
categorised 'lesser races' as lesser citizens. This allowed them to be stripped of
many rights and eventually helped to facilitate the mass extermination of 'lesser
races' in the Holocaust.[21]

The many attempts to use scientific methods to prove the existence of 'races' –
such as craniology, phrenology, IQ testing, blood testing, DNA testing – have all
failed to find any demonstrable link between biology and 'race'.[22] One problem
that racial science encountered was that there is considerable biological variation
within each set of people who were considered to be a 'race'. Another problem
is where to draw the line between one 'race' and another. Some racial scientists
made distinctions between White, Black, Brown, Yellow and Red races, which
roughly corresponded to continents – Europe, Africa, the Middle East and West
Asia, East Asia and the Americas. But these distinctions became less clear as one
moves away from the obvious cases. Should people from Greece, for example,
be included as Europeans? This would allow European civilisation to be traced
to Ancient Greece. Or should they be considered as Middle Eastern? Swarthy
Greeks (and not all Greeks are swarthy) are closer in complexion to their Middle
Eastern or North African neighbours and have dark hair and brown eyes. These
characteristics differentiate them from pale-skinned, blond-haired and blue-eyed
northern Europeans. Distinguishing between different groups of people in this
way involves stereotypes regarding what 'Europeans' look like, and what differentiates them from 'Africans' and people from the Middle East.

We now know from studies of genetics that there is genetic variation within the human population, but this variation does not allow us to distinguish between different 'races'. Most genetic variation is between individuals, rather than between groups of people. Study of human genetics shows that there is more variation within any so-called 'race' of people than there is between this 'race' and any other randomly chosen 'race'.[23] The claim that 'races' do not exist might seem strange to anyone who enjoys watching television programmes such as *Who Do You Think You Are* or *Finding Your Roots*, or anyone who has paid a genetic tracing company to trace their ancestry. These programmes, however, do not prove the existence of 'races'. They provide sophisticated guesswork about the geographical origins of some fragments of DNA. So they can say things like 'there is a high probability that one of your ancestors was from West Africa'. But that is not the same thing as proving the existence of 'races'. In as far as the programmes or companies do refer to 'race' they take the existence of 'races' as a starting assumption. The attempts to find a biological basis for the division of humanity into different races failed because these divisions are humanly created, not biologically given.

Geoghegan's choice of definition of racism seems to have been adopted because it allows him to clearly differentiate racism from sectarianism, not because of its applicability to analysing Northern Irish society. His study does provide some insights (the chapter on the chauvinistic, and mutually antagonistic, nature of both Irish Nationalist and Ulster Unionist anti-racism, for example, provides many interesting observations), but the distinction that he makes between racism and sectarianism is irrelevant to these insights.

Visible minorities and racism

Brewer makes a significantly different argument than Geoghegan regarding the difference between racism and sectarianism. Brewer argues that there are fundamental *similarities* between racism and sectarianism. He notes that both racism and sectarianism produce 'inequality in a structured manner, rather than randomly', have their roots 'in colonial exploitation', and 'describe a set of social relations that permeate all levels of society, rather than simply refer to a set of individual attitudes or prejudices'.[24] The main difference between racism and sectarianism, he argues, is the nature of the social marker used to categorise humanity. Racism, he argues, relies on visible markers of differences (he calls them perceptual cues) such as skin colour. With sectarianism, religion is the marker of difference. This relies on stereotypical cues by which people in Northern Ireland are differentiated on the basis 'of generalizations and stereotypes regarding behaviour' (such as Catholics support Glasgow Celtic football team and Protestants support Glasgow Rangers; Catholics attend Catholic schools and Protestants attend state schools; Catholics call Northern Ireland's second city Derry, Protestants call it Londonderry).[25] Brewer argues that the different nature of the markers involved has significant consequences. Because racism relies on perceptual cues, it is more difficult for Black people – and other visibly different 'races' – to avoid racism than it is for Catholics or Protestants to avoid sectarianism. Religious affiliation, Brewer points out, is something that is learned and that can be changed, or disguised. Genetically inherited physical differences cannot be changed at will.

Initially this appears to be a strong argument in favour of taking skin colour (or other visible and relatively unalterable markers of difference) seriously in distinguishing between racism and sectarianism. The use of perceptual cues to distinguish between racism and sectarianism is, however, problematic. One obvious problem is that sectarianism sometimes involves perceptual cues. The assailants in the racist attack on Poles in Derry/Londonderry appear to have relied on a Celtic football top as a perceptual cue. Celtic and Rangers tops, however, are just one of a number of visible markers of difference that are employed to differentiate between Catholics and Protestants in Northern Ireland. Yes, these visible markers can be changed or disguised or not adopted, but they are still what Brewer calls perceptual cues. According to Brewer's definition, however, attacks on White East Europeans cannot be considered to be examples of racism, unless they rely on perceptual cues (such as accent).

Brewer's distinction between racism and sectarianism also runs into the problem of where we draw the line between Black and White. The importance of visible markers of difference seems obvious in cases of discrimination against dark-skinned people from sub-Saharan Africa. But at what point does difference become 'invisible'? Or, in other words, where can we draw the boundary between visibly different people and those who look the same as 'us'? Do we include people from Greece as part of 'us'? If so, do we also include lighter-skinned people from Turkey, Iraq, Egypt or India? In these less obvious cases, how do we decide if the discrimination is on the basis of identification through a perceptual cue, such as skin colour, or a stereotypical cue, such as being of Muslim faith?

Brewer appears to be assuming that in the case of people of colour the racists choose their victim on the basis of skin colour. Skin colour, however, is increasingly less reliable as a perceptual marker of difference in the UK context. In the 1970s and 1980s the far right slogan 'There Ain't no Black in the Union Jack' summed up a commonplace view that 'Black' and 'British' were mutually exclusive categories.[26] A number of recent studies suggest that the experience of living alongside immigrant communities mean that many 'White British' people now see no necessary contradiction between 'Black' and 'British'.[27] In research carried out in Bristol and Norfolk, for example, Steve Garner found that many of his White middle-class and working-class interviewees drew an 'us' and 'them' distinction between respectable and hard-working people (us) and welfare scroungers (them). The former category included people of Afro-Caribbean and Asian descent. The latter category included White British, White Poles, Black and White Portuguese and Black asylum seekers.[28] In an era in which people of colour enjoy a significant profile in public life in the UK as television presenters, sportsmen and women, politicians, musicians and comedians, it is difficult to sustain the idea that 'Black' and 'British' are mutually exclusive. There are, no doubt, some people in Northern Ireland who view *all* people of colour as outsiders, but this clear-cut Black/White = Them/Us distinction is increasingly difficult to sustain. Consequently, the distinction that Brewer makes is losing whatever utility it once had.

Finally, Brewer's approach is also misleading because it focuses on the marker of difference, which takes our attention away from the underlying structures. Where he does refer to structures, it is to highlight the similarities between racism and sectarianism. Both, he argues, involve structured inequality, colonial roots and a set of relations that permeate all levels of society. The way in which Brewer discusses these similarities, however, is almost entirely abstract. We can say that each involve structured inequality, but that truism tells us nothing about the processes involved in creating and maintaining these inequalities. The way in which Catholics have been structurally disadvantaged in Northern Ireland is different to the way that inequality regarding immigrant minorities is structured, and both of these are different to the way in which Irish Travellers are structurally disadvantaged. The focus on surface appearances does provide a logical basis, however unsatisfactory this may be in practice, for differentiating between racism and sectarianism. This approach, however, is a barrier to developing an emancipatory anti-racism, because it focuses on the marker of difference, not the underlying processes.

Race Relations law

Connolly notes that there is some debate about whether sectarianism should be defined as racism. He says that there is 'some merit in doing so and it would thus be worth pursuing this debate further'.[29] Connolly, however, does not pursue the debate any further. Instead, he points out that the Race Relations (NI) Order 1997 'does not list religion as a basis upon which a "racial group" can be identified'.[30] On the pragmatic grounds that the law treats sectarianism as being distinct from racism, he does the same in his review of the literature on racism in Northern Ireland. This is a disingenuous evasion of the issue.

Elsewhere in the same report Connolly notes that the 'Race Relations (NI) Order defines a "racial group" as "a group of persons defined by reference to colour, race, nationality or ethnic or national origins"'.[31] And he also points out that the Order defines Irish Travellers 'as a "racial group"' in that they are 'a community of people commonly so called who are identified (both by themselves and by others) as people with a shared history, culture and traditions including, historically, a nomadic way of life on the island of Ireland'.[32] Connolly is well aware that Irish Nationalists/Catholics and Ulster Unionists/Protestants are commonly characterised as 'a community of people commonly so called who are identified (both by themselves and by others) as people with a shared history, culture and traditions'. In fact the dominant contemporary characterisation of the Northern Ireland conflict is that it is an ethnic conflict.[33] Connolly's evasion makes the task of reviewing the literature on racism more manageable, but it does so by avoiding the difficult theoretical work.

The case for treating sectarianism as racism

Robbie McVeigh has persistently pointed out the inconsistencies in the approach of those, including state authorities, who treat sectarianism and racism as distinct. He has drawn attention to a range of ways in which religion or religious identification has become an increasingly important element in racist practice and in Race Relations legislation in the UK. He has noted, for example, that 'in the aftermath of the Rushdie Affair, Muslim was often used as an ethnic label' to carry out racist attacks on people of South Asian origin, irrespective of their religious identity.[34] In relation to the law, he has pointed out that the ruling in the landmark *Mandela v. Lee* prosecution in England 'made two key points about the Race Relations Act (1976): first ethnicity was the most important and embracing of all dimensions of the Act; second religion was often a constituent part of ethnicity'.[35] In making these points about religion and ethnicity McVeigh has drawn attention to the increasing divergence between Northern Ireland and the rest of the UK.[36] In the rest of the UK religion has increasingly been interpreted as an important component of ethnicity, and ethnicity has increasingly been the most important 'racial' grounds invoked in Race Relations laws in the rest of the UK.

In Northern Ireland there has been a consistent attempt to treat racism and sectarianism as separate issues in official policy. Connolly, as we have seen, uses the exclusion of 'religion' as a criterion in the 1997 Race Relations (NI) Order as justification for his treatment of sectarianism as being distinct from racism. The disingenuous nature of this evasion is evident in the Northern Ireland *Racial Equality Strategy* (2005–10), the key document that outlined the Northern Ireland government's strategy for tackling racism. In the strategy the term racism is employed 'as shorthand for all forms of racial intolerance and discrimination including Islamophobia, anti-Semitism and sedentarism [anti-Traveller discrimination]'.[37] The document does not include sectarianism as a form of racial intolerance and discrimination. Nor does it define sectarianism. If, however, sectarianism can be excluded from Race Relations law in Northern Ireland on the grounds of excluding 'religion', what are the grounds for including Islamophobia (fear and prejudice directed against Muslims and Islam) and anti-Semitism (prejudice and discrimination against Jews) in the *Racial Equality Strategy*? Surely both involve, in Geoghegan's terms, the complex interaction between religion and politics, through which ideas about religious difference are used to infer political identities – such as support for Jihadist terrorism, or support for the state of Israel as a Zionist state?

McVeigh points out that the colonial roots of the Catholic/Protestant distinction mean that the religious dimension maps on to a native/settler distinction. He goes on to say that

> Moreover other labels – like 'Unionist' and 'Loyalist' or 'Nationalist' and 'Republican' – signify the political and ethnic elements which also constitute identities that appear formally theological … This already suggests that we are dealing with ethnicity – which recognises just such an amalgam of different elements – rather than faith. Tellingly in the jurisprudence of 'fair employment', 'perceived religious identity' came to be more important than 'religious identity'. The ethnicity paradigm offers a holistic reading of inequality and discrimination in Northern Ireland that the 'religious conflict' approach cannot.[38]

Connolly uses the law as justification for him not engaging with the question 'is sectarianism racism?' McVeigh uses the same law to make the case for saying that sectarianism is racism. McVeigh's implicit challenge to Connolly turns on the key concept of 'ethnicity'. In order to understand and assess McVeigh's argument we need to explore the concept of 'ethnicity' in more detail.

The distinction between 'race', 'nation' and 'ethnic group' is a common source of confusion in any attempt to understand racism and sectarianism in Northern Ireland. In large part this is because the concepts of 'ethnic group', 'race' and 'nation' are all ways of conceiving of humanity as composed of groups of people who are differentiated from each other by their common descent. As Steve Fenton puts it:

> Common to all [three] is an idea of descent or ancestry and very closely implicated in all three we find the idea of shared culture. Ideas about culture will include myths about the past, beliefs about 'the kinds of people we are' and the idea that 'culture', language, dress and custom define a group … Ethnic group, race and nation are all viewed, by themselves or by observers, as peoples who have or lay claim to shared antecedents.[39]

It is hardly surprising that many ordinary people confuse 'race', 'nation' and 'ethnic group', because all three terms are continually conflated in the criminal justice system, in the media and in academia. One strategy for dealing with this confusion is to focus on what is specific about each term. The most common way of distinguishing between 'race', 'nation' and 'ethnic group' is to say that the concept of 'race' views humanity as divided according to their biologically inherited origins; 'nation' divides humanity with reference to their origins in a particular territory; and 'ethnic' divides them with reference to common cultural inheritance. Geoghegan does a version of this when he distinguishes between racism as based on dividing humanity according to physical and biological criteria and sectarianism as based on differentiating people on the basis of religion as a cultural marker of difference. These distinctions between 'race' (biology), 'nation' (territory) and 'ethnic' (culture) are clear, but they are denotive distinctions. They are useful if you are trying to compile a dictionary, but they lead us into confusion when they are used to examine the real world. In everyday speech people commonly use and interpret words connotatively. In everyday speech, words are wrapped up in associations and nuances that are given meaning by context, tone and other factors outside their literal meaning. The language of 'race' is rich in connotation.[40]

In this part of the chapter we examine the problem of the intertwining of 'race', 'nation' and 'ethnic group' in more detail in two different ways. In the first part we examine the historical example of the conception of 'race' articulated by Douglas Hyde. This conception was an important and influential strand of Irish Nationalist ideology in the late nineteenth and early twentieth centuries, but it is one that conflates 'race', nation and ethnic group. In the second part we briefly outline the rise of the concept of 'ethnic group' as an alternative to 'race'.

The conflation of biology, culture and territory

In the nineteenth century, and the early years of the twentieth century, 'race' was not conceived solely, or even mainly, in terms of biology. Take this example from a speech – *The Necessity for De-Anglicising Ireland* – made by Douglas Hyde in Dublin in 1892:

> we must strive to cultivate everything that is most racial, most smacking of the soil, most Gaelic, most Irish, because in spite of the little admixture of Saxon blood in the north-east corner, this island is and will ever remain Celtic at the core, far more Celtic than most people imagine … On racial lines, then, we shall best develop, following the bent of our own natures; and, in order to do this, we must create a strong feeling against West-Britonism, for it – if we give it the least chance, or show it the smallest quarter – will overwhelm us like a flood, and we shall find ourselves toiling painfully behind the English at each step following the same fashions, only six months behind the English ones.[41]

In this short extract we see the equating of 'race' with biology ('Saxon blood'), culture ('Gaelic', 'Celtic', 'the same fashions') and territory ('the soil', 'Irish', 'this island'). This amalgamation of biology, culture and territory in discourses of 'race' was commonplace in Anglo-American culture in the Victorian era.

When Hyde talks about *cultivating* everything that is most racial (and most smacking of the soil), he is articulating a biological view of 'race' which owes more to horticulture and animal husbandry than to the scientific study of primates or humans. Breeding, in this view of 'race', is about more than just biology. It is about the combination of biology – good stock – and nurturing of the stock. In this view nature is not contrasted to nurture. It is the combination of nature and nurture that helps to create the most vigorous 'races'. This conception also informed the distinction between people who were civilised – those who were cultivated in their tastes and knowledge – and people who were uncivilised – those who were wild, untamed or primitive. The idea of the civilised and uncivilised was applied to humanity globally and used to justify colonialism – as in the idea of 'the civilising mission of the White man'. It was also applied domestically by elites in Europe, and in the Anglo-American world, to talk about social class. Gentlemen were men of breeding, men who were cultivated through education. The lower orders were those who lacked breeding. In the Victorian era talk of 'race' shaded very easily into talk of social class.[42] Elements of this class snobbery can be seen in Hyde's complaints about the culture of the masses, when he refers to the best-selling literature of his day as 'penny dreadfuls' and 'shilling shockers'.

In the conservative Romantic view of culture (which Hyde is articulating in his speech), this cultivation of humans has natural limits. Hyde suggests that it goes against nature for the Irish to neglect their own culture and instead imitate an alien culture. This Romantic view of culture developed in opposition to the Enlightenment view, which tended to think in terms of a universal humanity. In the Enlightenment view of humanity, all human beings share a common humanity by virtue of our capacity for reason. In the Enlightenment view there is only one 'race', the human race. Enlightenment thinkers tended to talk about humanity in universal terms, for example referring to the Rights of Man. Conservative Romantics tended to think in more racial terms. They generally thought of humanity as composed of many particular 'races'. The opposition between the Enlightenment view of humanity and the conservative Romantic one is well captured in one of Count de Maistre's comments on the French Revolutionary Declaration of the Rights of Man and of the Citizen. De Maistre complained that 'there is no such thing in the world as Man. In the course of my life, I have seen Frenchmen, Italians, Russians, etc … But, as for Man, I declare that I have never met him in my life. If he exists, I certainly have no knowledge of him.'[43] In de Maistre's view, the universal right to liberty and equality proclaimed in the declaration cannot exist because there is no universal humanity, only many particular 'races' of men.[44]

This particularist view of humanity does not necessarily involve ideas about the inferiority or superiority of particular 'races'. Hyde is not attempting to claim that Gaelic culture is superior to Anglo-Saxon culture. He even praises the best that England has to offer. At the beginning of his speech he advocates de-Anglicisation 'not as a protest against imitating what is best in the English people, for that would be absurd, but rather to show the folly of neglecting what is Irish'. Cultivating the Irish 'race' through English culture, in the conservative Romantic view articulated by Hyde, will never lead the Irish to attain greatness, because it is only as Irish people that they can truly attain greatness. Cultivating English culture will always mean that the Irish are mere imitators, following several months behind the English fashions. This is because it is only by being true to their nature as Irish people that they can hope to be truly cultivated. In horticultural terms we might say that a lily can be cultivated to blossom more fully, but it will never be a rose. One is not better than the other. They are simply different by nature.

In Hyde's view the issue of culture is not just about the vigour of the Irish as a 'race'. It is also about the recognition of the Irish in the eyes of the rest of the world. In the same speech he warned his audience that Anglicisation was a problem for the movement for Home Rule because 'in Anglicising ourselves wholesale we have thrown away with a light heart the best claim which we have upon the world's recognition of us as a separate nationality'. If the Irish neglect their culture, Hyde suggests, there will be little to distinguish them from Anglo-Saxons as a 'race'. If the Irish are not a distinct 'race', he argues, there is then little basis for the Irish to argue that they should be granted the freedom to act as a distinct nation.

The idea (presented by Geoghegan but shared by many) that 'race' is about biology and physical appearance takes one particular version of racism – racial science – and treats this as if it is the only version. Racial science was influential. But even at its high point of influence in the Victorian era, it was not the only form of racial thinking. Hyde freely mixes ideas about cultural difference with ideas about biological difference and presents these as being part of the case for making claims about rights to a nation-state. His view of 'race' was unexceptional at the time. In Anglo-American discussions of 'race' in the Victorian era, Elazar Barkan notes, 'the term "race" ... [was] used to refer to any geographical, religious, class-based or color-based grouping ... its scientific usage was multiple, ambiguous and at times self-contradictory'.[45] Hyde's views on 'race' were unexceptional, but he was influential. He was one of the leading figures in the Gaelic Revival and was later to become the first president of the Irish Free State.

The fluidity of the concept of 'race' can be seen in the way that Black radicals in the USA in the early part of the twentieth century, such as Marcus Garvey and W. E. B. du Bois, viewed the Irish as a 'race'. These leading figures supported the Irish independence movement, in which they perceived

> a shared interest in anticolonialism and antiracism tied to a deep antipathy for 'perfidious Albion', a desire to overturn a series of racial representations that were deeply gendered and tightly tied to colonial oppression, a hope that Wilsonian idealism and the postwar drive for colonial self-determination might overturn the dominance of white over black or Anglo-Saxon over Celt, and a sense of global dispersion and racial community that made their struggles similarly diasporic.[46]

Garvey and du Bois endorsed the idea that the Irish were a Celtic 'race', different to and oppressed by the Anglo-Saxons. This endorsement, however, coexisted with a debate in radical Black circles about the degree to which the Irish were also White. Ironically (given Brewer's and Geoghegan's presentation of the issue of 'race') the achievement of Irish independence was one of the factors that led du Bois and others to 'shed the clumsy imprecision of Romantic racialism and helped to move the lines of racial classification from "the fifty races of the world" to five: the black, brown, red, yellow, and white'.[47] Du Bois did not invent colour as a form of racial classification, but he did help to popularise it.

The rise of the concept of 'ethnicity'

Hyde does not use the terms ethnic or ethnicity in his speech, or in any of his other speeches or writings. To many people reading Hyde's speech today the absence of the term ethnic or ethnicity appears odd. The main emphasis of Hyde's speech – de-Anglicisation and the promotion of the Irish language – is on culture. Why then does he not use the terms ethnic or ethnicity? The simple reason is that in the Victorian era no one in the English-speaking world used these terms. They would not have been recognised by Hyde's audience. In contemporary contexts where the term ethnic is used, the Victorians would most likely have used the term 'race' or nation. In this subsection we shall identify some of the factors that led to the decline of 'race' as a term and the rise of 'ethnic' in its place.

In the UK the term 'ethnic' did not come into widespread use in academic writing until the 1970s and did not come into more popular use, in the media and among policy-makers, until the 1980s. The roots of the rise of the concept of the 'ethnic group', however, go back further. In the 1930s a number of biologists and anthropologists in the UK and USA questioned the utility of the concept of 'race' because attempts at racial classification 'led to endless irresolvable inconsistencies and contradictions'.[48] In what is generally regarded as one of the most influential anti-racist texts of the 1930s, We Europeans, Julian Huxley and Alfred Haddon proposed replacing the term 'race' with the term 'ethnic'. They argued that 'ethnic' was a more useful concept because it acknowledged that 'the decision as to what is a "race" is a personal matter resting largely on subjective impressions'.[49] After the Second World War this understanding was taken up by the United Nations Educational, Scientific and Cultural Organization (UNESCO), under Julian Huxley's leadership.[50] In 1950, for example, UNESCO published a Statement on Race that had been drawn up by leading scholars in the fields of sociology, psychology, biology, cultural anthropology and ethnology. These scholars argued that when most people use the term 'race', they do not do so in the scientific sense of the word, but rather in an ordinary everyday or folk sense. As they put it, for 'most people, a race is any group of people whom they choose to describe as a race. Thus, many national, religious, geographic, linguistic or cultural groups have, in such loose usage, been called [a] "race".'[51] The statement went on to suggest that 'it would be better when speaking of human races to drop the term "race" altogether and speak of ethnic groups'. This suggestion was not widely adopted at the time, and the term ethnic does not even appear in the UNESCO *Statement on the Nature of Race and Race Differences* published in 1951.

Although the 1951 statement did not use the term 'ethnic', its authors did concur on the key points that underpinned the 1950 suggestion to drop the term 'race' and use the term 'ethnic group' instead. The preamble to the 1951 statement notes that its authors recognised that humanity is distinguished as much by cultural differences as by biological ones, and that 'it was clear to all of us that many of the factors leading to the formation of minor races of men have been cultural'. The authors of the 1951 statement also had no 'hesitation or lack of unanimity in reaching the primary conclusion that there were no scientific grounds whatever for the racialist position regarding purity of race and the hierarchy of inferior and superior races to which this leads'.[52] As the 1951 statement puts it, 'the chief conclusions of the first statement were sustained, but with differences in emphasis and with some important deletions'.[53] Both statements agree that there was no biological basis to ideas of racial superiority. Both recognised the use of the concept of 'race' to refer to groups differentiated by culture rather than biology. The two statements differed, however, in the emphasis that they gave to the latter point. The 1950 statement recommended dropping 'race' in favour of 'ethnic group' because its authors believed that the term 'ethnic group' better described what most people actually meant when they used the term 'race'. The authors of the 1951 statement, in which more scientists were involved, wanted to differentiate between the use of the concept of 'race' in science and its misuse in folk conceptions and abuse by racists. Later documents produced by UNESCO appear to fudge this difference of opinion by using both of the terms.

We might expect that the discrediting of racial hierarchy would mean that ideas about racial difference would become consigned to the dustbin of history, but that has not been the case. At the heart of official anti-racism, from the international level of the UN to local Race Relations officers, there is ambivalence about the existence of races. We can see this ambivalence in Article 1 of the 1978 UNESCO Declaration on Race and Racial Prejudice.[54] The declaration opens with the statement that 'All human beings belong to a single species and are descended from a common stock.' This seems to be a clear rejection of the idea that humanity is made up of different races. The declaration then appears to go on to contradict the opening clause when it says that 'All individuals and groups have the right to be different, to consider themselves as different and to be regarded as such.' So, in the first clause all humans belong to a single species, but in the second they are divided up into different groups. The declaration's concern is not with the division of humanity into different groups, which it accepts and even defends as a right. Its main concerns are that group differences should not be used as a 'pretext for any rank-ordered classification of nations or peoples', 'serve as a pretext for racial prejudice' or 'justify either in law or in fact any discriminatory practice whatsoever'.

The declaration rejects the hierarchical ordering of humanity into superior and inferior races, ethnic groups, nations or peoples. It rejects prejudice against any of these groups. And it rejects discrimination against any of these groups. It does not, however, reject the idea that humanity is divided into different racial, ethnic or national groups. What it does is to argue that the division of humanity into different groups is not based on biology, but instead is based on 'geographical, historical, political, economic, social and cultural factors'. As Kenan Malik puts it, the UNESCO view turns 'the evolutionary ladder of Victorian racial theory on to its side, and … [conceives] of humanity as horizontally rather than vertically segmented'.[55] Instead of a view of the world in which some races or ethnic groups are superior to others (vertically segmented), UNESCO presents a view in which the world is composed of different, but equally valid and valued, races or ethnic groups (horizontally segmented).

The suggestion of dropping the term 'race' and using the term 'ethnic group' instead has only been partially adopted. The term 'race' has been retained for a whole range of reasons. One important reason is that many of the statements and laws – at the international and state level – aimed at tackling racial discrimination use the language of 'race'. This retention of the concept of 'race', however, has gone alongside the adoption of the concept of 'ethnic group'. One of the results has been ambivalence over the meaning and appropriate use of the term 'race'. Another has been the continual conflation of the terms 'race' and 'ethnic group'.

Is sectarianism racism?

McVeigh does a very good job of drawing attention to inconsistencies in the application of the definition of 'racial group' in Race Relations law and racial equality policy. If law and policy covers discrimination and harassment against Irish Travellers as an ethnic group, and if the same law and policy covers Muslims and Jews, there is no logical reason why discrimination and harassment directed at people *because* they are Catholics or Protestants should not also be covered by the same laws. By this reasoning sectarianism is racism. However, if sectarianism is racism, then what are we to make of this statement by McVeigh? 'Sectarianism pervades life in Northern Ireland. Not surprisingly, it also structures the way in which racism is reproduced and experienced.'[56] If sectarianism is racism, then we can rewrite this sentence, substituting the word racism for the word sectarianism. If we do so, however, we have a sentence that says that racism 'structures the way in which racism is reproduced and experienced'. The idea that racism can structure racism appears nonsensical. And what about this statement by McVeigh:

[I]t is clear that the experience of racism in Britain and sectarianism in Northern Ireland are not identical. There are key differences: levels of racist and sectarian violence; the political mobilisation of sectarianism and racism; the relevant strength of different ethnic blocs involved in the two situations and so on.[57]

At first glance, it appears that McVeigh is guilty of his own inconsistencies. He appears to want to have it both ways: sectarianism is racism, but it is also different to racism. His criticisms of inconsistencies in law and policy are well made, but his identification of ways in which sectarianism in Northern Ireland differs from racism, in Northern Ireland and in the rest of the UK, also makes sense.

Racisms not racism

Garner provides a useful way to cut through the confusions regarding racism and sectarianism when he argues that 'racism is a phenomenon manifesting itself in such a diverse spectrum of ways across time and place' that it is useful to use 'the plural, *racisms*, to denote the variations on the main themes'.[58] Garner's approach allows us to treat racism that involves visible markers of difference, sectarianism that involves religious markers of difference, discrimination against Irish Travellers and racism against immigrants from Eastern Europe as different *forms* of racism. In this framework, racism becomes a broad overarching term that encompasses a range of different forms. From this perspective, we can say that one of the problems with Brewer's and Geoghegan's attempts to distinguish between racism and sectarianism is that they are actually comparing sectarianism and a *particular form* of racism. When Brewer talks about racism, it might be more accurate to use the term colour-coded racism. Racism that relies on skin colour as a marker of difference is simply one of many forms, rather than the only form that racism takes. When Geoghegan uses the term racism, he appears to have in mind scientific racism.

Racisms vary according to which groups are the focus (or the ways in which they are a focus) of hostility over time. In the early twenty-first century, for example, there is widespread fear and hostility towards Muslims across Europe and in the USA.[59] This focus on Muslims is new in many countries. In the UK, for example, existing hostility in some quarters towards Pakistanis has shifted to highlight their religious identification as Muslim rather than their country of origin or their skin colour. In other words, many individuals who were categorised and stereotyped as Pakistani in the 1970s, 1980s and 1990s became categorised and stereotyped as Muslim in the twenty-first century.[60] In the UK a number of different scholars have pointed to parallels between the treatment of the Irish as a 'suspect community' in Britain in the 1970s and 1980s and similar treatment of Muslims in Britain in the early twenty-first century.[61] One study, for example, found that both the Irish (in the past) and Muslims (in the present) tended to be presented in the press as either 'law-abiding' or 'extremist'. And the law-abiding were always defined in relation to the extremist; hence the sense of being 'suspect' even among law-abiding Irish or Muslims. This sense of being viewed as suspect 'resulted from negative responses in everyday encounters, from neighbours, at work, in shops, on the street; police activity; and from security operations at ports and airports'.[62] These studies suggest that there has been hostility towards particular groups in Britain on the basis that this group is viewed as a threat to law and order. It is the group that is vilified and all individuals who are identified as belonging to this group can find themselves treated with suspicion, regardless of whether or not they are hostile or sympathetic to 'extremists'. These studies also point out that the particular stigmatised group has changed, from the Irish to Muslims.

Racisms do not just vary according to the way in which the target group is identified – by skin colour or by religion, for example – but also in terms of the way that specific groups are conceived. We can see this variation in shifts in the portrayal of the Irish in English political cartoons in the nineteenth century. Curtis points to a change in caricatures of the Irish between the early nineteenth century and late nineteenth century 'from a drunken and relatively harmless peasant into a dangerous ape-man or simianized agitator'.[63] He notes the gradual development of a caricature of the Irish as ape-like – with large jaw-bone, heavy protruding forehead and extensive body hair. And he argues that this portrayal became more prevalent with the rise of Irish Fenianism (which was dedicated to the removal of British rule from Ireland though the use of violence) in the 1860s. Violent resistance, he suggests, 'seemed to reveal the beast that lurked within Irish character'.[64] This characterisation of the Irish as bestial continued into the twentieth century and gradually faded from prominence after the Irish War of Independence. Curtis's analysis suggests that the intensity of hostility towards particular 'racial' or ethnic groups is related to the extent to which that group is perceived to be a threat in society. Understanding racisms as phenomena that evolve is important because it draws our attention to the ways that 'races' and racisms are made and can be unmade. In this vein, scholars of the Irish experience, for example, have drawn attention to the ways in which 'the Irish' were not always White, but were made White.[65]

Racisms also vary between different countries. McVeigh argues along these lines when he says that '[r]acism assumes different forms in different situations – sectarianism might be very different to anti-Black racism in Britain but a form of racism for all that – just as South African racism is undoubtedly racism despite being different in many ways to racism in Britain'.[66] In addition to varying between countries and varying over time, racisms also vary within a country at any particular moment in time. Back's study of young people and racism in inner-city London, for example, found that attitudes towards 'race' and racism were significantly different in the two areas where he conducted his research. In one area, which experienced non-White immigration from the 1970s onwards, there was a widespread association between immigration and urban decline. In this area racist attitudes were expressed through 'the assertion that the area had lost its sense of community' and 'the idea that the neighbourhood was being swamped by minorities'.[67] In the other district, which had a longer experience of non-White immigration, he found that both White and Black residents talked about harmonious community relations and rejected 'the legitimacy of racism … racism was both acknowledged as socially significant but rejected as inapplicable to the situation found in the neighbourhood'.[68]

One of the problems with the approach taken by Brewer and Geoghegan is that their distinctions between racism and sectarianism employ definitions of racism (and sectarianism) that take no account of the historically and contextually variable nature of racisms. Garner's approach allows us to acknowledge the existence of racism without having to rely on a definition of racism that is tied to time or place. Garner's approach enables us to cut through some of the confusions that have bedevilled attempts to compare racism and sectarianism. It allows us to differentiate between sectarianism and other forms of racism. It also allows us to acknowledge that there is an affinity between sectarianism and other forms of racism.

Racisms and Race Relations law and policy

UK Race Relations law and policy acknowledges that racism can take a variety of forms. The first piece of legislation that prohibited racial discrimination and incitement to racial hatred in the UK, the Race Relations Act 1965, outlawed discrimination on the grounds of colour, race, ethnic or national origins.[69] Michael Banton notes that the UK is not unique in specifying these grounds. The United Nations International Convention on the Elimination of All Forms of Racial Discrimination (1966) 'lists race, colour, descent, national and ethnic origin' and all 'the main international human rights conventions and British anti-discrimination policy statements list race and colour separately'.[70] The specifying of colour, race, ethnic or national origins as invalid grounds for discrimination date back to the United Nations Universal Declaration of Human Rights (1948). Article 2 of the declaration states that 'Everyone is entitled to all the rights and freedoms set forth in this Declaration, without distinction of any kind, such as race, colour, sex, language, religion, political or other opinion, national or social origin.'[71]

Banton argues that the way racial discrimination has been defined in Race Relations law (on the basis of groups categorised by colour, race, ethnic or national origins) is more effective than technical definitions (such as that provided by Geoghegan) or approaches (such as that provided by Brewer) that argue that racism is directed only against physically distinct categories of people. A key reason why he argues that the law has often been more effective than many social scientists at identifying and stigmatising racism is because the law has interpreted the meanings of 'colour, race, ethnic or national origins' in terms of their meaning to the general public. Consequently the law has been able to 'acknowledge that in different countries the general public varies in its use of the idea of race as a pointer to classification' and has also been able to acknowledge that the meaning of 'race' 'also changes over time' and changes in 'relation to other classifiers', such as ethnic group.[72] UK Race Relations law, whether through conscious choice or not, has followed the UNESCO observation that for 'most people, a race is any group of people whom they choose to describe as a race. Thus, many national, religious, geographic, linguistic or cultural groups have, in such loose usage, been called [a] "race".'[73]

Race Relations law and policy in the UK, and at an international level, acknowledges that racism takes different forms which change over time and are different in different countries. In the case of UK law and policy, this acknowledgement of different forms of racism is based on the understanding that the meaning of 'race' is subjective. UK law and policy, however, only recognises the shifting meaning of 'race' in relation to the identifying of a target group. (We shall go on to examine the problems presented by this limitation in the next chapter.) If UK Race Relations law and policy is flexible enough to acknowledge different forms of racism, and if the category of ethnic origins has been interpreted to also include religion as an important component of the ethnic identity of some ethnic groups, why was Race Relations law in Northern Ireland not extended to cover sectarianism as a form of racism? We will investigate this question in the next section.

Racism, sectarianism and exceptionalism

When the UK's Race Relations Act 1965 was enacted, it outlawed discrimination on the grounds of colour, 'race', ethnic or national origins. Significantly, however, it did not cover grounds of religion or belief and it only covered England, Wales and Scotland, not Northern Ireland. In the parliamentary debate that led to the Act, amendments were proposed to widen its scope to cover religious prejudice. A secret memorandum, written by the Secretary of State for the Home Department (the Home Office) and circulated to the Labour Cabinet, notes that some members of the Home Affairs Committee expressed a concern that

> [A] charge of racial discrimination might be met by the suggestion that the person in question was refused services, not on grounds of race, but because he was, for example, a Muslim; and that ... it would be expected that the provisions against incitement would protect religious as well as racial minorities.[74]

The memorandum indicates that politicians were aware that, in terms of everyday understandings, there was some overlap between 'race' and religious identification and that not including religion within the Act would provide a means for some people to evade prosecution. The Secretary of State rejected the inclusion of religious grounds, however, citing concerns about free speech and stating that he was 'anxious not to have to face a charge of preventing religious or political controversy except where a clear case for doing so can be made out'.[75]

The Cabinet minutes and memoranda do not indicate why Northern Ireland was excluded from the Act. Anthony Dickey investigated the background to the 1965 Act and found that the Stormont government requested that religion be excluded as grounds for prosecution under the Act, and that it not be extended to Northern Ireland.[76] McVeigh argues that this request was granted because 'it would be embarrassing to have anti-religious discrimination legislation everywhere in the UK other than the place where it was needed most'.[77] Whatever the reason, the exclusion of Northern Ireland from the Act has had several effects.

One consequence was the fact that the law was not available as a means of redress for the anti-Catholic discrimination that was prevalent in the region. The Campaign for Social Justice, a precursor to the Northern Ireland Civil Rights Association (NICRA), began its life as lobby group that petitioned the Stormont and Westminster governments and attempted to seek redress through formal legal and political channels. It found, however, that its attempts to do so were frustrated at every turn. When, for example, they contacted the UK Prime Minister in 1964 to complain about anti-Catholic discrimination in Northern Ireland, he wrote back to say that

> the matters you raise appear to be within the field of responsibility of the Parliament and Government of Northern Ireland, and are not, therefore, matters upon which the Prime Minister can properly comment. Nor is it possible for the Prime Minister to advise on the possibility of initiating legal proceedings in Northern Ireland.[78]

The failure to include the region in the 1965 Race Relations Act was in keeping with this general Westminster convention of deferring to Stormont in matters pertaining to Northern Ireland. The lack of legal redress was a contributory factor in the development of street protests and popular mobilisation as the approach to challenging discrimination in the region. In this regard, the exclusion of Northern Ireland from the Act was a contributory factor in the politicisation of the civil rights issue and the subsequent eruption of violence in the region.

One consequence of the exclusion of religion from the Act, at the request of Stormont, was the creating and maintaining of the distinction between racism and sectarianism. Once violence had escalated in the region, from 1968 onwards, the Westminster government continued to exclude a clause on religion (or religion as a criterion for acknowledging a 'racial group') and it did not extend the Act to cover Northern Ireland. Instead of extending the 1968 Race Relations Act, the Westminster government pressurised Stormont to adopt a Northern Ireland Community Relations Commission (NICRC) and a Minister for Community Relations.[79] Although the former was modelled on the Community Relations Commission, established under the 1968 Act, this was the only element of the Act that was drawn upon. When the Race Relations Act was updated in 1976, religion was again excluded, and again the Act was not extended to Northern Ireland. Instead, a Northern Ireland Fair Employment Agency was established to provide redress against employment discrimination on religious grounds.[80]

If Northern Ireland is widely considered to be exceptional, it is not solely due to factors internal to the region. The exemption of Northern Ireland from Race Relations legislation in the 1960s and 1970s, and the deliberate exclusion of religion as a criterion from the Acts, are two obvious ways in which political decisions made in Westminster made Northern Ireland different, and thus acted to further bolster the perception of Northern Ireland as exceptional. This has consequences not just for this small part of the UK, but for the whole of the UK. It is notable that, with very few exceptions, the literature on racism in the UK skirts around Northern Ireland. The highly influential, radical left Centre for Contemporary Cultural Studies (CCCS), for example, included Northern Ireland as a factor in the crisis of the British state in the late 1960s and the 1970s, but this factor is not explored in any depth.[81] Paul Gilroy, a leading figure in CCCS, noted that the police in England made extensive comparisons between the policing of the Black population of England and the policing of Catholics in Northern Ireland. Instead of pursuing this, however, he says that the 'fact that these parallels are constantly drawn should not be taken to signify that the six counties supply another laboratory from which control techniques can be transplanted. This has a conspiratorial ring and could obscure the obvious differences between police operations there and on the mainland.'[82] Robert Miles's observation in relation to Scotland that '[a]lmost without exception, analyses of the expression of racism in Britain refer in fact only to England' has been even more true with regard to Northern Ireland.[83] It is our contention that the understanding of racism in the UK is poorer because of the exclusion of the part of the UK state where discrimination against a sizeable racialised minority (Catholics) has been long-standing and extensive. The study of state policy on racism in the UK would benefit from comparative studies of different parts of the UK, and from treating policy on sectarianism in Northern Ireland as part of this analysis.

Conclusion

In this chapter we have explored some of the conceptual difficulties involved in trying to distinguish between racism and sectarianism. Geoghegan's attempt to distinguish between the two suffers from the fact that it relies on a denotive meaning of racism, which does not directly correspond to how the term racism is used in practice in the media, policy documents or the criminal justice system in contemporary Northern Ireland, the UK or the Republic of Ireland. Brewer's attempt to distinguish the two is limited by its narrow definition of racism as colour-based. One consequence of these narrow definitions is that they cannot be applied to discrimination against White East Europeans, the largest immigrant population in contemporary Northern Ireland. If we reformulate McVeigh's question 'is sectarianism racism?' to instead ask 'is sectarianism a *form* of racism, as defined within Race Relations law and policy in the UK?' then the answer is 'yes'. Racism does take different forms, in different countries, at different times in history, for different racialised groups and in different parts of the same country. Some of the confusions that have dogged the discussion of racism and sectarianism can be avoided if we think of sectarianism as being a form of racism and if we think of racism not as a singular phenomenon, but as taking many different forms.

We also explored McVeigh's examination of the inconsistencies in the application of the definition of 'racial group' in Race Relations law and racial equality policy. These inconsistencies are, in part, due to the attempt to maintain the convenient fiction of Northern Irish exceptionalism. Acceptance of this exceptionalism in the academic field of ethnic and racial studies has prevented academics and activists from asking more searching questions about the nature of the UK state. McVeigh does a good job of pointing to ways in which the term 'ethnic' facilitates attempts to examine sectarianism as a form of racism. The term 'ethnic' has played a role in challenging the idea that there is an objective, biological basis to 'race'. Its reliance on subjective understandings of 'race', however, presents its own problems. In the next chapter we will explore the Race Relations approach in more detail.

Notes

1 Duncan Morrow, 'Foreword', in *A good relations framework: an approach to the development of good relations* (Belfast: Community Relations Council, 2004), 5.
2 McVeigh, 'Sectarianism in Northern Ireland', 5.
3 Geoghegan, *A difficult difference*, 4.
4 Brewer, 'Sectarianism and racism', 359.
5 Geoghegan, *A difficult difference*, 5.
6 'Celtic shirts spark racist attack on Polish family', *Belfast News Letter*, 24 May 2006; 'Poles forced to flee home', *Derry Journal*, 23 May 2006.
7 Robbie McVeigh, 'Is sectarianism racism? Theorising the racism/sectarianism interface', in *Rethinking Northern Ireland*, ed. David Miller (Harlow: Longman, 1998), 184.
8 James Walvin, *Questioning slavery* (London: Routledge, 1996); Basil Davidson, *The African slave trade* (London: Back Bay, rev. edn, 1980).
9 W. E. B. du Bois, *The souls of black folk* (Philadelphia, PA: Pennsylvania State University, 1902); Douglas S. Massey and Nancy A. Denton, *American apartheid: segregation and the making of the underclass* (Cambridge, MA: Harvard University Press, 1994); Thomas C. Holt, *The problem of race in the 21st century* (Cambridge, MA: Harvard University Press, 2001).
10 Daryl Glaser, *Politics and society in South Africa* (London: Sage, 2001).

11 Ronald Takaki, *Strangers from a different shore: a history of Asian Americans* (Boston: Little Brown, rev. edn, 1998); Erika Lee, 'The "Yellow Peril" and Asian exclusion in the Americas', *Pacific Historical Review* 76.4 (2007): 537–562; Sean Brawley, *The White Peril: foreign relations and Asian immigration to Australasia and North America, 1919–1978* (Sydney: University of New South Wales Press, 1995).

12 Jane Samson, *Race and empire* (Harlow: Pearson, 2005); Hugh Tinker, *Race, conflict and the international order: from empire to United Nations* (London: Macmillan, 1977); Paul Gordon Lauren, *Power and prejudice: politics and diplomacy of racial discrimination* (Boulder, CO: Westview Press, 1988).

13 George M. Fredrickson, *Racism: a short history* (Princeton, NJ: Princeton University Press, 2002); Neil MacMaster, *Racism in Europe: 1870–2000* (Basingstoke: Palgrave Macmillan, 2001).

14 Ben Pitcher, *Consuming race* (Abingdon: Routledge, 2014); Kheven Lee LaGrone, 'From minstrelsy to gangstar rap: the "nigger" as commodity for popular American entertainment', *Journal of African American Men* 5.2 (2000): 117–131.

15 Lei Guo and Summer Harlow, 'User-generated racism: an analysis of stereotypes of African Americans, Latinos, and Asians in YouTube videos', *Howard Journal of Communications* 25.3 (2014): 281–302; David Parker and Miri Song, 'Ethnicity, social capital and the Internet: British Chinese websites', *Ethnicities* 6.2 (2006): 178–202; Lisa Nakamura, *Digitizing race: visual cultures of the Internet* (Minneapolis: University of Minnesota Press, 2008).

16 Ludi Simpson, '"Race" statistics: theirs and ours', *Radical Statistics* 79/80 (2002); Ann Morning, 'Ethnic classification in global perspective: a cross-national survey of the 2000 census round', *Population Research and Policy Review* 27.2 (2008): 239–272; Alastair Bonnett and Bruce Carrington, 'Fitting into categories or falling between them? Rethinking ethnic classification', *British Journal of Sociology of Education* 21.4 (2000): 487–500.

17 Stephen Jay Gould, *The mismeasure of Man* (London: Penguin, 1992); Geoffrey G. Field, 'Nordic racism', *Journal of the History of Ideas* 38.3 (1977): 523–540.

18 It was not Darwin but a sociologist, Herbert Spencer, who coined the term 'survival of the fittest'. Spencer was a key figure in Social Darwinism. His thinking on human evolution was initially influenced by Lamarck, not Darwin. See, for example, Derek Freeman et al., 'The evolutionary theories of Charles Darwin and Herbert Spencer', *Current Anthropology* 15.3 (2008): 211–237; Rutledge M. Dennis, 'Social Darwinism, scientific racism, and the metaphysics of race', *The Journal of Negro Education* 64 (1995): 243; Bernard Semmel, *Imperialism and social reform: English social-imperial thought 1895–1914* (New York: Anchor Books, 1968), 18–42.

19 Cited in Kenan Malik, *Strange fruit: why both sides are wrong in the race debate* (Oxford: Oneworld, 2008), 152.

20 Field, 'Nordic racism'; John Connelly et al., 'Nazis and Slavs: from racial theory to racist practice', *Central European History* 32.1 (1998): 61–63; Michael Burleigh and Wolfgang Wippermann, *The racial state: Germany 1939–1945* (Cambridge: Cambridge University Press, 1991); Dorothy M. Figueria, 'Aryan ancestors, pariahs and the lunatic fringe', *Comparative Civilizations Review* 25 (1991): 1–27.

21 Burleigh and Wippermann, *The racial state: Germany 1939–1945*, 43–51.

22   On different forms of racial science, see, for example, Gould, *The mismeasure of Man*; Malik, *Strange fruit;* Roland Littlewood and Maurice Lipsedge, *Aliens and alienists: ethnic minorities and psychiatry*, ed. Maurice Lipsedge (London and New York: Routledge, 3rd edn, 1997)

23   Littlewood and Lipsedge, *Aliens and alienists*; Gould, *The mismeasure of Man*; Malik, *Strange fruit.*

24   Brewer, 'Sectarianism and racism', 353.

25   Ibid., 360.

26   Paul Gilroy, *There ain't no black in the Union Jack* (Abingdon: Routledge, 2002).

27   See, for example, Christopher Kyriakides, Satnam Virdee and Tariq Modood, 'Racism, Muslims and the national imagination', *Journal of Ethnic and Migration Studies* 35.2 (2009): 289–308.

28   Steve Garner, 'A moral economy of whiteness: behaviours, belonging and Britishness', *Ethnicities* 12.4 (2012): 445–464. Kyriakides, Virdee and Modood found similar ambivalent views regarding Muslims in research carried out in Bristol and Glasgow. See Satnam Virdee, Christopher Kyriakides and Tariq Modood, 'Codes of cultural belonging: racialised national identities in a multi-ethnic Scottish neighbourhood', *Sociological Research Online* 11.4 (2006); Kyriakides, Virdee and Modood, 'Racism, Muslims and the national imagination'.

29   Connolly, *'Race' and racism in Northern Ireland*, 7.

30   Ibid.

31   Ibid., 5.

32   Ibid., 5–6.

33   For a range of different authors who operate within an ethnic conflict interpretation, see, for example, Fidelma Ashe. 'Gendering ethno-nationalist conflict in Northern Ireland: a comparative analysis of nationalist women's political protests', *Ethnic and Racial Studies* 30.5 (2007): 766–786; Steve Bruce, 'Victim selection in ethnic conflict: motives and attitudes in Irish republicanism', *Terrorism and Political Violence* 9.1 (1997): 56–71; Jocylean Evans and Jon Tonge, 'Unionist party competition and the Orange Order vote in Northern Ireland', *Electoral Studies* 26 (2007), 156–167; Donald L. Horowitz, 'Explaining the Northern Ireland Agreement: the sources of an unlikely constitutional consensus', *British Journal of Political Science* 32.2 (2002), 193–220; Neil Jarman, 'From outrage to apathy? The disputes over parades, 1995–2003', *The Global Review of Ethnopolitics* 3.1 (2003), 92–105; Cillian McGrattan, 'Learning from the past or laundering history? Consociational narratives and state intervention in Northern Ireland', *British Politics* 5.1 (2010): 92–113.

34   McVeigh, 'Is sectarianism racism?', 189.

35   Ibid., 188.

36   McVeigh, *Sectarianism in Northern Ireland.*

37   OFMDFM, *A racial equality strategy for Northern Ireland: 2005–2010*, 7.

38   McVeigh, *Sectarianism in Northern Ireland: towards a definition in law*, 3.

39   Steve Fenton, *Ethnicity* (Cambridge: Polity, 2nd edn, 2010), 12.

40   Peter J. Aspinall, 'Approaches to developing an improved cross-national understanding of concepts and terms relating to ethnicity and race', *International Sociology* 22.1 (2007): 41–70.

41 Douglas Hyde, 'The necessity for de-Anglicising Ireland', 1892, www.gaeilge.org/deanglicising.html (accessed 10 January 2017).

42 David Cannadine, *Ornamentalism: how the British saw their empire* (London: Penguin, 2001); Alastair Bonnett, 'How the British working class became white: the symbolic (re)formation of racialized capitalism', *Journal of Historical Sociology* 11.3 (1998): 316–340.

43 Robin Corey, 'Isn't it Romantic? Burke, Maistre, and conservatism', *Coreyrobin. com*, 2003, http://coreyrobin.com/2012/03/03/isnt-it-romantic-burke-maistre-and-conservatism/ (accessed 10 January 2017).

44 On the Romantic reaction to the Enlightenment and 'race', see Tzvetan Todorov, *Imperfect garden: the legacy of humanism* (Princeton, NJ: Princeton University Press, 2002); Kenan Malik, *The meaning of race: race, history and culture in Western society* (Basingstoke: Macmillan, 1996).

45 Elazar Barkan, *The retreat of scientific racism: changing conceptions of race in Britain and the United States between the world wars* (Cambridge: Cambridge University Press, 1992), 2.

46 Matthew Pratt Guterl, 'The new race consciousness: race, nation, and empire in American culture, 1910–1925', *Journal of World History* 10.2 (1999): 337.

47 Ibid., 350.

48 Barkan, *The retreat of scientific racism*, 3.

49 Quoted in ibid., 297.

50 Anthony Q. Hazard Jr, *Postwar anti-racism: the United States, UNESCO, and 'race', 1945–1968* (New York: Palgrave Macmillan, 2012).

51 UNESCO, *Four statements on the race question* (Paris: UNESCO, 1969), 31.

52 Ibid., 36.

53 Ibid.

54 UNESCO, Declaration on Race and Racial Prejudice (Paris: UNESCO, 1978).

55 Malik, *The meaning of race*, 156.

56 Robbie McVeigh, '"There's no racism because there's no black people here": racism and anti-racism in Northern Ireland', in *Divided society: ethnic minorities and racism in Northern Ireland*, ed. Paul Hainsworth (London: Pluto Press, 1998), 20.

57 McVeigh, 'Is sectarianism racism?', 185

58 Steve Garner, *Racisms* (London: Sage, 2010), 11; emphasis added.

59 EUMC, Allen and Nielsen, *Summary report on Islamophobia in the EU after 11 September 2001*.

60 Ruari Shaw Sutherland, 'Reductio ad Hitlerium: the "new racism" – a challenge for the anti-racist movement ?', *Concept* 3.2 (2012); Pnina Werbner, 'The translocation of culture: "community cohesion" and the force of multiculturalism in history', *The Sociological Review* 53.4 (2005): 745–768; Kenan Malik, *From fatwa to jihad: the Rushdie affair and its legacy* (London: Atlantic Books, 2009).

61 McGovern, *Countering terror or counter-productive?*; Nickels et al., *A comparative study of the representations of 'suspect' communities*.

62 Nickels et al., *A comparative study of the representations of 'suspect' communities*, 24.

63 L. Perry Curtis, *Apes and angels: the Irishman in Victorian caricature* (Newton Abbot: David & Charles, 1971), vii.

64 Ibid., 37.
65 See, for example, Theodore W. Allen, *The invention of the white race, volume 1: racial oppression and social control* (London: Verso, 1994); Steve Garner, *Racism in the Irish experience* (London: Pluto Press, 2004); Noel Ignatiev, *How the Irish became white* (London: Routledge, 1995).
66 McVeigh, 'Is sectarianism racism?', 185.
67 Les Back, *New ethnicities and urban culture: racisms and multiculture in young lives* (Abingdon: Routledge, 1996), 239.
68 Ibid.
69 Tariq Modood, Jan Dobbernack and Nasar Meer, 'Great Britain', in *Addressing tolerance and diversity discourses in Europe: a comparative overview of 16 European countries*, ed. Ricard Zapata-Barrero and Anna Triandafyllidou (Barcelona: CIDOB/GRITIM-UPF, 2012), 156–157.
70 Michael Banton, 'The race relations problematic', *British Journal of Sociology* 42.1 (1991): 119.
71 United Nations, Universal Declaration of Human Rights (1948). See also Article 14 of the European Convention on Human Rights (1950).
72 Banton, 'The race relations problematic', 125.
73 UNESCO, *Four statements on the race question*.
74 Secretary of State for the Home Department, *Racial discrimination and incitement to racial hatred* (London: HMG, 1965), 4.
75 Ibid.
76 Anthony Dickey, 'Anti-incitement legislation in Britain and Northern Ireland', *New Community* 1.2 (1972): 133–138.
77 McVeigh, 'Is sectarianism racism?', 179.
78 Cited in Gianluca De Fazio, 'Legal opportunity structure and social movement strategy in Northern Ireland and southern United States', *International Journal of Comparative Sociology* 53.1 (2012): 12.
79 Maurice Hayes, *Community relations and the role of the Community Relations Commission in Northern Ireland* (London: Runnymede Trust, 1972); Bill Rolston, 'Community politics', in *Northern Ireland: between civil rights and civil war*, ed. Liam O'Dowd, Bill Rolston and Mike Tomlinson (London: CSE Books, 1980).
80 Robert D. Osborne, 'Equality of opportunity and discrimination: the case of religion in Northern Ireland', *Administration* 29.4 (1981): 331–355.
81 CCCS, *Policing the crisis: mugging, the state, and law and order* (London: Macmillan, 1978).
82 Paul Gilroy, 'Police and thieves', in *The empire strikes back: race and racism in 70s Britain*, ed. Centre for Contemporary Cultural Studies (London: Hutchinson, 1982), 171.
83 Robert Miles and Lesley Muirhead, 'Racism in Scotland: a matter for further investigation', *Scottish Government Yearbook 1986* (1986): 108.

3

Racisms and the Race Relations approach

In August 2005 Frank Kakopa, his wife and his two children, aged 6 and 12, arrived at Belfast City Airport on a flight from Liverpool for a weekend holiday break. Kakopa and his family had previously lived in the Republic of Ireland, and now they lived near Liverpool. They wanted to visit Northern Ireland, a part of the UK they had not visited before. The family had booked a hire car and bed and breakfast accommodation in advance and were planning to visit the Giant's Causeway, one of Ireland's most famous tourist sites. Even though the flight was internal to the UK, Kakopa was stopped by officers from the UK Border and Immigration Agency (BIA). As he passed through the airport he was asked for proof of identity. He produced his UK driver's licence, the children's passports, a pay slip with his UK national insurance number and a bank statement. The immigration officials were not satisfied. They took him aside and questioned him further. They then separated him from his distraught wife and children and took him to another part of the airport. They kept saying to him 'Prove who you are'. He was then walked past his family and taken to a prison van and locked in the back with other detained men, all of whom were Black. The van was then driven more than twenty miles away to Maghaberry Prison. Once at the prison Kakopa was strip-searched and then locked in a cell with a convicted criminal. He asked for permission to call his family to let them know where he was. His request was denied. In fact, he was denied the right to make *any* phone call. He was detained in prison for two days and when he was released, without any charges having been brought against him, he was put on the street outside the prison and given a prisoner's pass so that he could get a bus back to Belfast.[1] Is Frank Kakopa's treatment at Belfast City Airport an example of racism? Kakopa is from Zimbabwe in southern Africa and, like all the other people he saw detained at the airport that day, is Black. Is the treatment of the other Black people, detained on the same day as Kakopa, also an example of racism?

In the previous chapter, we examined the question 'is sectarianism racism?' and we concluded that, within the framework of UK Race Relations policy, sectarianism can be considered to be *a form of* racism (the separation between the two in Northern Ireland has political roots, and this separation produces the inconsistencies that McVeigh highlights). We argued that it is useful to think in terms of *racisms*, as that allows us to acknowledge that racism takes different forms, and that sectarianism can be considered a form of racism. In this chapter we explore the question 'what is racism?' We do so through the prism of Race Relations theory and practice, because they constitute the dominant approach to tackling racism in the UK. We focus on the *conception of racism* that under-pins Race Relations policy and theory (in the next chapter we examine the Race Relations conception of anti-racism). Our analysis examines both UK Race Relations policy and Northern Ireland's specific policy. We do so for two main reasons: first, because policy in Northern Ireland is largely derived from the rest of the UK, and secondly, in order to challenge the tendency to treat Northern Ireland as exceptional.

The Race Relations (Northern Ireland) Order of 1997 was the first explicit extension of Race Relations policy to the region. We argue, however, that com-munity relations policy (which has a much longer history) is essentially a form of Race Relations policy. We draw on the work of scholars of sectarianism and other forms of racism in Northern Ireland and government policy on good rela-tions, community relations and Race Relations to substantiate this argument. In the first part of the chapter, we introduce Race Relations policy and theory. In the second part, we look at the issue of how to define racism and why we might need a definition of racism. In the third part, we focus on two key ways in which racism is conceptualised in Race Relations policy. In the fourth part, we focus on the conceptualisation of racism in Race Relations theory. We make this dis-tinction between policy and theory for the sake of clarity of presentation, rather than to present the idea that the two exist in isolation from each other. What we characterise as the Race Relations approach involves a close relationship between theory and policy.

The Race Relations approach

We use the term 'Race Relations approach' to refer to Race Relations policy, and the theories that inform and justify this policy. The first articulation of the Race Relations approach emerged at the time of the First World War in the city of Chicago. From its beginnings, it involved a practical policy dimension and an intellectual attempt to theorise Race Relations. Robert E. Park was a key figure in the development of the Chicago School of sociology and became one of the most influential figures in early US sociology. He also played a leading role in creating the Chicago Urban League, which was set up to assist Black migrant workers moving from the Deep South, where plantation slavery had been the dominant mode of agricultural production, to take up work in the growing industrial sector in Chicago. Park sought social, rather than biological, explanations for racism, and he advocated measures to improve relations between 'races'.[2] He warned of a developing Black racial consciousness in the USA and cautioned that the idea of White superiority was a danger to American society, and to international politics. In an article published in 1917, for example, he counselled:

> One of the best indices to the possibilities of increased racial friction is the Negro's own recognition of the universality of the white man's racial antipathy toward him … even before the Japanese-Russian conflict [of 1905], 'Ethiopianism' and the cry of 'Africa for the Africans' had begun to disturb the English in South Africa. It is said time and again that the dissatisfaction and unrest in India are accentuated by the results of this same war. There can be no doubt in the mind of any man who carefully reads American Negro journals that their rejoicing over the Japanese victory [in the Japanese-Russian conflict] sounded a very different note from that of the white American.[3]

In 1919, when 'race' riots broke out in Chicago, his warnings seemed prescient. The riots led to the formation of the Chicago Commission on Race Relations (CCRR), which was charged with investigating the cause of the riots and suggesting measures to prevent a repeat. One of Park's students, Charles Johnston, was the driving intellectual force behind the CCRR, and the key author of its report of 1922.[4]

Since the 1940s, Race Relations theory and policy has been further developed and internationalised, through the United Nations and within nation-states.[5] In the UK the Race Relations approach has been developed through think tanks, research centres, government legislation and national and local government policy.[6] The close relationship between Race Relations policy and theory has meant 'that in practice, researchers have been pulled in a variety of directions, by both political and academic pressures'.[7] There has been, for example, political pressure for academic research to 'be put to the service of policy, as though there was a consensus about ends, and the only questions which need to be researched were about means'.[8] Academic pressures have, to some extent, moderated this instrumentalist approach to the production of knowledge. Scholars who do not root their research findings in social science theory leave themselves open to the criticism that they lack intellectual independence and are simply lackeys of government.[9] The fact that social science is a competing set of perspectives on society, combined with the pressures for an intellectual defence of research, has generated considerable debate. This has involved debate between advocates of a Race Relations approach and their critics, but also debate *among* scholars who endorse a Race Relations approach. Consequently, scholars who employ the concept of 'race relations' do not necessarily agree with each other on some important conceptual issues.

There is considerable debate among advocates of a Race Relations approach about how to define basic terms, such as 'race', 'racism' or 'race relations'. Take, for instance, the question of whether sectarianism in Northern Ireland is a form of 'race relations'. In an article published in 1972, Robert Moore asked 'if the social relations of Northern Ireland, and especially the class relations modified by sectarianism, are, in fact, race relations', and on examining the evidence answered in the affirmative.[10] John Brewer, writing two decade later and using a different definition of 'race relations', disagreed. Brewer argues that sectarianism is better characterised as ethnic conflict. The boundary between the two 'groups', he says, is derived from 'each group possessing a belief in its own culture, common descent and identification'.[11] This boundary is 'socially marked by religion', rather than by phenotypical markers of difference such as skin colour, hence it is sectarian rather than 'racial'.[12] There is also disagreement about central issues, such as whether racisms can be eradicated or only managed. Michael Banton, for example, argues that in the debate over the drafting of the UN International Convention on the Elimination of Racial Discrimination (ICERD), there were two incompatible views on the nature of 'racial' discrimination. In the first conception, 'racial discrimination was an outward form or manifestation of a pathological internal condition produced by a certain kind of social structure. It was restricted to particular historical and geographical circumstances, and there-fore could be eliminated.'[13] In the second, 'racial discrimination was a normal characteristic of social relations ... Official action could reduce it ... but it would not eliminate discrimination.'[14]

Northern Ireland did not explicitly adopt UK Race Relations policy until 1997, but the region has tended to shadow developments in the rest of the UK, though in veiled forms specifically adapted to Northern Irish conditions. In the previous chapter we noted that one of the UK government's responses to the outbreak of serious social unrest in Northern Ireland in 1969 was to pressurise the Unionist government in Stormont to adopt a Minister for Community Relations and a Northern Ireland Community Relations Commission, the latter of which was modelled on the Community Relations Commission established under the 1968 UK Race Relations Act. We also noted that when the UK Race Relations Act was updated in 1976, religion was again excluded, and again the Act was not extended to Northern Ireland. Instead, a Northern Ireland Fair Employment Agency was established to provide redress against employment discrimination on religious grounds – in parallel with the anti-discrimination provisions that had been introduced in the rest of the UK.

This link is acknowledged by Hugh Frazer and Mari Fitzduff in a report that contributed to the revival of community relations policy in the 1980s. In that report they note that:

> The term community relations seems to have been coined around the early sixties in Britain and pertained to solutions being sought there in relation to the problem of racial disharmony, apparently arising from the immigration of various African and Asian peoples to the United Kingdom. Earlier definitions of the objectives of com-munity relations seem to have primarily concerned themselves with emphasising the idea of a harmonious existence between differing groups, with the intended goal

of integrating minority groups into the wider community as quickly as possible. Later definitions of objectives have put a far greater emphasis on the idea of equality of basic rights and opportunity for all groups, whilst simultaneously encouraging cultural diversity.[15]

The merging of Race Relations and community relations into the policy area of good relations in the twenty-first century implicitly acknowledges the close affinity between race and community relations policy.

Despite the variety of forms of policy and disagreement between scholars, it is possible to talk about a Race Relations approach. All of the scholars and policy actors who advocate this approach take social interactions between 'races' as their central focus (we will go on to see that examining relations between 'races' does not necessarily involve accepting the idea that humanity is composed of biologically distinct 'races'). The leading intellectual advocates of a Race Relations approach adopt what Michael Banton refers to as a Kantian epistemology, rather than a Hegelian one (we will elaborate on this distinction in Chapter 5).[16] The leading scholars of the Race Relations approach also believe that theory has a role to play in helping government to tackle racism. Banton, for example, is a pioneer of Race Relations theory in the UK. He founded, and was the director for almost a decade, of the Social Science Research Council's Research Unit on Ethnic Relations at Bristol University. He later went on to serve as a member of the United Nations Committee on the Elimination of Racial Discrimination. Paul Connolly is a Professor of Education at Queen's University in Belfast, and has written a number of influential reports on racism and sectarianism for government in Northern Ireland. He has served as chairperson of the Ministerial Advisory Group on Advancing Shared Education for the Department of Education Northern Ireland.

Defining racism

We might expect that if a government wants to tackle a social problem, or if scholars want to research a particular social phenomenon, they should start by defining the problem that they want to tackle or phenomenon that they want to research. This, however, has not been the case with sectarianism. In the words of Robbie McVeigh, sectarianism has been under-theorised in the academic literature on Northern Ireland. Academics who gained research funding to investigate the conflict, he says, 'were tied very firmly to the British State's (non-)definition of sectarianism. This allowed for little more than exercises in sectarian headcounting.'[17] The Committee for the Administration of Justice (CAJ) (a Belfast-based human rights and civil liberties pressure group) has highlighted the lack of a definition of sectarianism as a problem. In a written submission (dated March 2004) to the Westminster-based Hate Crime in

Northern Ireland Inquiry, the CAJ noted that 'the most common hate crime in Northern Ireland (sectarian motivated crime or incidents) has not been formally recorded or monitored to date, and the PSNI is only now consulting on definitions'.[18] In a subsequent (undated) submission to the inquiry, the CAJ urged that 'It is vital, if sectarian hate crime is to be tackled effectively, that there be clear definitions that allow for effective monitoring, recording and investigation.'[19] The policing representatives called to the inquiry were grilled about the lack of a definition. The final report of the inquiry was scathing when it stated that 'Nothing could illustrate the dysfunction of Northern Ireland society better than the absence, until recently, of an agreed, official definition of sectarian hate crime.'[20]

The government, and state agencies such as the PSNI, need a definition of sectarianism (and of racism) in order to be able to demonstrate that they are tackling the problem. A sense of nervousness about a lack of an agreed definition of sectarianism is evident in a number of documents. The document used to monitor the implementation of the good relations policy states that 'Sectarianism, whilst not clearly defined, is a term almost exclusively used in incidents of bigoted dislike or hatred of members of a different religious or political group.'[21] In a consultation document on good relations, produced in 2013, the government defined sectarianism as 'threatening, abusive or insulting behaviour or attitudes towards a person by reason of that person's religious belief or political opinion; or to an individual as a member of such a group'.[22] The provisional nature of this definition, however, is signalled in the same paragraph when the government says that it 'will seek to find an appropriate consensus around a definition of sectarianism'.[23]

The authors of the *Racial Equality Strategy* were more fortunate. The police had been monitoring racial incidents since the extension of the UK's Race Relations Act to Northern Ireland in 1998, and a range of different definitions of racism were available that they could work from. They chose to cut and paste a definition of racism from the UNESCO Declaration of 1978, which states that the term racism refers to

> Any theory which involves the claim that racial or ethnic groups are inherently superior or inferior, thus implying that some would be entitled to dominate or eliminate others, presumed to be inferior, or which base value judgements on racial differentiation, has no scientific foundation and is contrary to the moral and ethical principle of humanity. Racism includes racist ideologies, prejudiced attitudes, discriminatory behaviour, structural arrangements and institutionalised practices resulting in racial inequality as well as the fallacious notion that discriminatory relations between groups are morally and scientifically justifiable; it is reflected in discriminatory provisions in legislation or regulations and discriminatory practices as well as in anti-social beliefs and acts; it hinders the development of its victims, perverts those who practise it, divides nations internally, impedes international

co-operation and gives rise to political tensions between peoples; it is contrary to the fundamental principles of international law and, consequently, seriously disturbs international peace and security.[24]

Definitions such as this lead Garner to argue that 'the complexity of racism … [means that it] cannot easily be reduced to a formula of the type "racism is…"'.[25] The UNESCO definition identifies five aspects of racisms. First, racism is a *theory* that humanity is composed of racial or ethnic groups that are inherently superior or inferior. Secondly, racism *includes* various features (racist ideologies, prejudiced attitudes, discriminatory behaviour, structural arrangements and institutionalised practices). Thirdly, these features *produce* racial inequality and the false idea that science and morality provide justifications for racial discrimination. Fourthly, racism is *reflected* (manifested or expressed) in society in various ways (discriminatory provisions in legislation or regulations, discriminatory practices and anti-social beliefs and acts). Fifthly, racism has some *effects* (impacts or consequences) on the victims (it hinders their development), on those who practice racism (it perverts them), on nations (it divides them internally), on international cooperation (it impedes it) and on relations between peoples (it gives rise to political tensions).

If we look at the case of Frank Kakopa we can see that some of these aspects of racism were evident in his treatment by UK immigration officials. Kakopa claimed that 'only Black African passengers were stopped and checked and that no Caucasian persons were subjected to the same or similar treatment as him'.[26] If Kakopa's claim is correct then the BIA officials were guilty of discriminatory behaviour. An investigation by the Northern Ireland Human Rights Commission (NIHRC) found evidence that many immigration officials made decisions about who to take aside for more rigorous questioning based 'on "feeling", "suspicion" and, in some cases, stereotyped views about certain nationalities'.[27] The evidence from the NIHRC shows cases of prejudiced attitudes and it also suggests that not only is Kakopa's claim correct, but that the discriminatory behaviour he was subjected to may be an example of institutionalised practice. The BIA's chief inspector, Elwyn Soutter, told reporters that his officers 'question everyone, but inevitably EU citizens can quickly satisfy us. It is not terribly surprising to find it is people who are black or of other ethnicities who are detained.'[28] Soutter denied that immigration officials practise discrimination, but admitted that their actions did result in racial inequality in outcome. The blocking of Kakopa's visit to Northern Ireland and his detention had the negative effects of humiliating and degrading him. From this, we can see that the UNESCO definition has its uses. It enables us to check any incident against the list of criteria laid out in the definition. It is, however, about as useful for helping us to *understand* racism as a shopping list is for helping us to understand shopping.

The UNESCO definition allows the Northern Ireland government to develop a set of indicators that it can use to monitor the extent of racism in society. The definition, however, has only a very limited use in the development of an understanding of racism. Steve Garner points out that the kind of definition provided by UNESCO tells us nothing about the relative importance of any of the aspects of racism listed, and it tells us very little about the relationship between the different aspects.[29] In Chapter 1 we noted that Paul Connolly (like UNESCO) used a definition that treats racism as an umbrella term that refers to a broad range of things – ideas, beliefs, actions, customs, practices and policies. In Connolly's definition, however, the *outcome* of actions is key to understanding racism. In other words, he gives greater significance to this particular aspect of his definition.

Banton points to three other complications that face any attempt to develop definitions for the study of racism. The first is the issue of case selection; the second is the purpose for which the definitions are used; and the third is the epistemological approach taken by the researcher. Banton says that ordinary everyday use of definitions involves 'a form of argument from the paradigm case'.[30] Dictionary definitions, for example, take this approach. A paradigm case is a clear and unambiguous case, such as the brutal (sectarian) attack on James Turley or the intimidating (racist) attack on the Awoyelu family home mentioned in Chapter 1, that illustrates the definition. Banton warns, however, that in social science it 'may be better to start from what may be thought borderline cases'.[31] When we used the example of the attack on the Polish family in Derry/Londonderry in the previous chapter, we were using a 'borderline case' in the sense that Banton uses the term. Using this attack as an example against which to test Geoghegan's and Brewer's definitions enabled us to point out that what appears to many people to be clear and unambiguous – the difference between racism and sectarianism – is not always clear and unambiguous. If the definitions that we use conflict with the reality that we are trying to describe, then this indicates that there is a problem with the definition that we are using.

The second issue, the purposes to which definitions are being put, is a problem in the study of any area of social life, such as racism and sectarianism, where there is significant interplay between policy and theory. The way that the terms 'racism' and 'sectarianism' are defined by organisations operating in the realm of Race Relations policy are not necessarily useful as definitions in Race Relations theory. Banton points out that 'the expressions racism, sexism, anti-Semitism, and Islamophobia have important uses in political contexts, especially for victim groups. They find these expressions empowering because they offer a vocabulary for criticizing those who discriminate against them and encourage sentiments of solidarity among members of their groups.'[32] McVeigh points to the political use of definitions in Northern Ireland when he says that 'For different reasons, many actors – including the British government and minority ethnic communities in Northern Ireland – would prefer to separate racism and sectarianism, analytically and practically.'[33] In the previous chapter, we noted that the British government has made political use of definitions as part of a broader attempt to keep Northern Ireland as 'a place apart'. We also noted that the government in Northern Ireland also made political use of definitions. The *Racial Equality Strategy*, for example, clumsily includes Islamophobia, anti-Semitism and sedentarism as examples of racism, while specifically excluding sectarianism from its definition. McVeigh argues that the interests of government and racialised minorities converge on the issue of distinguishing between racism and sectarianism. This distinction has been encouraged in various ways, by organisations representing racialised minorities, as 'part of the struggle for minority ethnic people to forge a distinctive place for themselves in Northern Ireland alongside the dominant sectarian blocs'.[34]

The third issue, the epistemological approach taken by the researcher, is fundamental to social science as a field of knowledge. Banton distinguishes two distinctly different approaches to understanding the social world: one that we can trace back to the German Enlightenment philosopher Emmanuel Kant, the other to a second German Enlightenment philosopher, Georg W. F. Hegel. Conventional social science, including the academic study of racisms, is largely derived from the Kantian approach to epistemology. We shall explore further the distinction between the Kantian approach of conventional social science and the Hegelian-inspired approach of Marxists in Chapter 5.

Racism and Race Relations policy

Racisms are commonly associated with prejudice. In Northern Ireland, the association between racisms and prejudice can be seen in documents produced by a diverse range of organisations. We can see it in government documents and policy, in literature produced by organisations mandated by government to tackle racism, in the work of academic researchers, and in the work of non-governmental campaign groups.[35] In the Northern Ireland government's *A Shared Future* document, for example, the first policy objective that is outlined is to 'eliminate sectarianism, racism and all forms of prejudice'.[36] In the *Programme for Cohesion, Sharing and Integration*, a consultation document aimed at updating the Shared Future policy, the government says that it will work 'directly with a reinvigorated Racial Equality Forum and other stakeholder groups ... To tackle the visible manifestations of racism, sectarianism intolerance and other forms of prejudice.'[37] One of the key aims outlined in the CSI programme is to promote 'Zero tolerance for crimes motivated by prejudice and all forms of hate crime'.[38] The importance that Race Relations policy (and sectarianism-focused community relations policy) attaches to prejudice can also be seen in the Good Relations Indicators that were drawn up by civil servants as a means of monitoring both the extent of racisms in Northern Ireland and their changes over time. Of the twelve indicators, three are explicit indicators of prejudice and two others are implicit indicators of prejudice.[39] The view that prejudice is the problem can also be seen in the emphasis that anti-racist policy places on education and training as means to tackle racisms.[40]

Race Relations policy acknowledges prejudice as a significant factor, but there are different ways in which prejudice is considered to play a role in racisms. In this section we look at two of these: the idea that prejudice causes racist behaviour and practices, and the idea that prejudice is only one element and that its significance depends on wider environmental or institutional factors.

Prejudice and racisms

The notion that prejudice is the underlying problem – it is at the root of racisms – is expressed in many of the documents produced by government and anti-racist organisations. In this view, actions such as discrimination or violent assaults are *manifestations* of these prejudices. It is not just obvious examples of racisms, such as the violent attack on James Turley, the smashing up of the Polish family's home in Derry/Londonderry, or the attack on the Awoyelu family home. Other, more subtle forms of racism are also considered to arise from prejudice. Colin Knox, in a study of the effectiveness of the *Race Equality Strategy*, argues that attitudinal questions which ask directly about prejudice, such as 'How prejudiced are you against other ethnic groups?', 'underestimate the extent of racism in Northern Ireland because respondents are unwilling to admit to being prejudiced or racist, as this is a socially undesirable viewpoint'.[41] He argues that questions on social distance, such as 'Would you accept people from other ethnic groups as colleagues?' (or friends, or relatives by marriage), are a more reliable measure of racial prejudice. Social distance questions indicate whether people are willing to have meaningful contact with ethnic minorities. These questions point to less blatant forms of behaviour, such as social avoidance of ethnic minorities, which can result in racialised minorities feeling socially isolated or unwelcome in their local community. The implicit assumption in these questions, however, is that this behaviour is motivated by prejudice.

Frank Kakopa complained to the Commission for Racial Equality (CRE) that his treatment by the BIA was an example of racism. The CRE agreed and referred his case to the Equality Commission for Northern Ireland (ECNI).[42] Eileen Lavery, head of enforcement at the ECNI, thought that his treatment was racist. She told the BBC that Kakopa had an enormous amount of documentation which demonstrated his status as a tax-paying UK resident, so 'Why pick on him? Other than I think because he is black.'[43] Kakopa told the ECNI that only Black African passengers were stopped.[44] The argument that the BIA officers who only stopped and checked Black African passengers must have been motivated by racial prejudice is plausible. The fact that they detained Kakopa despite his valid proof of identification suggests wilful disregard for him as a human being and significant prejudice against, and distrust of, Black Africans. The 'racism is prejudice' explanation is plausible, but it is not the only plausible explanation for the actions of the BIA officials.

The BIA argued that just because the outcome of their actions appeared to be racist, it did not mean that the actions of their officers were an example of racism. The wrongful detention of Frank Kakopa, they argued, was a mistake, not an example of racism. In the view of the BIA the outcome was a result of the fact that Black people are much more likely to be illegal immigrants, not of racism on the part of the BIA. The BIA's chief inspector, Elwyn Soutter, said: 'We are detecting 800 to 900 illegal immigrants a year … We occasionally get our facts wrong, but that is an inevitable by-product' of the detection process.[45] He said that 'It is not terribly surprising to find it is people who are black or of other ethnicities who are detained' because, unlike EU citizens, they were unable to demonstrate their right to be in the UK.[46] The BIA agreed an out-of-court settlement, in which it apologised to Kakopa for 'the significant injury to his feelings and the hurt and distress he suffered' and accepted that he had been 'unlawfully and falsely imprisoned'.[47] The BIA did not accept a charge of racism. In fact, it told the ECNI that it was committed 'to equality of opportunity and the elimination of unlawful discrimination on the grounds of colour, race, nationality or ethnic or national origins'.[48]

The counter-argument advanced by the BIA, that its officers are not racist, is also plausible. The idea that Black Africans are more likely than White Europeans to be illegal immigrants is not a prejudice, it is a fact. One retort to the BIA could be 'Well you would deny racism, wouldn't you?' The BIA was hardly likely to admit to racism. The fact that it paid compensation to Kakopa, rather than go to court, indicates that it knew it was likely to be found guilty. This is also plausible, but BIA could respond by saying that 'The compensation was for wrongful imprisonment. We took a gamble in making the out of court offer to Mr Kakopa, because the courts might have granted him a smaller amount, or they could have penalised us more harshly. We were guilty of wrongful imprisonment. We weren't guilty of racism.' This is typical of the kinds of arguments that go back and forth in a case where an individual or organisation stands accused of a racist crime. The view that prejudiced attitudes lead to racist behaviour persistently faces a problem in the courts, because the prejudice motivation has to be proven. In court, it is often difficult to prove prejudiced motivation.

The view that prejudice lies at the root of racism also raises the question, 'Where does this prejudice come from?' If racial prejudice is inherent to us as human beings, then we would expect all White people in Northern Ireland to be prejudiced against Black people, but this is not the case. We know that it is not the case because attitude data shows it and because intermarriage, and other forms of intimate social interaction between Black and White people, shows it. Prejudiced views must come from somewhere, but they are not innate. Colin Knox suggests that prejudiced views are stoked up by some political elites who attempt to scapegoat immigrants for problems in Northern Irish society. As he puts it:

> Some politicians have called for 'local jobs for local people' and accused minority ethnic representative groups of whipping up hysteria to attract greater funding … The most likely predictor of racist attitudes is how people perceive the role of migrant workers in the Northern Ireland economy. The mantra 'local jobs for local people' merely reinforces the notion, particularly during a recession, that migrants are 'taking' local jobs and, in turn, contributes to racist attitudes.[49]

Prejudices against ethnic minorities or immigrants are often a response to genuine concerns and real-world problems, such as rising unemployment. They are prejudices because they mis-identify the source of the problems, but they are not innate prejudices. They are a *reaction* to something external to the individual psyche of the person expressing the prejudice. If we want to understand racism, we need to understand why social issues such as unemployment or a shrinking welfare budget become interpreted in racial terms.

The contexts of racisms

Dissatisfaction with the view that individual prejudice leads to racism has led to a shift in Race Relations policy towards highlighting the broader context in which racist acts take place. The watershed was the inquiry into the Metropolitan Police Service's (MPS) handling of the murder of Stephen Lawrence. The inquiry, led by Lord Macpherson, concluded that the MPS investigation into the murder of the Black teenager involved 'fundamental errors. The investigation was marred by a combination of professional incompetence, institutional racism and a failure of leadership by senior officers. A flawed MPS review failed to expose these inadequacies.'[50] The report of the inquiry led to the passing of an Act that extended 'further the application of the Race Relations Act 1976 to the police and other public authorities'.[51] The purpose of extending the Act to the police and other public authorities was to help tackle what Macpherson described as 'institutional racism' in public life. The term 'institutional racism' has a range of different uses.[52] Underlying all of these, as Paul Connolly puts it, is 'a desire to challenge the belief that racism was essentially an individual phenomenon borne out of individual prejudice. Rather, the aim of those who used the term was to focus attention on the discriminatory effects of institutions and broader social structures.'[53]

The 'institutional racism' understanding does not deny that prejudice exists, or that it has a role to play in racism; rather it suggests that prejudice is not the only factor involved. Jenny Bourne summarises this view neatly in her critical discussion of the use of the term 'institutional racism' in the report of the Stephen Lawrence inquiry. '[I]f you work in an organisation,' she says,

> whose structures, culture and procedures are racist, it is inevitable that individuals who work there should be contaminated by such racism. The converse, though, is

not necessarily true: individuals who are prejudiced cannot, merely by virtue of their attitude, contaminate the organisation – unless they are allowed to act out their prejudice in discriminatory ways.[54]

In other words, prejudice, in and of itself, does not lead to racist action. The prejudiced person also has to inhabit an environment that enables them to act on their prejudice.

In the years since the report of the Stephen Lawrence inquiry was published, the idea that racisms require a conducive environment in order for prejudice to be translated into action has become central to UK government approaches to understanding racism (and is found in the Northern Ireland government's approach to tackling racism and sectarianism). It is an understanding, however, that is not confined to government. Richard Montague and Peter Shirlow, for example, in a report for the United Against Hate campaign, argue that people's concerns about scarce resources in times of austerity are genuine, but if anti-immigrant rhetoric about migrants 'taking our jobs' becomes socially acceptable then 'perpetrators of hate crime can feel that it is therefore "OK" to attack newcomers to Northern Ireland'.[55] The idea that racism and sectarianism have become socially acceptable also underlies Duncan Morrow's description of Northern Ireland as 'a criminally hating society'.[56]

Joseph Liechty and Celia Clegg use the concept of 'systemic sectarianism' in a similar way to the concept of 'institutional racism', in the sense that they use the concept to draw attention to the environment that facilitates sectarianism. They argue that sectarianism does not just involve prejudice, it is also enabled by 'our sane and rational responses', such as movement away from areas of mixed housing to exclusively Catholic or Protestant areas to avoid sectarian violence.[57] During the violent conflict in Northern Ireland thousands of people moved away from 'mixed' residential areas to live alongside co-religionists, not because they were motivated by prejudice against people of a different religion, but from a desire to live in a safer environment. The effect of these rational responses, however, is to further entrench division. Liechty and Clegg argue that in a context in which there are high levels of segregated housing, schooling and leisure activities it only requires a few prejudiced people to sustain sectarianism as a system. Challenging sectarianism, they suggest, requires a conscious effort from society. As they put it: 'sectarianism does not really require any direct, active response at all from most of us, it simply requires that we do nothing about it'.[58]

A similar idea, of sane and rational responses contributing to racisms, is articulated in the idea of 'unwitting racism' that was a central part of the Macpherson Inquiry report. The report, for example, argues that racism 'can arise from well intentioned but patronising words or actions. It can arise from unfamiliarity with the behaviour or cultural traditions of people or families from minority ethnic communities.'[59] Quintin Oliver and Paul McGill, in a report for the

ECNI, point out that the claim that an organisation treats everyone equally is not an adequate defence against a charge of institutional racism. Macpherson, they say, 'was clear that a "colour blind" response is flawed because it fails to take account of the nature and needs of the people involved'.[60] In this understanding of racisms, being impartial is not good enough; we need to be sensitive to the different cultural needs and understandings of different ethnic and racial groups if we are to go beyond institutional racism. In this view, institutions have to be proactive and consciously reflect on their own actions and processes if they are to eliminate racisms. Or, to put it in the terms of Liechty and Clegg, all that institutional racism requires for its survival is that we do nothing about it. In this view, tackling racisms requires eternal vigilance and critical institutional self-reflection.

This institutional, structural or systemic explanation for racisms now informs the Northern Ireland government's discussion of racism and sectarianism. When attempting to explain the roots of racism and sectarianism in the *Shared Future* document, the authors point out that 'the area that now comprises Northern Ireland has been deeply divided along sectarian lines over centuries – regardless of whether paramilitaries have been active'.[61] In doing so, the drafters of the document are suggesting that paramilitary violence is symptomatic of sectarian division, rather than its cause. The document then goes on to say that the problem is not fundamentally one of inequality between Catholics and Protestants, because 'since the civil rights movement of the 1960s the opportunity gap has, rightly, been narrowed – yet communal polarisation remains undiminished'.[62] This phrase is a reference to the argument that discrimination against Catholics in Northern Ireland, in the allocation of jobs, housing, job promotion and other societal resources, was what led to the civil rights movement of the late 1960s and subsequently to the Troubles. After dismissing paramilitaries and inequality as explanatory factors, the document goes on to say that the 'underlying difficulty is a culture of intolerance, which we will need to remedy if we are to make Northern Ireland a more "normal" society'.[63]

The Macpherson Inquiry's understanding of institutional racism led to three significant changes in the approach of Race Relations that are relevant to Frank Kakopa's case. First, it gave a more prominent role to the concept of a 'racial incident'. Secondly, it introduced a new term of 'unwitting racism'. Thirdly, it placed an onus on institutions to be proactive in tackling institutional racism. Regarding the first of these, the inquiry led to police forces, including the PSNI, adopting the definition of a racist incident as 'any incident which is perceived to be racist by the victim or any other person'.[64] It also recommended that 'the term "racist incident" must be understood to include crimes and non-crimes in policing terms. Both must be reported, recorded and investigated with equal commitment.'[65] (We will explore the implications of this change in more detail in the chapter on hate crime.) Frank Kakopa perceived his treatment to be racist, as did the CRE and the ECNI. Consequently, his treatment by the BIA should be recorded as a racial incident by the PSNI, even if the PSNI do not believe that an actual crime took place.

The second change in Race Relations policy prompted by the Macpherson Inquiry was the introduction of the term 'unwitting racism' to draw attention to ways in which institutions can act in a racist manner, despite the best intentions of their personnel. Macpherson stressed that, because racism is often unwitting, it 'is incumbent upon every institution to examine their policies and the outcome of their policies and practices to guard against disadvantaging any section of our communities'.[66] This approach to understanding Race Relations led Paul Connolly, in his summary of the literature on racism, to stress that 'it is the outcomes of particular activities that are important rather than whether those responsible for such activities intentionally mean to discriminate or not'.[67] From this perspective, we can say that because the outcome of the BIA's actions was that only Black Africans were detained, the BIA was guilty of institutional racism.

The third change prompted by the inquiry was to place the onus on public bodies to be proactive in tackling institutional racism. As Oliver and McGill put it, 'A far more radical, top-to-bottom approach is implied by Macpherson, often involving a total change in organisational culture and always requiring a concerted anti-racism programme and a review of all services in partnership with minority ethnic groups.'[68] This onus on public bodies might help to explain why, as part of the outcome of the Frank Kakopa case, the BIA agreed to meet with the ECNI 'to discuss its practices and procedures to ensure that immigration officers working in Northern Ireland comply fully with the Race Relations Order'.[69]

The 'institutional racism' approach, with its emphasis on the environment that enables racisms to be produced, appears to be an advance on the 'racism is prejudice' approach. It allows us to acknowledge that racialised minorities can be disadvantaged even in cases where the intention is not to do so (because of the unwitting nature of many racisms). And it provides an explanation for why racism has persisted despite more than fifty years of Race Relations law and policy in the UK (because tackling racisms requires more than just the prohibition of discrimination, it also requires a positive tackling of the conditions that give rise to racisms).

Racism and Race Relations theory

Formal politics is a messy business. Different competing interests are at play in the development of Race Relations policy. In Northern Ireland a range of different organisations have an interest in, and an input into, the development and implementation of good relations policy. Some of the key state actors include the UK government, the Northern Ireland government, the PSNI, the Public Prosecution Service for Northern Ireland (PPSNI), the Northern

Ireland Housing Executive and local government.[70] There are also a number of quasi-autonomous state organisations, such as the ECNI, NIHRC, Community Relations Council and Northern Ireland Strategic Migration Partnership. Some of the key civil society organisations include the Northern Ireland Council for Ethnic Minorities (NICEM), CAJ and South Tyrone Empowerment Programme, as well as the churches and trade unions. In addition there are a number of 'ethnic' organisations, such as the Chinese Welfare Association, the Polish Community Council, An Munia Tober (representing the interests of Irish Travellers) and the Northern Ireland Filipino Community.[71] We should also add the main political parties, with their different conceptions of the nature of the problems of sectarianism and racism, into this mix. When we consider the competing agendas behind the range of different interest groups involved in the development and implementation of policy, we would probably expect that there would be some inconsistencies in the conception of racisms embedded in good relations policy (which is a form of Race Relations policy).[72]

The purpose of Race Relations policy is to *tackle* racisms. The central concern of Race Relations theory, on the other hand, is to *understand* and *explain* the phenomena commonly referred to as forms of racism. Consequently, we find that scholars are less content to settle for inconsistencies and are usually more interested than policy actors in trying to understand the social processes that underpin racisms. In this section we will focus on the work of Michael Banton and John Rex to explore the conceptual underpinnings of Race Relations theory. We have chosen Banton and Rex as representatives because they are both pioneers of Race Relations theory in the UK who have had, and still have, a significant influence on both theory and policy. We have already noted (in the section on definitions in this chapter) that Race Relations theorists are informed by a Kantian approach to developing theory. This is true for both Banton and Rex. Both scholars also explicitly draw on the work of the classical German sociologist Max Weber, but do so with different emphases. Both have also criticised each other's work. Banton has, for example, criticised Rex for 'maintaining that racist belief systems were to be identified by their functions in maintaining structured inequalities' on the grounds that this 'failed to take sufficient account of the complexities of whole societies and situations'.[73] Rex has argued that Banton does not pay adequate attention to issues of power and conflict. He warns Banton that 'a sociologist should never merely ask "What system operates here?" without referring to the balance of power which underlies it. To fail to do this too often results in the representation of ruling-class ideologies as though they were simply unquestionable social facts.'[74] Despite these differences, the two scholars have developed their respective work in dialogue with each other, and they substantially agree on many main points. Banton, for example, describes their work as complementary when he says that 'Rex and I wanted to keep the focus of attention on the analysis of interaction between racialised categories. I described my approach as anascopic (looking up from the "micro") and his as catascopic (looking down from the "macro").[75]

This section is divided into two parts. In the first we examine the question 'If there is no biological basis to racial distinctions why do people think and act as if there is?' We use this question as a means to explore the way in which Race Relations theory explains how people come to think in terms of 'races' and 'ethnic groups'. In the second part we examine the question 'Why do racisms take different forms?' We use this section to outline Rex and Banton's argument that examining the social context in which racisms arise is a more fruitful way of approaching the differing forms of racisms than an approach that differentiates on the basis of the victim group that is targeted.

The social construction of 'race'

The prevailing consensus among social scientists is that 'race' is a social construct, not something given by nature. Recognising that 'racial' distinctions have no biological basis and that they are socially generated does not, however, automatically lead to a rejection of the Race Relations approach. Many of the people who acknowledge that 'race' is a social construct also advocate a Race Relations approach. We have seen that Macpherson, Connolly and UNESCO, for example, reject the idea that humanity is divided into different 'races', but also talk as if 'races' still exist. Banton acknowledges that racial distinctions are socially created and maintained or adapted when he says that the social 'significance attached to phenotypical variation differs from one society to another and changes over time'.[76] In Banton's view something that is objectively true, a person's outward physical appearance, is subjectively interpreted in different ways in different social contexts. In his view, 'race' is subjectively real because people believe that it is real. Because they believe that 'races' exist they therefore act as if they exist, and consequently we can talk about 'race relations' because some people act towards other people (have relations with them) as if 'races' did exist.

The subjective perception of 'race', when shared by a significant proportion of society, is so socially powerful that it even affects people who know that 'races' are social constructs. As Banton puts it:

> racial classifications of everyday life are social constructions based in the popular consciousness. Racial relations are therefore to be identified by shared subjective definitions ... Even if an individual realized that there was no objective basis for the distinction, and that appearances were socially generated, he or she was [or, can be] regarded as still trapped by others' perceptions.[77]

Banton goes on to say that the study of 'race relations' is not, as those who accuse him of reifying 'race' claim, the study of relations between different 'races', but rather it involves 'analysis of interaction between racialised categories'.[78] In other words, it is possible to study 'race' relations because people are racialised (i.e.

have adopted a racial category by choice, or are categorised as a member of a 'racial' group by others), and interact with others based on an understanding that humanity is composed of different 'racial' groups.

Brewer utilises a similar conception when referring to sectarianism in Northern Ireland. Sectarianism, he argues, relies on a process of ethnic differentiation in which the boundaries between groups are 'socially constructed and … not given in nature'.[79] Catholics and Protestants exist as different ethnic groups because, subjectively, 'people perceive themselves as sharing an identity on the grounds of culture, descent and territory, and invoke this as the mechanism for differentiation'.[80] This subjective ethnic differentiation is 'continually produced and reproduced through social processes, such as socialisation, boundary maintenance and social closure, which reinvoke the marker and maintain the differentiation'.[81] In other words, subjective ethnic differentiation is given an objective existence through practices such as teaching children about their ethnic culture and heritage (socialisation); the use of intimidation to encourage people to 'stick with their own kind' (boundary maintenance); and ethnically selective access to societal resources, such as jobs or housing (social closure). Through these practices, sectarianism (as Liechty and Clegg put it) becomes a self-reproducing system. We can illustrate this through the example of residential segregation. People move to be with their 'own community' for different reasons; some of these people may oppose segregation in principle, but faced with the reality of sectarian intimidation in a 'mixed' area may accept it as a pragmatic solution. Once established, however, segregation acts as a form of boundary maintenance that serves to keep 'communities' apart physically in the here and now. This segregation also leads to a situation where social contact with other people takes place largely, or even entirely, within the context of one's 'own community'. Consequently, children grow up with little meaningful contact with individuals from the 'other community'. Segregation thus, in various ways, serves to wittingly, and unwittingly, perpetuate ethnic differentiation.[82]

The Race Relations approach understands 'race relations' to be intersubjective relations (i.e. relations between individuals, based on shared subjective understandings). This understanding of society, as intersubjectively constructed, acknowledges the power of our subjective conception of the world. Ideas, such as the belief that humanity is composed of different 'races', do have real consequences when people act on them. In a sense, all of us, not just Race Relations theorists, think like this. We do not have direct access to the world. It is filtered through the concepts that we use to make sense of our sensory experiences. This intuition leads some to argue that education can play an important role in changing the way that people think and consequently their behaviour. Advocates of education as a means of tackling racisms often argue that challenging sectarian ideas and ways of thinking should be combined with schemes that enable 'cross-community' social contact, so that sensory experiences are changed alongside modes of thinking.[83]

The social constructionist understanding of society enables us to understand how subjective understandings, when they are part of what Banton calls popular consciousness, can have a powerful impact on objective reality. So far, we have been able to explain 'racial' differentiation, but we have not explained why 'racial' difference so often involves racisms, rather than, for example, peaceful multicultural coexistence. Banton, Brewer and Rex suggest some ways to explain the place of conflict in 'race relations'.

Racisms as contextual

Rex argues that if we want to understand 'race relations', we need to understand the wider social situation that these relations are located within. As he puts it:

> while the sense of belonging together because of shared cultural characteristics and beliefs in common ancestry brings men together in quasi-groups, the actual relations which arise between such quasi-groups may take a variety of forms, depending not on ethnicity itself, but upon other variable factors, including what characteristics are honoured, what legal rights are assigned to or obtained by the groups and what control they have over property.[84]

Rex is arguing that a shared subjective belief in common ancestry brings individuals together as a type of group (which can be characterised as an ethnic group or a racial group), with a subjective sense of being distinct from other ethnic or racial groups. The relations between these groups, however, depends on factors outside the groups themselves. A shared belief in common ancestry, even when this gives rise to groups based on this shared belief, does not intrinsically give rise to racism. The difference between 'race relations' situations characterised by good relations (the aim of good relations policy) and those situations characterised by some form of racism cannot be explained by the nature of ethnicity itself. Brewer acknowledges this when he says that

> a boundary marker becomes 'heated up' ... or mobilized, when actors develop identity investments because of their economic or political interests. Thus, religion in Northern Ireland is simply a boundary marker socially appropriated to define groups who are in conflict over other things; the most readily available and meaningful marker to distinguish descendants of the settler and indigenous communities in Northern Ireland.[85]

In other words, religion or ethnicity is not a driver of conflict. Economic or political interests drive conflict. Religious distinctions can provide a basis for self and group identification, but this does not in-and-of-itself lead to conflict. We know that religious differences per se are not key, because various Protestant denominations are differentiated from each other by religious belief. These religious differences, however, have not become 'heated up' because they do not map on to divergent economic or political interests. A 'cool' religious diversity among Protestants, however, has not been a permanent feature of Protestantism in

Ireland. At the end of the eighteenth century differences between Presbyterians and Protestants affiliated to the established Church of Ireland 'heated up' when some Presbyterians, from the merchant class, played a leading role in founding the United Irishmen (the first organisational form of Irish Republicanism). These Presbyterians combined with, mainly peasant, Catholics in a rebellion against British rule, and against mainly Church of Ireland landowners and state functionaries.[86] In this historical example, divergent economic and political interests led to religious differences becoming 'heated up', but it was Church of Ireland Protestants (who enjoyed a privileged position relative to all others) who were opposed, both by Catholics and by some Protestants (mainly Presbyterians).[87]

Rex identified nine different 'historical situations in which it is frequently the case that the problem of relations between men [*sic*] are defined as problems of race relations'.[88] Six of these occur in the context of colonial territories and the other three in situations that sometimes arise when migrants from the colonial ('Third') world 'settle in metropolitan countries together with poor and politically persecuted refugees from non-colonial countries'.[89] One example from the context of colonial territories is frontier situations where there is interaction between sets of people who are at different levels of technological development (a paradigm example that he gives is 'when the barbarians were pressing at the edges of the Roman Empire').[90] (There are some parallels between Rex's discussion of a frontier situation and Robbie McVeigh and Bill Rolston's discussion of 'the beginnings of English colonisation of Ireland in the twelfth century and the Plantations of the seventeenth century – [during which] English colonial intervention in Ireland was justified in terms of the civilisation of England and the barbarism of Ireland'.)[91] Another colonial situation that Rex identifies is the use of unfree labour, such as in the slave plantations of the southern states of America prior to the abolition of slavery in the USA. Two examples of migration situations that Rex identifies are ones where migrants enter at the bottom of the social ladder as a new 'underclass', and ones where 'in times of crisis a group which is culturally or physically distinguishable is blamed for the existence of a threat to the society's wellbeing ... a process known as scapegoating'.[92]

Rex makes a distinction not just between situations in colonial territories and situations of immigration into Western nation-states. He also distinguishes between situations where the social differentiation is on the basis of ownership of property (e.g. land, housing, factories, machinery), where it is on the basis of access to legal rights, and where it is on the basis of social status. Brewer acknowledges the first of these further distinctions when he says that in Northern Ireland, religion acts as a marker of ethnic differentiation that 'articulates the conflict between the relative economic privilege of one community and the relative economic dispossession of another'.[93] He points to different legal rights, or more correctly, differential access to civil liberties, when he says that 'Catholics in the working-class ghettos (as distinct from those in middle-class suburbs) are subject to intimidation from a source that Protestants do not experience; namely the security forces, whose presence in working-class Catholics areas in many large towns approaches saturation'.[94] And if we can consider enjoying national self-determination as a form of social status, then we can say that Brewer refers to religion as a marker of ethnic differentiation which articulates 'the desire of one for political union with the United Kingdom and the aspiration of the other for unity with the Irish Republic'.[95]

Banton notes that Rex's distinction between different 'race relations situations' provides us with conceptual tools that enable us to talk about different forms of racism that do not rely on 'ethnic' or 'racial' distinctions. As he puts it: 'For the purposes of social science such forms [of hostility] are better classified according to their origins and modes, not by the objects of hostility' (such as Jews, Muslims or Irish Travellers).[96] Brewer, in his article on racism and sectarianism, has the conceptual materials that would allow him to analyse sectarianism as a form of racism, and still distinguish it from other forms of racism operating in Northern Ireland. He could, for example, differentiate between sectarianism and other forms of racism on the grounds of political aspiration. Immigrants, and other 'groups' who do not align themselves to Irish Nationalism or Ulster Unionism, do not make claims for national self-determination.[97] Using this framework we could, for example, differentiate between the treatment of the Black Africans who were detained at the same time as Frank Kakopa (who were very probably detained for a much longer period of time and quite likely deported) and Kakopa himself (who was released), on the grounds of different access to legal rights. The fact that Brewer chose instead to highlight the distinction between sectarianism and other forms of racism not only feeds into the presentation of Northern Ireland as a place apart, it also diverts the focus of attention away from the social processes involved in the racialisation of Northern Irish Catholics and immigrants, and instead focuses on outward phenotypical appearances.

Conclusion

We have argued that there are a whole range of reasons why racism does not lend itself to a definition of the form 'racism is…' Rather than attempt to provide a dictionary-style definition of racism, we have chosen instead to demonstrate the richness and complexity of the phenomenon. A crucial reason why definitions are not straightforward is that they are, in part, shaped by the purposes for which they are developed. We have explored some of the differences in definitions of racism in Race Relations policy and in Race Relations theory. In doing so, we were not trying to evaluate the approach to definitions in the spheres of policy and theory and decide which one to award more marks to. Neither approach to defining racism is better than the other. Or, more correctly, we cannot judge which is better in the abstract. Which is better depends on the criteria that we use to make the judgement. The approach taken in the development of policy would make for poor theory; the approach taken by theorists would very likely lead to frustration in policy-making. What we can do is look at the consequences of defining racism in particular ways. Distinguishing between racism and sectarianism on the basis of the boundary marker, for example, obscures the social processes at work. This focus on the boundary marker leaves the researcher at the risk of being overtaken by events, as has happened to Brewer's distinction between racism and sectarianism when significant numbers of immigrants from Eastern Europe arrived in Northern Ireland.

We have highlighted the emphasis that Race Relations policy places on prejudice as a key explanation for racist behaviour. We have also pointed to a, more recent, acknowledgement in Race Relations policy that prejudice on its own is insufficient as an explanation for the existence of racisms. The concept of 'institutional racism' in Race Relations policy developed out of a critique of the limitations of the earlier emphasis on the prejudice of individuals. The concept of 'institutional racism' draws attention to the importance of social structures for either enabling, or frustrating, the translation of prejudice into action. Race Relations theory also draws attention to the role of social structures in enabling or frustrating the development of racisms. The social constructionist understanding of society found in Race Relations theory helps to explain how intersubjective relations between people – shared subjective understandings – can be powerful structuring factors in society. This social constructionist understanding draws attention to ways in which ideas, when they are shared by a large number of people in society, can shape the ways that individuals and groups act in society – even to the extent of shaping the actions of people who do not share these structuring beliefs.

We have also built on the analysis in the previous chapter in which we argued that it is useful to think of sectarianism as a form of racism, and that racism takes a number of different forms. This understanding of *racisms* helps to make sense of the parallel development of community relations policy in Northern Ireland and Race Relations policy in the rest of the UK. We have also shown that thinking of sectarianism as a form of racism does not have to involve an outright rejection of Brewer's analysis of racism and sectarianism. If we reject his highlighting of the boundary marker as key to differentiating between racism and sectarianism, but maintain his understanding of 'race' as a social construct and his acknowledgement that racisms are shaped by social structures, we can see that his analysis is consistent with key elements of Race Relations theory.

Notes

1 Susan McKay, "'They were chaining people up like animals'", *Irish Times*, 24 November 2007.

2 Z. Magubane, 'Science, reform, and the "science of reform": Booker T. Washington, Robert Park, and the making of a "science of society"', *Current Sociology* 62.4 (2014): 568–583; Martin Bulmer, 'Charles S. Johnson, Robert E. Park and the research methods of the Chicago Commission on Race Relations, 1919–22: an early experiment in applied social research', *Ethnic and Racial Studies* 4.3 (1981): 289–306; Mary Jo Deegan, 'The Chicago School of ethnography', in *Handbook of ethnography*, ed. Paul Atkinson et al. (London: Sage, 2001), 11–25; Cheryl Hudson, '"The negro in Chicago": harmony in conflict, 1919–22', *European Journal of American Culture* 29.1 (2010): 53–67.

3 The article was reprinted in Robert E. Park and Ernest W. Burgess, *Introduction to the science of sociology* (Chicago: University of Chicago Press, 1921), 722.

4 Chicago Commission on Race Relations, *The negro in Chicago: a study of race relations and a race riot* (Chicago: University of Chicago Press, 1922).

5 Hazard, *Postwar anti-racism*; Michael Banton, *The international politics of race* (Cambridge: Polity Press, 2002); Michael Banton, *International action against racial discrimination* (Oxford: Clarendon Press, 1996); Peter Lengyel (ed.), *Dimensions of the racial situation*, International Social Science Journal 23.4 (1971), special issue; UNESCO, *Four statements on the race question*.

6 Ambalavaner Sivanandan, 'Race and resistance: the IRR story', *Race & Class* 50.2 (2008): 1–30; Robert Moore, 'Race relations and the rediscovery of sociology', *British Journal of Sociology* 22.1 (1971): 97–104; Banton, 'The race relations problematic'; John Rex and David Mason, *Theories of race and ethnic relations* (Cambridge: Cambridge University Press, 1986); Tahir Abbas and Frank Reeves (eds), *Immigration and race relations: sociological theory and John Rex* (London: I. B. Tauris, 2007); Stephen Small and John Solomos, 'Race, immigration and politics in Britain: changing policy agendas and conceptual paradigms 1940s–2000s', *International Journal of Comparative Sociology* 47.3–4 (2006): 235–257; John Rex, *Race, colonialism and the city* (London: Routledge and Kegan Paul, 1973); Philip N. Sooben, *The origins of the Race Relations Act 1976* (Warwick: University of Warwick, 1990).

7 Small and Solomos, 'Race, immigration and politics in Britain', 250.

8 Ibid.

9 Maintaining intellectual independence has become increasingly difficult in UK academia due to the demand that research be policy relevant, and that policy be evidence-based. See, for example, Ruth Levitt, *The challenges of evidence: provocation paper for the Alliance for Useful Evidence* (London: NESTA, 2013); Holger Strassheim and Pekka Kettunen, 'When does evidence-based policy turn into policy-based evidence? Configurations, contexts and mechanisms', *Evidence & Policy: A Journal of Research, Debate and Practice* 10.2 (2014): 259–277; Christina Boswell, *The political uses of expert knowledge: immigration policy and social research* (Cambridge: Cambridge University Press, 2009).

10 Robert Moore, 'Race relations in the Six Counties: colonialism, industrialization, and stratification in Ireland', *Race* (now *Race & Class*) 14.1 (1972): 21.

11 Brewer, 'Sectarianism and racism', 356.

12 Ibid.

13 Banton, *International action against racial discrimination*, 60.

14 Ibid.
15 Hugh Frazer and Mari Fitzduff, *Improving community relations* (Belfast: Community Relations Council, 1992), 17.
16 Oliver Cromwell Cox has theorised 'race relations', but he does so within a post-Marx Marxist framework. He is not a proponent of what we refer to as a Race Relations approach. See Oliver Cromwell Cox, *Caste, class and race: a study in social dynamics* (New York: Monthy Review Press, 1970). For a critical appraisal of Cox by another post-Marx Marxist scholar, see Robert Miles, *Racism after 'race relations'* (London: Routledge, 1993), 30–35.
17 Robbie McVeigh, 'The undertheorisation of sectarianism', *Canadian Journal of Irish Studies* 16.2 (1990): 121.
18 Northern Ireland Affairs Committee (NIAC), *The challenge of diversity: hate crime in Northern Ireland, volume 2: oral and written evidence* (London: House of Commons, 2005), sec. Ev36.
19 Ibid., sec. Ev39.
20 NIAC, *The challenge of diversity: volume 1*, 9.
21 OFMDFM, *A shared future and racial equality strategy: good relations indicators baseline report* (Belfast: OFMDFM, 2007), 164.
22 OFMDFM, *Together: Building a united community* (Belfast: OFMDFM, 2013), 19.
23 Ibid.
24 Article 2(1) and (2) of the UNESCO Declaration on Race and Racial Prejudice (1978), reproduced on page 82 of the 2005 *Racial equality strategy*.
25 Garner, *Racisms*, 10.
26 Equality Commission Northern Ireland, *Frank Kakopa -v- Immigration Service* (Belfast: ECNI, 2007).
27 Nazia Latif and Agnieszka Martynowicz, *Our hidden borders: the UK Border Agency's powers of detention* (Belfast: Northern Ireland Human Rights Commission, 2009), 73.
28 McKay, '"They were chaining people up like animals"'.
29 Garner, *Racisms*, 5–12.
30 Michael Banton, 'Progress in ethnic and racial studies', *Ethnic and Racial Studies* 24.2 (2010): 186.
31 Ibid.
32 Ibid.
33 McVeigh, '"There's no racism because there's no black people here"', 24.
34 Ibid., 22.
35 See, for example, Quintin Oliver and Paul McGill, *A wake-up call on race: implications of the Macpherson Report for institutional racism in Northern Ireland* (Belfast: Equality Commission for Northern Ireland, 2002); Richard Montague and Peter Shirlow, *Challenging racism: ending hate* (Belfast: United Against Hate, 2014); OFMDFM, *A racial equality strategy for Northern Ireland: 2005–2010*; Paul Connolly and Michaela Keenan, *Racial attitudes and prejudice in Northern Ireland*, vol. 1 (Belfast: NISRA, 2000); Connolly, *'Race' and racism in Northern Ireland*; NIAC, *The challenge of diversity, volume 1*; NIAC, *The challenge of diversity, volume 2*; Vani K. Borooah and John

Mangan, 'Love thy neighbour: how much bigotry is there in Western countries?', *Kyklos* 60.3 (2007): 295–317; Knox, 'Tackling racism in Northern Ireland'.

36 OFMDFM, *A shared future: policy and strategic framework for good relations in Northern Ireland* (Belfast: OFMDFM, 2005), 10.

37 OFMDFM, *Programme for cohesion, sharing and integration: consultation document* (Belfast: OFMDFM, 2010), 6.

38 Ibid., 49.

39 OFMDFM, *A shared future and racial equality strategy: good relations indicators baseline report*.

40 See, for example, Equality Commission for Northern Ireland, *Racial equality in education: a good practice guide* (Belfast: ECNI, 2001); Iseult Honohan and Nathalie Rougier (eds), *Tolerance and diversity in Ireland, north and south* (Manchester: Manchester University Press, 2015); Ulrike Niens, Ed Cairns and Suzanne Bishop, 'Prejudiced or not? Hidden sectarianism among students in Northern Ireland', *The Journal of Social Psychology* 144.2 (2004): 163–180; Ulrike Niens, Una O'Connor and Alan Smith, 'Citizenship education in divided societies: teachers' perspectives in Northern Ireland', *Citizenship Studies* 17.1 (2013): 128–141; OFMDFM, *Programme for cohesion, sharing and integration: consultation document*; Central Council for Education and Training in Social Work (Northern Ireland), *Training to challenge racism in social work practice in Northern Ireland* (Belfast: CCETSW(NI), 2000).

41 Knox, 'Tackling racism in Northern Ireland', 16.

42 Susan McKay, 'Tourists discover North's deep-seated prejudices', *The Irish News*, 30 October 2007.

43 'Tourist arrested for being black', *BBC News Online*, 28 October 2007.

44 ECNI, *Frank Kakopa -v- Immigration Service*.

45 McKay, '"They were chaining people up like animals"'.

46 Ibid.

47 Wilson Nesbitt Solicitors, 'Innocent jailbird wins compensation for race bias', *Wilson-Nesbitt.com*, n.d.

48 Stephen Breen, 'I was jailed in Ulster because I am black', *Belfast Telegraph*, 29 October 2007.

49 Knox, 'Tackling racism in Northern Ireland', 24.

50 Sir William Macpherson, *The Stephen Lawrence Inquiry* (London, 1999), sec. 76.1.

51 Race Relations (Amendment) Act, 2000.

52 See, for example, Karim Murji, 'Sociological engagements: institutional racism and beyond', *Sociology* 41.5 (2007): 843–855; John Lea, 'The Macpherson Report and the question of institutional racism', *The Howard Journal* 39.3 (2000): 219–233; Macpherson, *The Stephen Lawrence Inquiry*; Bourne, 'The life and times of institutional racism'; Garner, *Racisms*, 102–116.

53 Connolly, *'Race' and racism in Northern Ireland*, 8.

54 Bourne, 'The life and times of institutional racism', 19.

55 Montague and Shirlow, *Challenging racism*, n.p.

56 Duncan Morrow, chief executive of the Northern Ireland Community Relations Council, in a speech at the PSNI Hate Crime Conference, 13 February 2006.

Duncan Morrow, 'Hate crime, policing and human rights in a violently divided society' (Community Relations Council, 2006), www.community-relations.org.uk/about-the-council/background-info/hate-crime-speech/.

57 Joseph Liechty and Cecelia Clegg, *Moving beyond sectarianism: religion, conflict and reconciliation in Northern Ireland* (Dublin: Columba Press, 2001), 14.
58 Ibid., 15.
59 Macpherson, *The Stephen Lawrence Inquiry*, sec. 6.17.
60 Oliver and McGill, *A wake-up call on race*, 4.
61 OFMDFM, *A shared future*, 8.
62 Ibid.
63 Ibid.
64 See, for example, PSNI, *Incidents and crimes with a hate motivation recorded by the police in Northern Ireland: quarterly update to 31 March 2014* (Belfast: PSNI, 2014).
65 Macpherson, *The Stephen Lawrence Inquiry*, sec. 47.13.
66 Ibid., sec. 46.27.
67 Connolly, *'Race' and racism in Northern Ireland*, i.
68 Oliver and McGill, *A wake-up call on race*, 7.
69 ECNI, *Frank Kakopa -v- Immigration Service*.
70 PPSNI, *Hate crime policy* (Belfast: PPSNI, 2010); Northern Ireland Housing Executive, *Towards a community relations strategy: a consultation paper* (Belfast: NIHE, 1999); OFMDFM, *Together*; Colin Knox and Joanne Hughes, 'Local government and crommunity relations', in *Facets of the conflict in Northern Ireland*, ed. Seamus Dunn (Basingstoke: Macmillan, 1995), 43–60; Máiréad Nic Craith, *Culture and identity politics in Northern Ireland* (Basingstoke: Palgrave Macmillan, 2003); PSNI, *Policy response to hate incidents* (Belfast: PSNI, 2005).
71 The number, and sometimes remit, of organisations is continually changing due to demographic changes, changing personnel and the vagaries of funding. Lists of organisations are available online from NISMP, www.migrationni.org/support-organisations, and from the Community Intercultural Programme, www.craigavon-intercultural.org/content/groups-offering-support-ethnic-communities
72 On political parties and racism and sectarianism, see, for example, Aidan McGarry, Paul Hainsworth and Chris Gilligan, *Elected representatives/political parties and minority ethnic communities in Northern Ireland* (Derry/Londonderry: INCORE, 2008); Karin Gilland Lutz and Christopher Farrington, 'Alternative Ulster? Political parties and the non-constitutional policy space in Northern Ireland', *Political Studies* 54.4 (2006): 715–742; Paul Mitchell, Geoffrey Evans and Brendan O'Leary, 'Extremist outbidding in ethnic party systems is not inevitable: tribune parties in Northern Ireland', *Political Studies* 57.2 (2009): 397–421; Catherine McGlynn, Jonathan Tonge and James W. McAuley, 'The party politics of post-devolution identity in Northern Ireland', *The British Journal of Politics & International Relations* 16.2 (2014): 273–290; Jocelyn Evans and Jonathan Tonge, 'Problems of modernizing an ethno-religious party: the case of the Ulster Unionist Party in Northern Ireland', *Party Politics* 11.3 (2005): 319–338; Aidan McGarry, Paul Hainsworth and Chris Gilligan, 'Political parties and minority ethnic communities in Northern Ireland: election manifestos 1994–2007', *Translocations* 3.1 (2008): 106–132; Paul

Hainsworth, 'Politics, racism and ethnicity in Northern Ireland', in *Divided society: ethnic minorities and racism in Northern Ireland*, ed. Paul Hainsworth (London: Pluto Press, 1998).

73 Banton, 'Progress in ethnic and racial studies', 187.

74 Rex, *Race, colonialism and the city*, 225.

75 Banton, 'The race relations problematic', 117.

76 Ibid., 116–117.

77 Ibid., 116. Banton attributes the origins of this idea to Robert E. Park and E. W. Burgess of the Chicago School of sociology.

78 Ibid., 117.

79 Brewer, 'Sectarianism and racism', 357.

80 Ibid.

81 Ibid.

82 For interesting studies of residential segregation, see Peter Shirlow, '"Who fears to speak": fear, mobility, and ethno-sectarianism in the two "Ardoynes"', *Global Review of Ethnopolitics* 3.1 (2003): 76–91; Madeleine Leonard, 'Teens and territory in contested spaces: negotiating sectarian interfaces in Northern Ireland', *Children's Geographies* 4.2 (2006): 225–238; F. W. Boal, 'Territoriality on the Shankill–Falls divide, Belfast', *Irish Geography* 6.1 (1969): 30–50; John Darby, *Intimidation and the control of conflict in Northern Ireland* (Syracuse, NY: Syracuse University Press, 1986); Niall O'Dochartaigh, 'Conflict, territory and new technologies: online interaction at a Belfast interface', *Political Geography* 26.4 (2007): 474–491.

83 See, for example, Joanne Hughes, 'Contact and context: sharing education and building relationships in a divided society', *Research Papers in Education* 29.2 (2014): 193–210; Paul Connolly, 'What now for the contact hypothesis? Towards a new research agenda', *Race Ethnicity and Education* 3.2 (2000): 169–193.

84 John Rex, *Race and ethnicity* (Milton Keynes: Open University Press, 1986), 14.

85 Brewer, 'Sectarianism and racism', 357.

86 Jim Smyth, *The men of no property: Irish radicals and popular politics in the late eighteenth century* (Basingstoke: Macmillan, 1998).

87 The United Irishmen rebellion is an important historical reference point for Irish Republicans. Both pro-peace process Sinn Féin and anti-peace process Republican dissidents cite the rebellion as part of their Republican tradition.

88 Rex, *Race, colonialism and the city*, 203.

89 Ibid., 204.

90 Ibid.

91 Robbie McVeigh and Bill Rolston, 'Civilising the Irish', *Race & Class* 51.1 (2009): 3.

92 Rex, *Race, colonialism and the city*, 204.

93 Brewer, 'Sectarianism and racism', 358.

94 Ibid., 363.

95 Ibid., 358.

96 Banton, 'Progress in ethnic and racial studies', 186.

97 For an interesting example of this kind of distinction in the Canadian context, see Elke Winter, '"Immigrants don't ask for self-government": how multiculturalism is (de)legitimized in multi-national societies', *Ethnopolitics* 10.2 (2011): 187–204.

4

Anti-racism and disavowed racism

The term racism is unambiguously a negative one, morally and politically. Sectarianism and other forms of racism are often referred to as evil. Anna Lo, MLA, for example, can often be heard describing racism and sectarianism as 'twin evils of prejudice and intolerance'.[1] In 2001 a report on racism commissioned by the Northern Ireland government concluded that 'racist harassment is a particularly pernicious and evil part of society'.[2] Racisms are commonly characterised as forms of extremism. The British MP Paul Murphy, when he was the Secretary of State for Northern Ireland, urged that 'all of us across civic society should have a zero tolerance towards racism, sectarianism and any other such extremism'.[3] Mainstream politicians are not the only people who view racisms as unambiguously negative. Garner, in research he conducted with White working-class people in England, found that many of his interviewees were adamant that they were not racist. These 'repeated claims by white working-class interviewees', he says, 'that neither they nor the things they say are racist, indicate that being racist is an undesirable position'.[4] Garner goes on to point out that the consensus that racisms are unambiguously bad is so widely understood today that 'Even far-right parties in the twenty-first century officially deny that they are working toward racist objectives.'[5] The moral consensus on the wrongs of racism can be seen in the way that many people prefix critical comments about racialised minorities by saying 'I'm not a racist, but…'

Racist ideas and practices, however, have not always been viewed as unambiguously negative. Take this example of a speech on the merits of the British Empire made by Lord Rosebery in 1900.

> We are a conquering and imperial race. All over the world we have displayed our mettle … An Empire such as ours requires as its first condition an imperial race – a race vigorous and industrious and intrepid … The survival of the fittest is an absolute truth in the conditions of the modern world … [in the] struggle before us … depends the future, and the immediate future, of the race; and what is Empire but the predominance of race?[6]

Lord Rosebery did not feel any need to prefix his comments with 'I'm not a racist, but…' The predominance of the Anglo-Saxon race was something that

he celebrated, not something that he felt defensive about. The concerns that he expressed in his speech were not about the racial domination of colonised peoples; he championed such domination. His few references to colonised peoples were derogatory. He referred to 'savage territories' and 'naked tribes of savages'. He expressed concern that the British Empire was facing increasing competition from France, Germany and the United States in the colonial world. He did not express concern about the colonised in the colonial world.

Lord Rosebery was not a doddery old member of the House of Lords who was on the margins of political life in the UK. During the 1880s and 1890s he was a leading figure in the imperialist faction of the Liberal Party. He served as the Foreign Secretary, twice – in 1886 and between 1892 and 1894. He moved from the role of Foreign Secretary to take up the role of Prime Minister for a year. Less than five years before the speech we have just quoted, Rosebery was in the most powerful position in UK politics, and at a time when the UK was the most powerful nation that the world had ever known.[7] The empire that he referred to was so vast that it was sometimes referred to as the empire on which the sun never set. He made his speech in his role as the newly elected Rector of the University of Glasgow, one of the oldest and most prestigious universities in the world. His speech was delivered to a largely student audience and Rosebery sought to encourage them to take up service in the empire upon their graduation.

Rosebery's views were unexceptional in the year he delivered his speech. In the late nineteenth century, and the early years of the twentieth century, belief in the superiority of the White (or Aryan or Nordic) 'race' was commonplace among Anglo-European elites. It provided a justification for colonial domination, for Jim Crow laws that codified Black disadvantage in the USA and for the Whites-only immigration policy in Australia.[8] During the twentieth century the English-speaking world shifted from a situation in which White supremacy could be openly espoused by leading figures in public life to one where condemnation of such views is vociferous, and virtually everyone wants to proclaim: 'I'm not a racist.'

One of the most common explanations for the shift from White supremacy to anti-racism is the notion that popular disgust at the Nazis' mass extermination of the Jews led to anti-racism becoming established as a moral outlook that was adopted internationally. As George M. Fredrickson puts it:

> Hitler, it has been said, gave racism a bad name. The moral revulsion of people throughout the world against what the Nazis did, reinforced by scientific studies undermining racist genetics (or eugenics), served to discredit the scientific racism that had been respectable and influential in the United States and Europe before the Second World War.[9]

This conventional explanation of the development of anti-racism is misleading in a number of ways. The Second World War was a watershed in the development of official anti-racism, but it merely crystallised a number of trends that were already apparent. The emergence of a Race Relations approach, and the coining of the term 'racism', both pre-date the Second World War. Opposition to the Nazis and the discrediting of racial science were factors, but not the only factors. The most misleading aspect of the conventional explanation is the emphasis that it gives to intellectuals and ideas, in isolation from anti-racist practice. The work of intellectuals was accompanied by, and in many respects driven by, movements opposing White supremacy. Anti-racist theory was developed in a context where the issue of racial oppression was being raised by the demands of the racialised – in the colonial world and in the USA – for liberty and equality. The official rejection of White supremacy was, in many ways, a defensive attempt to depoliticise the issue of 'race'. It ran alongside attempts to frustrate the desire for human freedom that was being articulated by the racially oppressed.

Ben Pitcher highlights one of the contemporary confusions that underpins the crisis of anti-racism today when he says that it is increasingly difficult to think of the politics of 'race' as 'an explicit, straightforward struggle between racists and anti-racists'.[10] He argues that the success of radical grassroots anti-racist campaigning in the 1960s and 1970s has given rise to the incorporation of 'anti-racism as an *oppositional* discourse [which] has been institutionalized by the state'.[11] The co-option of anti-racism has led to a situation in which 'a key dynamic of the contemporary politics of race involves the disavowal – but not necessarily the overcoming – of racist practice'.[12] We agree both that the radical grassroots anti-racist movements of the 1960s and 1970s were important and that the relationship between racism and anti-racism is not straightforward. We argue, however, that the coexistence of an avowed anti-racism and a disavowed racism has been characteristic of official state anti-racism from its origins. In the second part of this chapter, we elaborate on our argument through an examination of the mutual development of official state anti-racism and disavowed racism. We do so through a brief consideration of the internationalisation of the Race Relations approach through the UN, and the incorporation of Race Relations into domestic UK policy.

In the third part of this chapter we outline a number of different forms of anti-racism. Anti-racists agree that racism is wrong, but they do not all agree on why, exactly, racisms are wrong. The condemnation of racism and sectarianism because they are evil casts the issue in moral terms. The problem with describing racism as evil lies not in the casting of the issue in these terms – as Anna Lo and many other advocates of official anti-racism do – but in the failure to recognise that there is no consensus in society about what is morally just and unjust. There is widespread agreement across the Western world today that racism (in its various forms) is something that should be *opposed*. There is not, however, consensus on *why* racism should be opposed. In the third part of the chapter we briefly outline and explore four forms of anti-racism that are found in Northern Ireland currently. We identify ways in which each of these four forms act as limitations on the development of an emancipatory anti-racism.

The origins of the term 'racism'

The term 'racism' was coined in the 1930s. From the beginning, it identified racism as something negative, as something to be opposed. The term did not magically appear from nowhere, but was the expression of a wider tendency. As Elazar Barkan puts it, the appearance of the term racism 'to denote racial prejudice suggests that the debunking of race theories and their crude political analogies began sometime earlier'.[13] In the previous chapter, we noted that Race Relations theory and policy first developed in the USA around the time of the First World War. Race Relations theory questioned the idea that there was a biological basis to 'race' and sought explanations for it in social factors. We can see, therefore, that only a few years after Rosebery's speech, the idea of White supremacy was already being called into question. Various factors created the conditions in which the term 'racism' emerged and was subsequently taken up as part of a growing political opposition to racisms.

Barkan provides a detailed account of one element in the process of naming and challenging racisms; the intellectual endeavour of pioneering scientists and anthropologists who interrogated the claims of racial science. These scientists and anthropologists questioned key tenets of racial science, such as the idea that it was possible to classify humanity into relatively discrete 'racial' groups; that biological factors alone could account for variations in phenotype; that 'race' could account for variations in intellectual capacity; or that miscegenation created biological degeneracy. Barkan notes that the key figures in this challenge to racial science were not necessarily leading scientists, although many were, but were individuals who were able to command influence through their ability to address both specialist scientific audiences and the general public. These key figures both belonged to the establishment and were in some way outsiders, as women, Jews, or political radicals. This 'status of partial outsider,' he argues, 'encouraged a greater sensitivity to racial attributes, and led to active criticism of racism'.[14]

The idea of 'race' was not just called into question on the issue of phenotypical differences. It was also problematic because the ideology of White supremacy was really an ideology of the elite. Alistair Bonnett notes that in Victorian Britain:

> Whiteness was fetishised and idealised as an 'extra-ordinary', almost superhuman identity; an identity developed, in the main, for and by the bourgeoisie. The Victorian working class, most particularly the urban and immigrant working class, were positioned as marginal to this construction.[15]

We can see this in Rosebery's speech at Glasgow University. He not only extolled the virtues of the Anglo-Saxons as a conquering and imperial 'race', he also expressed concerns that the urban working class in Scotland and England were unfit as an imperial 'race' and were 'a progeny doomed from its birth to misery and ignominy'.[16] At the turn of the nineteenth and twentieth centuries the issues of empire, welfare and mass democracy were closely tied together.[17] In Weimar Germany, for example, a leading advisor to the government on social policy, Othmar von Verschuer, was 'an advocate of sterilization for the mentally and "morally" subnormal, and he emphasized the biological basis of class structure. He condemned democracy as a quantitative rather than a qualitative social system, which posed undue financial burdens on the national elite.'[18] (Verschuer went on to play a leading role in Nazi 'racial hygiene' policy, eventually becoming Josef Mengele's supervisor at Auschwitz.)[19] On the political left, the working-class socialist movements were divided on the issues of 'race' and nation. Satnam Virdee notes that in Britain, many socialists and trade unionists supported empire and immigration controls and argued that extension of the franchise and welfare reform demonstrated that socialism and nationalism were compatible. Among the more radical sections of the working class, within whose ranks Irish and Jewish 'outsiders' were over-represented, racism was challenged and internationalism promoted through making arguments for workers of the world to unite against their common oppressor, the capitalists.[20]

The idea of 'race' was also undermined by Japan's decisive military victory over imperial Russia at the 1905 Battle of Tsushima. The event was of global significance. As Pankraj Misra puts it, 'For the first time since the Middle Ages, a non-European country had vanquished a European power in a major war; and the news careened around a world that Western imperialists – and the invention of the telegraph – had closely knit together.'[21] Many of the leading figures in what was to become known as 'Third World' nationalism – Kemal Ataturk (Turkey), Jawaharlal Nehru (India), Sun Yat-sen (China), U. Ottama (Burma) – were inspired by this event. White elites were worried. Lord Curzon, Viceroy of India, declared that 'the reverberations of that victory have gone like a thunderclap through the whispering galleries of the East'.[22] Japan's victory shattered the ideology of White supremacy by demonstrating that White imperial power could be not only defeated, but spectacularly so, by a non-White nation-state. We have already seen, in the previous chapter, that the response to Japan's victory among Black Americans was one of the events that Robert E. Park cited as a warning that good race relations needed to be taken seriously. Park was one of a number of figures who were concerned that White supremacy was encouraging 'race consciousness' among Blacks and that this might help to galvanise collective Black resistance to racism. Such fear of the power of the Black masses was one of the spurs to the development and institutionalising of official anti-racism.

Rosebery, as we noted in the introduction, expressed concerns about increasing challenges to the hegemony of the British Empire from France, Germany and the United States. This competition between the dominant global power and the aspiring powers spilled over into the First World War. Its reverberations were felt around the world. In the USA, for example, increased manufacturing production, stimulated by the war, was one of the factors that drew many Black Americans from the Deep South to centres of industry, like Chicago, in the North. Almost half a million Black Americans enlisted and served in the US military during the war. Prior to the war Black soldiers accounted for about 3 per cent of the US armed forces; by the end of the war they constituted more than 33 per cent of a much-enlarged force. The war armed and provided military training for a cohort of Black Americans, and some of these demobbed soldiers were involved in the Chicago riots.[23] The barbarity of the war also challenged the claims of White elites to represent civilisation, or led to disenchantment with civilisation itself.[24] Michael Adas, for example, notes that in Africa and Asia the war 'gave credence to Gandhi's contention that the path for humanity cleared by the industrial West was neither morally or socially enabling nor ultimately sustainable'.[25] This viewpoint was initially influential among intellectuals in the colonial world, such as Gandhi, who had been educated in the West. Through the agitations of these intellectuals, such ideas 'were taken up by the peasants and urban laborers who joined them in the revolt against the European colonial order'.[26] The Bolshevik Revolution was another source of fear for defenders of the existing, Anglo-European global and domestic orders. In one of the most influential defences of White supremacy in the interwar period, *The Rising Tide of Color Against White World-Supremacy*, Lothrop Stoddard warned his readers that

> in every quarter of the globe, in Asia, Africa, Latin America, and the United States, Bolshevik agitators whisper in the ears of discontented colored men their gospel of hatred and revenge. Every nationalist aspiration, every political grievance, every social discrimination, is fuel for Bolshevism's hellish incitement to racial as well as to class war.[27]

The First World War, in numerous ways, was a watershed in the way that 'race' was perceived. At the end of the war, in 1919, when the Paris Peace Conference was convened to discuss a settlement and how to prevent a future war, Japan put the question of racial equality on the agenda. The Japanese government's motivation in doing so was to secure a position for itself as a major Western power, rather than to champion the cause of oppressed peoples around the world.[28] The proposal, nevertheless, excited Black political activists and 'Third World' nationalists. The rejection of the proposal, vetoed by US President Woodrow Wilson, provoked outrage. There were protests in China, Egypt, India and Palestine. The infamous Amritsar Massacre, in the Indian Punjab, was a British over-reaction against one of the many protests that sprang up in India in response to the outcome of the conference. In the USA Black radicals condemned the rejection of racial equality, and White supremacists revived the Ku Klux Klan and proclaimed their determination to prevent demands for 'racial' equality being accepted. Paul Gordon Lauren notes that this clash in opinion between Black activists and White supremacists 'exploded into open violence during the long, hot summer of 1919 ... in Chicago, Knoxville, Omaha, and the nation's own capital Washington, D.C. ... Lynchings, burnings, floggings, shocking terror, and destruction accompanied what some called nothing short of a "race war".'[29] This was the wider context in which Race Relations theory and policy began to make headway in the USA. White elites globally began to express concern about the demographic growth of Black populations internationally and worried that the global balance of power might shift from White to non-White.[30]

In the 1930s, when the term 'racism' was coined, the rise of Nazi Germany was an important factor driving the discussion. *We Europeans*, one of the most important books that helped to undermine scientific racist arguments, was 'an explicit attempt to fight Nazi pseudo-scientific theories of race'.[31] The book, co-authored by Julian Huxley (a biologist) and Alfred C. Haddon (an anthropologist), provided an early attempt to argue for replacing the term 'racial' with 'ethnic', on the grounds that there was no biological basis to 'racial' distinctions. The most important aspect of the book at the time, Barkan argues, 'was its anti-racist statements, a fact well reflected in the reviews'.[32] Kenan Malik notes that by the mid-1930s, 'Huxley was a leading antiracist who spent much of his considerable talents in publicising the fight against Nazism', and the book that he co-authored with Haddon 'became one of the most influential antiracist books of the time'.[33] Both Malik and Barkan, however, also note that Huxley was ambivalent about the existence of 'race' and about 'racial' equality. Frank Furedi notes that Huxley, 'who was appointed first Director of UNESCO [in 1946], still took it upon himself to defend Britain's imperial record as late as 1944. He implored his readers not to forget that "Africa remained for the most part in an early stage of barbarism".'[34]

During the 1930s anti-colonial movements developed and became increasingly assertive. In part, these protest movements were fuelled by the economic depression, which called into question the claims made for the benefits of empire for those who were colonised. In India, for example, the UK government had responded to pressure from the Indian nationalist movement by conceding, in the Government of India Act 1935, the legitimacy of the demand for Dominion status (as enjoyed by Australia, Canada and other White nation-states of the empire). The concessions, however, proved to be a case of too little, too late. The independence movement continued to demand national self-determination and in the 1937 provincial elections the Indian National Congress became the majority party in seven out of eleven provinces.[35] Nationalist movements became increasingly active, not just in India but across the British Empire during the 1930s and 1940s. This growth of anti-colonial nationalism raised concern among the UK political elite that 'race consciousness' could provide a unifying ideology across the empire and lead to a situation of the West against the rest.[36] The widespread reaction, among colonised peoples, against the invasion of Ethiopia by fascist Italy in 1935 was a cause of concern for defenders of empire. Du Bois, the American campaigner against racism, wrote that people of colour around the world interpreted the invasion as further evidence of the arrogance of White supremacy. He warned that the lesson of the invasion

> as Negroes see it, is that if any colored nation expects to maintain itself against white Europe it need appeal neither to religion nor culture but only to force. That is why Japan today has the sympathy of the majority of mankind because that majority is colored. Italy's action in Ethiopia deprives China of her last hope for aid from Europe. She must now either follow Japan or fall into chaos ... The result of Italy's venture must inevitably tend to destroy in India whatever faith there is in the justice of white Europe.[37]

Du Bois touched on a raw nerve. He articulated two ideas that concerned White elites: the idea that people of colour across the world would draw the lesson that it was only by force that they would gain independence, and the idea that the leading White nations were going to face a challenge from a unified force of the coloured nations of the world, possibly led by Japan.

The context in which the term 'racism' was coined and initially took hold was one in which White supremacy was increasingly contested by radical Black activists and 'Third World' nationalists. It was also, however, one in which White supremacy was vigorously asserted, through the ideological propaganda and racist activity of organisations such as the National Socialists in Germany and the Ku Klux Klan in the USA. In this highly charged environment, Furedi suggests, Anglo-American elites began to develop a new 'racial pragmatism' in which public displays of racism were to be avoided because they were potentially destabilising. This pragmatism did not challenge racism, he says; instead it 'was an approach that self-consciously ignored the fundamental question of racial oppression and focused its concern on the etiquette of race relations'.[38]

The term 'racism' is negatively loaded. The coining of the term, and the growth in its use, indicate that White supremacy was becoming a problematic ideology. Confronting this ideology in thought, however, meant confronting institutionalised practices such as Jim Crow laws in the USA, the colour bar in the colonies and immigration controls in Anglo-American states. In the 1930s, reform of these measures would have been a fundamental challenge to Anglo-American elites. It was easier to focus on extreme examples, such as Nazi Germany or the Ku Klux Klan, than the systemic allocation of Black people to inferior positions in Western nation-states and in the global order. White elites were not anti-racist, but ... they did want to dampen down racisms.

Anti-racism and disavowed racism

The Race Relations approach to tackling racisms became internationalised during and after the Second World War. The shift from 'race' as a source of pride for elites in the West to embarrassment with racism and the development of official anti-racism was mediated through shifting global power relations and the rise of radical anti-racist movements. The twentieth century witnessed the long decline of the British Empire and the rise of the USA as the dominant global power. The high point of the global supremacy of the UK was in the late nineteenth century. By the time that Lord Rosebery was making his speech to students at Glasgow University, at the turn of the twentieth century, the UK was already facing challenges from other major powers. By the end of the Second World War the USA had emerged as the pre-eminent global power. The issue of 'race' and the shift to anti-racism was an integral part of the US displacing the UK.

From the beginning of the war the US was already putting in place the outlines of a new global order. In 1939 the UK state was bankrupt, uncertain of its capacity to defeat Nazi Germany and desperate for US support in the war effort. The US exacted a price for its support of the UK. It made clear that the UK would have to withdraw from its colonies after the war. This can be seen in the Atlantic Charter, signed by Churchill and Roosevelt in August 1941. (The charter helped to prepare the way for the founding of the UN.) Clause three of the charter states that the signatories 'respect the right of all people to choose the form of government under which they will live, and they wish to see sovereign rights and self-government returned to those who have been forcibly deprived of them'. The charter also makes a commitment to free trade and access to mineral resources, a move that was aimed at removing the UK's use of the resources of its colonies for its own advantage.

The Declaration of the United Nations, signed by 26 Allied-aligned governments at the beginning of 1942, was modelled on principles laid down in the 1776 American Declaration of Independence. The US state presented these as principles that should govern the globe.[39] The UN declaration committed the signatories 'to defend life, liberty, independence and religious freedom, and to preserve human rights and justice in their own lands as well as in other lands'. The declaration also committed its signatories to agreeing to the purposes and principles of the Atlantic Charter. Lawrence James, in one of the best-selling (and sympathetic) histories of the British Empire, notes the sense of confident ascendency of the US's new global mission when he says that

> Emotional anti-imperialism was endemic in America. The general line was that all empires, including the British, were parasitic tyrannies which were fast becoming obsolete. 'The age of empires is dead', proclaimed Under-Secretary of State, Sumner Welles. For him and millions of Americans the war was a crusade for democracy and human rights throughout the world.[40]

The assumption of American superiority worried the UK government. The commitment to the self-determination of peoples was a source of tension between the US and the UK during the war. Churchill, for example, claimed that it only applied to countries occupied by the Axis Powers. The US insisted that the UK would have to grant self-government to its colonies.[41]

In the early stages of the war the UK government was on the defensive. The British Army was defeated in almost every theatre in which it was deployed. It was routed in France in June 1940. The evacuation at Dunkirk saved many of the personnel, but the army had to abandon most of its equipment. The UK managed, by a narrow margin, to frustrate German attempts to neutralise its war effort by maintaining command of the air in the Battle of Britain. Elsewhere it had less success. In August 1940 it was defeated by the Italians in East Africa. In early 1941 it was defeated in North Africa by a combined Italian and German force. The British Army's attempts to go on the offensive in Greece and Crete both proved abortive. In Asia it lost Hong Kong to the Japanese at the end of 1941 and beat a hasty retreat from Burma in early 1942. The single biggest shock, however, was the fall of Singapore, which was experienced as a humiliating defeat at the hands of the Japanese Army. Both the UK and US governments were aware that colonial opposition to the British Empire was part of the reason for the defeats in Africa and Asia.[42] The empire appeared to be lost to the UK and the USA was in a position to easily displace the UK from its position of global supremacy by the end of the war.

Despite being on the defensive, however, the UK government mounted a challenge to the rise of the USA. Suke Wolton describes how, at an Institute of Pacific Relations conference in Canada in late 1942, Lord Hailey put the Americans on the defensive. The issue of 'race' was a central element in the UK's rearguard attempt to unsettle the US government from the moral high ground on which it had placed itself. The UK government had been monitoring public opinion in the USA in order to judge how to pitch its defence of empire. It was aware of demands that Black American organisations were raising for racial equality in the military and in factory production for the war effort. The stationing of US troops in Britain had also raised the UK government's awareness of the issue of segregation in the military.[43] Elites in the US were sensitive to criticisms of the 'race' issue. By the end of the 1930s, American elites had become increasingly aware that the unequal treatment of Black Americans in the US was problematic for a country that was attempting to take on a global leadership role while proclaiming a commitment to freedom, equality and human rights. This concern can be seen in a flurry of research and discussion around the issue of 'race' in the US immediately prior to, during and after the war. Notable among these was the commissioning of a major investigation into the 'Negro problem' by the Carnegie Foundation in 1938, and the response to its publication (as *An American Dilemma*) in 1944.[44] The UK criticised the USA's isolationist stance of the 1930s and its long-standing practice of 'racial' discrimination, and by doing so it sought to persuade the American government that it should work in partnership with the UK, not attempt to ride roughshod over it. As Wolton puts it, US sensitivity 'on segregation and isolationism meant that when these issues were raised ... the American delegates were forced onto the defensive. This allowed Hailey the space to argue for a positive role for Britain in the working out of the postwar order.'[45]

The outlines of international official anti-racism were sketched out during and following the war. White elites in the UK and USA conceded the idea of 'race' equality in principle, while in practice they sought to rewrite the meaning of 'race' and to maintain, as far as possible, existing power relations. This was attempted in various different ways. The idea of 'racial' superiority was condemned. White superiority was rewritten as a humanitarian obligation to promote development. The issue of colour was obscured through promoting the idea that there are many 'races', not just White and Black, but also Hindu, Muslim, Chinese, Malay, etc. Racism was naturalised through presenting it as a feature of all 'race relations' situations, not just ones of White domination. There were concerted attempts to individualise the issue of racism by treating it as an issue of prejudice, rather than something with structural sources. There was an attempt to relativise Western 'racial' domination by pointing to features of 'Third World' societies, such as the caste system in India, that were presented as comparable.[46]

The founding Charter of the United Nations, signed in June 1945, stated that one of the main purposes of the United Nations was to 'achieve international co-operation ... in promoting and encouraging respect for human rights and for fundamental freedoms for all without distinction as to race'.[47] This principle, however, was in conflict with the practice of the powerful nation-states of the West. The disjuncture between the UN commitment to rights and freedoms regardless of 'race' and the practice of Western states was a continual problem and source of embarrassment, particularly for the UK and the USA. In the case of the UK, this was because of discriminatory practices in the British Empire, which actually expanded after 1945. In the case of the USA, this was because of the blatant, legally enshrined, racial discrimination known as Jim Crow.

An illustration of the problematic nature of the issue of 'race' for the UK and the USA can be seen in the response to a complaint, filed by the Indian delegation to the UN in 1946, against the South African government's treatment of people of Indian origin. The Indian proposal was supported by delegates from African and Asian countries, by the Soviet Union and countries within the Soviet bloc and by some Latin American countries. It was opposed by Britain, Australia, Canada, the United States and the Netherlands. These 'White' nations were concerned that, if endorsed by the UN, the complaint would set a precedent which would be used to challenge their own racially discriminatory practices. The debates which ensued from the Indian complaint were to lead to the drafting of the UN's Universal Declaration of Human Rights (UDHR), which was agreed in 1948.

The UDHR was a compromise. Some states and anti-racist activists wanted a legally binding Bill of Rights. The UDHR, however, only elaborated in more detail the principles outlined in the UN Charter. It did not make them legally binding. One of the reasons why the outcome was a declaration rather than a treaty was the concern on the part of many nation-states that a treaty would lead to intervention into their own domestic affairs. This is relatively easy to understand in the case of the White Western states that had explicitly racist policies. These White countries also, however, sought to convince countries such as India, Ethiopia and the Philippines, which had some experience of being dominated by colonial powers, that it was in their interests to support a declaration rather than a legally binding treaty. The UK, for example, responded to the Indian complaint against South Africa by accusing the Indians of hypocrisy because they upheld a caste system and were guilty of permitting discrimination against the Muslim minority in India. It was arguments such as these which appear to have influenced the Indian delegation to step back from their initial attempts to give teeth to the principles of racial equality outlined in the UN Charter and to support the side of the debate which upheld the principle of non-interference in the domestic affairs of states instead.[48]

After 1948 the issue of racial discrimination moved from being a politically contentious issue in the UN General Assembly to being an issue for expert consideration under the auspices of UNESCO. Over the course of the 1950s UNESCO commissioned research and published books and pamphlets on 'race' issues. This work took place alongside the work of academic researchers who also conducted and published research and held conferences on 'race' issues. A majority of the scholars working on the topic, and the books and academic journals where their work was published, were based in the United States and the UK.[49]

The issue of racism became politicised again in the 1960s, due to the activity of racialised peoples. Within the UN the politicisation of racism was facilitated by the expansion of UN membership, the activities of states aligned to the Soviet Union and the action of the Civil Rights movement in the USA. The states that were aligned to the Soviet Union during the Cold War used the issue of racism to embarrass the USA during the 1960s. They highlighted blatant racial discrimination in the USA as an indictment of the capitalist West. After 1945 most of the new members of the UN were former colonies.[50] These states almost invariably supported moves to raise and advance the issue of racial equality (even if they did not align themselves politically and economically with the Soviet Union). The increased activity around the issue of racial equality can be seen in the adoption of the Declaration of the Granting of Independence to Colonial Countries and Peoples (1960), the International Declaration on the Elimination of All

Forms of Racial Discrimination (1963), the International Convention on the Elimination of All Forms of Racial Discrimination (1966) and the declaration of 1971 as the International Year to Combat Racism and Racial Discrimination. This activity in the UN both fed on and encouraged the protests by the Civil Rights movement in the USA.[51] This wider international context informed the development of the civil rights movement in Northern Ireland, which aimed to bring an end to sectarian discrimination in this region of the UK. And it also partially informed the response of the UK government to the breakdown in civil order in Northern Ireland in August 1969.

Race Relations policy became institutionalised in the USA and the UK in the 1960s. In the USA this happened through the 1964 and 1965 Civil Rights Acts. In the UK official anti-racism became enshrined through the Race Relations Acts of 1965 and 1968. The aim of the UK Race Relations Acts was the integration of Black immigrants into the UK. One side of the approach focused on enabling immigrants and included measures such as welfare provision and support for learning English. The other side focused on the barriers to integration presented by the wider society and included measures to tackle racial discrimination in employment and measures to tackle prejudice through educating the population as a whole about race relations.[52] This policy of integration was conceived, in the words of the Home Secretary Roy Jenkins, not as 'a flattening process of assimilation but equal opportunity, accompanied by cultural diversity, in an atmosphere of mutual tolerance'.[53] Jenkins articulated a view of anti-racism which conceived it as an approach that acknowledged the needs of immigrants and acknowledged cultural diversity, but also acknowledged some of the ways in which UK society perpetuated racial inequality.[54]

In Chapter 2 we noted that when the 1965 Act was passed it did not cover discrimination on grounds of religion or belief and it did not cover Northern Ireland. We also noted that these exclusions were at the request of the Stormont government. The avowed anti-racism of the Act was thus accompanied by the 'racially' discriminatory act of excluding Catholics in Northern Ireland from a means of legal redress for the discrimination that was prevalent in the region. There were other ways in which official anti-racism was accompanied by a disavowed racism. One obvious one was the parallel enactment of racist immigration controls. In the words of the Labour politician Roy Hattersley, 'Without limitation [on immigration] integration is impossible, without integration limitation is inexcusable.'[55] In other words, in order to tackle racism in the UK, Black immigrants from the former colonies needed to be integrated into UK society, but in order for this anti-racist measure to be successful racist immigration controls were required. Spencer highlights the racist nature of the immigration controls of the 1960s in the conclusion to his historical account of UK immigration policy when he says that

There was little dissent in the post-war debate from the view that 'colonial', or 'coloured' or 'new Commonwealth', immigration was undesirable and no question that white immigration from the Commonwealth and Eire was, and continued to be, desirable. The debate about immigration controls was not a debate about controls in general but only about the control of coloured 'immigration'.[56]

In the 1960s UK labour markets required immigrant labour, hence the desire for immigration from the Commonwealth and the Republic of Ireland. The success of official anti-racism, however, was premised on control of Black immigration. In the 1960s cultural difference was viewed as primarily an external import and the idea of a relatively culturally homogeneous island people was taken as given by many people. The UK was divided over the issue of 'race'. On one side were the Powellites, the National Front and others who opposed Black immigration and called for repatriation. This viewpoint was perhaps most clearly articulated in the NF slogan 'There ain't no black in the Union Jack'. On the other side were those who opposed racism. The opponents of racism, however, included the disavowed racists who advocated race relations policy, radical left groups that opposed racism because it divided the working class, sectionalists who advocated Black Power or other forms of anti-racist self-organisation and liberals who upheld principles such as equality of opportunity regardless of 'race'.[57] In the next section, we turn to looking at some of the forms of anti-racism that underpinned the anti-racisms of the 1960s, and that are still influential in Northern Ireland today. Each of these forms mount a challenge to racisms, but do so in ways that also place limits on the emancipatory dynamic of radical anti-racism.

The 'anti' of anti-racism

Since the Second World War there has been widespread agreement – among politicians, policy-makers and radical anti-racist activists – that racism (in its various forms) is wrong. There is, however, no consensus on why it is wrong. The 1978 UNESCO declaration, for example, identifies five different ways in which racism is wrong – it hinders the development of its victims, perverts those who practise it, divides nations internally, impedes international cooperation and gives rise to political tensions between peoples. Bonnett identifies seven different ways in which racism has been said to be wrong: because it is socially disruptive, is foreign, sustains the ruling class, hinders the progress of our community, is an intellectual error, distorts and erases people's identities and is anti-egalitarian and socially unjust.[58] Miles and Brown examine the Revd Martin Luther King Jr's 'Letter from Birmingham Jail' and identify seven different reasons why King says racism is wrong. These include the idea that racism is damaging not just to victims but to society as a whole, and the idea that racism relies on prejudice, myth and half-truths instead of creative analysis, objective appraisal and higher understanding. King also condemned racism on the grounds that it is unjust because it imposes laws on a minority that a majority will not accept for themselves.[59] The one thing that is common to all forms of anti-racism is their opposition to racism. The *reasons* for opposing racisms, however, differentiate them.

The fact that there are different reasons for opposing racism is not a problem in and of itself. The problem lies in the ways that some of these reasons impede the development of an emancipatory anti-racism. In this section we briefly outline and explore four of the most common reasons that are given, in contemporary Northern Ireland and beyond, for opposing racisms.

Nationalist anti-racism

Some anti-racists attempt to draw on national 'tradition' as a resource in opposition to racism. Bonnett notes that this form of anti-racism 'tends to rely on the evocation of "our" national history as marked by equality, tolerance and/or pluralism and the claim that another society is the natural home, as well as the prime source, of racist ideas'.[60] The UNESCO declaration, with its emphasis on states as bearing the prime responsibility for tackling racism, implicitly supports a nationalist approach to tackling racism. This is the case because in practice nation-states invariably interpret racism and anti-racism in terms which are congruent with national identity. But it is not just nation-states which promote a nationalist approach. Gilroy has criticised the Anti-Nazi League, one of the most high-profile anti-racist campaigns against the far right National Front in the UK in the late 1970s and early 1980s, on the grounds that: 'the ANL deliberately sought to summon and manipulate a form of nationalism and patriotism as part of its broad anti-fascist drive'.[61] The ANL characterised the NF as Nazis and contrasted them to a genuine British tradition of fighting against Nazi Germany.

In Northern Ireland there are two, mutually antagonistic, forms of nationalism – an Irish nationalist one and an Ulster Unionist (or British nationalist) one. Geoghegan provides an insightful analysis of anti-racist approaches that are articulated from within each of these two nationalist perspectives. He does so through a contextualised examination of anti-racist murals and leafleting and poster campaigns in two working-class districts of Belfast – the Irish Republican heartland area of West Belfast and the iconic Ulster Unionist area of the Shankill Road. Geoghegan points to one mural in West Belfast which 'highlights the parallel experience of anti-Irish discrimination in London in the 1960s and contemporary prejudices and racism in Belfast'.[62] He goes on to note that this mural does not make any mention of the racism of the Irish. Consequently, 'the absence of a reference to Irish racism in the mural might reinforce the sense that racism is a problem in other (loyalist) areas and does not happen in Catholic/nationalist communities'.[63] In the Shankill a 'Declare War on Racism' mural employs visual symbolism that is similar to that of the ANL. The mural shows war graves (it is ambiguous whether these are from the First or Second World Wars) with single words – Auschwitz, Bergen-Belsen, slavery, extermination –

painted on to the surface of the image. The mural points to Britain's fight against Nazi Germany and to the role of Ulster Protestants in that fight. Geoghegan suggests that the anti-racist 'us' which is invoked in these murals implicitly excludes the nationalist or Unionist 'them' from anti-racism. Geoghegan argues that the content of the murals reproduces sectarianised political identities and the location of the murals serves to reproduce sectarian constructions of space. In other words, in the context of Northern Ireland a nationalist approach to anti-racism is also a sectarianised approach.

These two nationalist anti-racisms are in many respects mirror images of each other. Both involve racialising 'us' – the people who constitute the respective nation. They present this 'us' in positive anti-racist terms – as a people who have a tradition of anti-racist practice. Absent from both is any critical reflection on how 'our' tradition has also been implicated in racisms.

Egalitarian anti-racism

Bonnett notes that one of the common arguments against racisms is that they are *anti-egalitarian and socially unjust*. He notes that this type of argument is employed in most forms of anti-racism and that 'this form of opposition to racism usually draws on what are often cast as "deeply held" political and/or religious convictions that all people are, at some fundamental level, equal'.[64] Martin Luther King drew on this sense of social justice in his 'Letter from Birmingham Jail'. He makes a distinction between laws, which can be unjust, and social justice, which is fundamental. He says, for example, that a 'just law is a man-made code that squares with the moral law, or the law of God. An unjust law is a code that is out of harmony with the moral law.'[65] For King, something is right and just not because it is legally sanctioned, but because it is morally just or is in tune with God's law. For King, all humans are equal in the eyes of God. The sources for his argument are religious – they include St Augustine, St Thomas Aquinas, Martin Buber and Paul Tillich – but his rationales do not have to rely on a religious source for their justification. Aquinas's argument, that any 'law that uplifts human personality is just. Any law that degrades human personality is unjust', appeals as much to a secular audience as to a religious one.[66]

This argument regarding why racism is wrong points to the contradiction between the ideology of equality and the reality of inequality found in liberal democratic societies. The ideology of equality (and of liberty) is evident in the American Declaration of Independence (1776) which pronounced: 'We hold these truths to be self-evident, that all men are created equal, that they are endowed by their Creator with certain inalienable Rights, that among these are Life, Liberty and the pursuit of Happiness.'[67] These principles of liberty and equality were, however, limited in practice. They did not extend to women or to enslaved Africans.[68] We should not, nevertheless, draw the conclusion that commitment to equality and liberty in a capitalist society is merely rhetorical.

Freedom is intrinsic to capitalism, but freedom of a limited kind. Karl Marx notes that in a capitalist society the wage-labourer, unlike the slave, or the serf, 'belongs neither to an owner nor to the soil, but eight, 10, 12, 15 hours of his daily life belong to whomsoever buys them. The worker leaves the capitalist, to whom he has sold himself, as often as he chooses.'[69] Wage-labourers work for a wage. We own our own labour-power. We are free to sell it to the highest bidder. This freedom is, however, of a limited kind. As wage-labourers we have no independent means of existence, and so we *must* sell our labour-power, or starve. The capitalist is also free. He or she is free to hire and fire workers 'as often as he sees fit, as soon as he no longer gets any use, or not the required use, out of' the worker.[70] The freedom of the worker and the capitalist disguises the relations of power that underpin the labour process in a capitalist society. The commitment to freedom is not rhetorical. It is real. Freedom is really a requisite of normally functioning capitalism. Freedom is a requirement, one that is often violated in practice, but that also asserts itself as an inherent aspect of the relationship between capitalist and worker. This freedom is also an antagonistic one. Our freedom to buy and sell our labour-power, as wage-labourers, is a constraint on the freedom of the capitalist. The capitalist's freedom to hire and fire is a constraint on the freedom of workers.

It is true that the framers of the Declaration of Independence had a limited commitment to equality and liberty in practice, but that does not mean that they had no commitment, and it does not mean that this commitment did not place constraints on them. This commitment was a source of tension between, for example, the slave-owning South and the wage-labour North. The ideological commitment to freedom also established a principle by which the framers of the American Constitution, and future governments, could be judged. They were also powerless to confine the reach of the principle to cover only those people who they considered worthy. The principles of liberty and equality (and fraternity) inspired revolts by African slaves in the Americas, and in the case of the Caribbean island of Saint Domingue led to the defeat of French colonialism, the abolition of slavery on the island and the creation of the Republic of Haiti.[71] The principles of liberty and equality also inspired the United Irishmen who attempted to unite Protestant, Catholic and dissenter in Ireland to overthrow British rule on the island and establish Ireland as a republic.[72] It is difficult to imagine how slavery would have been abolished, how anti-discrimination legislation and equal opportunities policies (for women and for ethnic minorities) would have been enacted, or how racism could be viewed as wrong without the widespread establishing of the idea that all human beings are created equal and have the right to liberty. The free market and the principle of equality in the eyes of the law are not just rhetorical ideas. They are real in practice.

Anti-racism and social cohesion

Another common argument against racisms is that they are *socially disruptive*. 'If racism is regarded as a destabilising influence upon "good community relations", "social cohesion", and "national unity",' Bonnett says, 'it follows that those institutions concerned to maintain or establish these supposed norms will identify it as subversive.'[73] In this conception of anti-racism, he argues, the 'model of an "integrated", "peaceful" and "tolerant" society tends to be offered as an alternative ideal towards which to strive'.[74] Race Relations theory and practice, from its origins, has had an overriding concern with maintaining social order in the face of social disruption (such as the Chicago riots of 1919). Social disruption is an inherent feature of capitalist society. Marx and Engels's words, written more than 150 years ago, still resonate today.

> Constant revolutionising of production, uninterrupted disturbance of all social conditions, everlasting uncertainty and agitation distinguish the bourgeois epoch from all earlier ones ... The need of a constantly expanding market for its products chases the bourgeoisie over the entire surface of the globe ... All old-established national industries have been destroyed or are daily being destroyed. They are dislodged by new industries, whose introduction becomes a life and death question for all civilised nations, by industries that no longer work up indigenous raw material, but raw material drawn from the remotest zones; industries whose products are consumed, not only at home, but in every quarter of the globe.[75]

Capitalism also, however, requires stability, reliability and predictability. 'Business transactions at every level,' notes Ellen Meiksins Wood, 'require consistency and reliable enforcement, in contractual relations, monetary standards, exchanges of property.'[76] These transactions, and wider relations between individuals and organisations, are regulated through the rule of law, which is enforced by nation-states. The financial crisis of 2008 demonstrated the importance of nation-states as stabilising mechanisms. As Paul Mason, economics editor for *BBC Newsnight*, put it: 'We have lived through an event most of us thought that we would never see. Global capitalism, on the precipice of collapse, has been rescued by the state. The alternative was oblivion.'[77]

Race Relations practice, from its origins in response to the Chicago riots of 1919, was motivated by a concern with social cohesion and good community relations. But, as the US and Northern Ireland civil rights examples show, anti-racism can also be socially disruptive. The anti-racism of the Civil Rights movement in the USA in the 1950s and 1960s, the demand for equality between Blacks and Whites, meant challenging the organisation of the state and society more broadly. It meant resisting segregation on buses, in cafés, in schooling and in other public spaces. It meant challenging Jim Crow laws that institutionalised racial discrimination. Likewise, the demand for equality on the part of the civil rights movement in Northern Ireland in the late 1960s was socially disruptive.

In both cases 'aggressive counter-mobilization and repression ensued' as part of an attempt to defend the discriminatory status quo.[78]

Capitalism creates disruption, change and innovation. It is based on competition between different capitalists. Capitalist societies also, however, require predictability, regularity and coordination. The nation-state is a key mechanism which plays this role of bringing order out of chaos. A key function of the state is that it acts in the interest of capital-in-general, rather than in the interest of any particular capitalist, or group of capitalists. The state stands above individual capitalists and acts in the interests of them all. All capitalists need the physical and legal infrastructure necessary for the exploitation of labour and the realisation of profit, but they would all prefer that the cost of building and maintaining that infrastructure is borne by someone other than them. Construction companies that build roads profit directly from this exploitation of labour. Supermarket chains don't. The supermarket chains, however, require this transport infrastructure in order to move goods from the factory door to the shop floor. They require this transport infrastructure to enable consumers to get from their homes to purchase goods in their shops. Capitalists require a legal infrastructure that guarantees ownership of property, and that regulates industrial relations between employer and employee. As John Holloway and Sol Piciotto put it, 'capital can exist only in the form of individual capitalists' with their own particular, often competing interests, and 'it is only due to the existence of an autonomized state standing above the fray that the social relations of an otherwise anarchic society are reproduced and the general interest of total social capital thus established'.[79]

In some historical circumstances the interests of capital-in-general, in particular nation-states, has taken the form of 'racial' domination in order to secure social cohesion and profitability. 'Racial' domination is the form that European colonial rule took. It is also the form taken in the plantation slave-labour system in the Deep South, in the Jim Crow domination in the Deep South after slavery was abolished and in Unionist-controlled Northern Ireland. In all of these circumstances extraordinary levels of coercion were necessary in order to maintain social stability, and in all of these cases anti-racism was a threat to that stability. The fact that the UK government did not include Northern Ireland in the Race Relations Act when it was first drawn up in 1965, or when it was further developed in 1968, indicates that the commitment to tackling ethnic and racial discrimination was motivated by a concern with social order, rather than as a matter of principle. Robert Moore suggests something along these lines when he says that, in relation to Northern Ireland and the southern states of the US, 'the price paid by a central government for maintaining the loyalty of the majority in peripheral territories and the coherence of a political union is that it does not ask many questions about what goes on within those territories'.[80]

Multicultural anti-racism

A key feature of multicultural anti-racism is the argument that racisms distort and erase people's identities. Bonnett notes that this distortion and erasure is 'usually considered to take place within the individual psyche as well as at a collective level'.[81] Multicultural anti-racism is implied in UNESCO's 1978 Declaration on Race and Racial Prejudice when it states that 'All individuals and groups have the right to be different, to consider themselves as different and to be regarded as such.'[82] This right to difference, Bonnett notes, is 'commonly focused upon the destructive power racism has upon people's notions of and ability to politically deploy "their own" history, culture and sense of social cohesion'.[83] Racisms and other oppressions, Charles Taylor suggests, should be opposed because racist actions, words or images present minorities with 'a confining or demeaning or contemptible picture of themselves' and this 'can inflict harm, can be a form of oppression, imprisoning someone in a false, distorted, and reduced mode of being'.[84] It is for this reason that the politics of multiculturalism is sometimes referred to as the politics of recognition.

The multicultural view involves a conception of human beings in which one's ethnic or racial identity is considered to be core to one's sense of self, and to provide a common collective bond with others. As Charles Taylor puts it, our identity provides a sense of belonging, it is a fundamental part of 'a person's understanding of who they are, of their fundamental defining characteristics as a human being'.[85] The process of socialisation, of gaining culture, in this view, binds us to others; it provides us with a sense of belonging. Consequently, individuals are afforded recognition, not for their unique individuality, but for them in as far as they are viewed as representative of an officially recognised category (such as 'ethnic minority', 'women', 'disabled'). As Wendy Brown notes, 'one's race, sexuality, culture, or gender is considered to generate the consciousness, beliefs, or practice – the difference – that must be protected or tolerated' or recognised.[86] This conception of the individual as belonging to a 'group' underlies the multicultural emphasis on respect and recognition. The 'groupist' thinking that is inherent in this view has led critics to accuse multiculturalists of reifying 'race'.

Malik draws attention to the racialisation involved in multicultural anti-racism when he says that this approach to culture conflates the fact that human beings are culture-bearing creatures with the claim that as humans we have to bear a particular culture. 'Clearly no human can live outside of culture', he says:

> To say that no human can live outside of culture, however, is not to say they have to live inside a *particular* one … To view humans as having to bear specific cultures … suggests that every human being is so shaped by a particular culture that to change or undermine that culture would be to undermine the very dignity of that individual. It suggests that the biological fact of, say, Jewish or Bangladeshi ancestry somehow makes a human being incapable of living well except as a participant of

Jewish or Bangladeshi culture. This would only make sense if Jews or Bangladeshis were biologically distinct, in other words, if cultural identity was really about racial difference.[87]

Racisms and anti-racisms are a product of their times. Egalitarian anti-racism was ascendant in the 1960s and 1970s, when social movements demanded equality. In our more depoliticised times, multicultural anti-racism has become dominant. This way of understanding what is wrong with racism infuses good relations policy in contemporary Northern Ireland. It is more concerned with psychic well-being than substantive or formal equality. In many respects, it is hostile to equality, which is sometimes presented as a form of racism. It is the outlook that leads advocates of tackling 'institutional racism' to claim that racism 'can arise from well intentioned but patronising words or actions. It can arise from unfamiliarity with the behaviour or cultural traditions of people or families from minority ethnic communities.'[88] Multicultural anti-racism involves the kind of conception of 'race' articulated by Douglas Hyde and the Gaelic League, not the kind articulated in racial science. It conceives of humanity as horizontally, rather than vertically segmented. It is a form of anti-racism that reifies 'race', but presents different 'races' as equally valued and valid. It is more concerned with representation in the sense of positive images or esteem for cultural symbols than representation in the sense of democratic accountability.[89]

We can see the different conception of what it means to be human, one that resists racialisation, in Martin Luther King's 'Letter from Birmingham Jail'. King provides a fundamentally different view on the demeaning nature of racism and its impact on identity when he says:

> when you suddenly find your tongue twisted and your speech stammering as you seek to explain to your six-year-old daughter why she cannot go to the public amusement park that has just been advertised on television, and see tears welling up in her little eyes when she is told that Funtown is closed to colored children, and see the depressing clouds of inferiority begin to form in her little mental sky, and see her begin to distort her little personality by unconsciously developing a bitterness toward white people.[90]

This poignant extract illustrates his different emphasis to that of the multicultural view. King points to the demeaning nature of racism and its impact on Black children. The picture that King paints is a good illustration of what Taylor means by a society mirroring back a demeaning or contemptible picture of racialised minorities. King, however, does not use the demeaning nature of racisms as an argument in favour of a Black identity. Instead he uses it to argue that racisms distort the common humanity that both the victims and perpetrators of racisms share. Racisms are confining and demeaning to the racist because adopting a racist worldview involves a distorted view of humanity. Racisms perpetuate the division of humanity, in part, by fostering bitterness between different 'races'.

The existence of injustice twists your tongue when you attempt to explain or rationalise it because it runs contrary to a deeper sense of justice and a sense that we belong to a common humanity.

Conclusion

Our examination of anti-racism highlights the fact that there are a number of different approaches to anti-racism, and that often these approaches are mutually incompatible. Even where there is significant overlap between approaches, there are often underlying differences in their understanding of why racism is a problem and what needs to be done about tackling it. We have pointed out that the forms of anti-racism that international institutions and nation-states officially endorse are motivated by concerns with social cohesion, rather than a desire for the emancipation of the racialised. Most forms of official anti-racism are also problematic, because they are often instrumental in promoting processes of racialisation. We have also noted that the two nation-states that did most to initiate and shape official anti-racism – the UK and the USA – were responsible for significant forms of racial discrimination. The UK attempted to develop official anti-racism in ways that would enable it to maintain its colonies. The USA attempted to develop official anti-racism in ways that did not create severe disruption to the American nation-state. Both the UK and USA continued to maintain institutionalised forms of racism while promoting anti-racism at the international level. There was a shift from racism as an influential ideology in the nineteenth century to anti-racism as an influential ideology in the latter half of the twentieth century. This shift, however, was not a complete inversion. There were many continuities between racialism and anti-racism. Recognising this fact helps us to maintain a critical focus in our attempts to analyse racisms in Northern Ireland.

The official approach to anti-racism agreed by the UN, and translated into policy by states in the form of Race Relations policy, is opposed to racism, but it upholds the racist idea that humanity is divided into different races. It is opposed to racism, but primarily because it is socially disruptive. It is opposed to racial inequality, but is often content to accept racial inequality in practice. It is opposed to racism, but tackles the issue from within the existing international framework of a world divided into nation-states. It rejects the division of humanity into different 'races'. 'Racial' groups, it declares, do not exist, but it endorses the division of humanity into different 'races', and even calls for society to celebrate the division of humanity into different 'races'.

Notes

1 Lo is a Member of the Northern Ireland Legislative Assembly, and is the only elected representative in the United Kingdom to have been born in China. She has been a tireless campaigner against racisms. See, for example, Andras Gergely, 'Battle for jobs feeds Northern Ireland xenophobia', *Reuters Online*, 19 August 2009.
2 Paul Connolly and Michaela Keenan, *The hidden truth: racist harassment in Northern Ireland* (Belfast: OFMDFM, 2001), 86.
3 'Extremists must be confronted to ensure real change: Murphy', *4NI Online*, September 2004.
4 Steve Garner, *White working-class neighbourhoods: common themes and policy suggestions* (York: Joseph Rowntree Foundation, 2011), 13.
5 Ibid.
6 Lord Rosebery, *Questions of empire: a rectorial address delivered before the students of the University of Glasgow: November the Sixteenth Nineteen Hundred* (New York: Thomas Y. Crowell & Co., 1901), 12, 23, 24, 30.
7 See, for example, D. A. Hamer, 'The Irish Question and Liberal politics, 1886–1894', *The Historical Journal* 12.3 (1969): 511–532; Semmel, *Imperialism and social reform*.
8 Field, 'Nordic racism'; Horne, 'Race from power: US foreign policy and the general crisis of "White Supremacy"'; Horne, *Race war!*; Frank Furedi, *The silent war: imperialism and the changing perception of race* (London: Pluto Press, 1998); du Bois, *The souls of black folk*; Brawley, *The white peril*; Marilyn Lake, 'The white man under siege: new histories of race in the nineteenth century and the advent of White Australia', *History Workshop Journal* 58 (2004); Gunnar Myrdal, *An American dilemma: the negro problem and modern democracy* (New York: Harper & Brothers, 1944); Alistair Bonnett 'From white to Western: "racial decline" and the idea of the West in Britain, 1890–1930', *Journal of Historical Sociology* 16.3 (2003): 320–348.
9 Fredrickson, *Racism*, 2–3.
10 Pitcher, *The politics of multiculturalism*, 3.
11 Ibid., 109; emphasis in the original.
12 Ibid., 170.
13 Barkan, *The retreat of scientific racism*, 3.
14 Ibid., 9.
15 Bonnett, 'How the British working class became white', 318.
16 Lord Rosebery, *Questions of empire*, 23.
17 Semmel, *Imperialism and social reform*.
18 Paul Weindling, 'Weimar eugenics: the Kaiser Wilhelm Institute for Anthropology, Human Heredity and Eugenics in social context', *Annals of Science* 42.3 (1985): 314, doi:10.1080/00033798500200221.
19 For a detailed analysis of Nazi 'racial' policy, see Burleigh and Wippermann, *The racial state: Germany 1939–1945*.
20 Satnam Virdee, *Racism, class and the racialised outsider* (Basingstoke: Palgrave Macmillan, 2014).
21 Pankaj Mishra, *From the ruins of empire: the revolt against the West and the remaking of Asia* (Harmondsworth: Penguin, 2013).

22 Cited in ibid.
23 Chicago Commission on Race Relations, *The negro in Chicago*; Lauren, *Power and prejudice*.
24 Olivier Compagnon, '1914–18: the death throes of civilization: the elites of Latin America face the Great War', in *Perspectives in First World War Studies* (Amsterdam: Brill, 2004), 279–295; Joseph T. Stuart, 'The question of human progress in Britain after the Great War', *British Scholar* 1.1 (2008): 53–78; Michael Adas, 'Contested hegemony: the Great War and the Afro-Asian assault on the civilizing mission ideology', *Journal of World History* 15.1 (2004): 31–63; Prasenjit Duara, 'The discourse of civilization and Pan-Asianism', *Journal of World History* 12.1 (2001): 99–130, doi:10.1353/jwh.2001.0009.
25 Adas, 'Contested hegemony', 63.
26 Ibid.
27 Lothrop Stoddard, *The rising tide of color against white world-supremacy* (New York: Charles Scribner's Sons, 1921), 220.
28 Naoko Shimazu, *Japan, race and equality: the racial equality proposal of 1919* (London: Routledge, 1998).
29 Lauren, *Power and prejudice*, 99.
30 Bonnett, 'From the crises of whiteness to Western supremacism'; Gerald Horne, 'The crisis of white supremacy', *Socialism and Democracy* 17.1 (2003): 123–139; Bonnett, 'From white to Western'.
31 Barkan, *The retreat of scientific racism*, 297.
32 Ibid.
33 Malik, *The meaning of race*, 125.
34 Furedi, *The silent war*, 7.
35 M. J. Akbar, *Nehru: the making of India* (London: Penguin, 1988); D. N. Panigrahi, *India's partition: the story of imperialism in retreat* (Abingdon: Routledge, 2004).
36 Horne, 'The crisis of white supremacy'; Horne, 'Race from power'; Furedi, *Colonial wars*; Furedi, *The silent war*.
37 W. E. B. du Bois, 'Inter-racial implications of the Ethiopian crisis: a negro view', *Foreign Affairs* 14.1 (1935): 89.
38 Furedi, *The silent war*, 79.
39 Hazard, *Postwar anti-racism*.
40 Lawrence James, *The rise and fall of the British Empire* (London: Abacus, 1998), 511–512.
41 Suke Wolton, *Lord Hailey, the Colonial Office and the politics of race and empire in the Second World War* (Basingstoke: Palgrave Macmillan, 2000), 97–103.
42 Horne, *Race war!*; Wolton, *Lord Hailey*; Stanley Wolpert, *Shameful flight: the last years of the British Empire in India* (Oxford: Oxford University Press, 2006); Furedi, *The silent war*.
43 Northern Ireland played a small role in this aspect of the Second World War. See Simon Topping, 'Laying down the law to the Irish and the Coons: Stormont's response to American racial segregation in Northern Ireland during the Second World War', *Historical Research* 86.234 (2013), 741–759; Simon Topping, '"The dusky doughboys": interaction between African American soldiers and the population

of Northern Ireland during the Second World War', *Journal of American Studies* 47.4 (2013): 1131–1154.

44 Myrdal, *An American dilemma*.

45 Wolton, *Lord Hailey*, 106.

46 See, for example, Andrew W. Lind (ed.), *Race relations in world perspective* (Honolulu: University of Hawaii Press, 1955). For critical accounts, see Wolton, *Lord Hailey*; Furedi, *The silent war*; Horne, *Race war!*; Lauren, *Power and prejudice*; Leah N. Gordon, 'The individual and "the general situation": the tension barometer and the race problem at the University of Chicago, 1947–1954', *Journal of Historical Sociology* 46.1 (2010): 27–51.

47 United Nations, *Charter of the United Nations* (1945), www.un.org/en/documents/ charter Article 1, Clause 3.

48 Lauren, *Power and prejudice*.

49 Hazard, *Postwar anti-racism*.

50 The UN began its life as a much smaller organisation than it is today. Fifty-one member states signed the UN Charter in 1945. These included colonial powers (the UK, France, Belgium, Netherlands), White settler states (Australia, Canada, New Zealand, South Africa) and European states that were not part of the Soviet bloc (Denmark, Greece, Luxemburg, Norway). Another significant bloc of states were those aligned to the Soviet Union (the USSR, Byelorussian Soviet Socialist Republic, Czechoslovakia, Poland, Ukrainian Soviet Socialist Republic and Yugoslavia). And there was a significant bloc of countries with a history of colonisation. The largest number of these was from Latin America (Argentina, Bolivia, Brazil, Chile, Colombia, Costa Rica, Cuba, Dominican Republic, Ecuador, El Salvador, Guatemala, Haiti, Honduras, Mexico, Nicaragua, Panama, Paraguay, Peru, Uruguay and Venezuela), followed by the Middle East (Egypt, Iran, Iraq, Lebanon, Saudi Arabia, Syria and Turkey), Asia (China, India and the Philippine Republic) and Africa (Ethiopia and Liberia). By 1960 the UN had 99 members and by 1968 there were 126. The vast majority of the new members joined when they gained their independence from their former colonial masters.

51 Tinker, *Race, conflict and the international order*; Banton, *The international politics of race*; Lauren, *Power and prejudice*; Hazard, *Postwar anti-racism*; Manning Marable, *Race, reform and rebellion: the second Reconstruction in black America, 1945–1990* (Jackson, MS: University Press of Mississippi, 2nd edn, 1991).

52 Small and Solomos, 'Race, immigration and politics in Britain'; Gideon Ben-Tovim and John Gabriel, 'The politics of race in Britain, 1962–79: a review of major trends and of recent debates', in *'Race' in Britain: continuity and change*, ed. Charles Husband (London: Hutchinson, 1982), 145–171.

53 Cited in Nicholas Deakin, *Colour, citizenship and British society* (London: Panther, 1970), 108.

54 Leo Kuper, *Theories of race relations* (Paris: UNESCO, 1972); Herbert Blumer, 'Reflections on theory of race relations', in *Race relations in world perspective*, ed. Andrew W. Lind (Honolulu: University of Hawaii Press, 1955), 3–21; Banton, 'The race relations problematic'.

55 Cited in Malik, *The meaning of race*, 18.

56 Ian R. G. Spencer, *British immigration policy since 1939: the making of multi-racial Britain* (London: Routledge, 1997), 154.

57 Ambalavaner Sivanandan, 'From resistance to rebellion: Asian and Afro-Caribbean struggles in Britain', *Race & Class* 23.2–3 (1981): 111–152; Bonnett, *Anti-racism*; Gilroy, *There ain't no black in the Union Jack*.

58 Bonnett, *Anti-racism*, 4–7.

59 Robert Miles and Malcolm Brown, *Racism* (London: Routledge, 2nd edn, 2003), 12–14.

60 Bonnett, *Anti-racism*, 5.

61 Gilroy, *There ain't no black in the Union Jack*, 171.

62 Geoghegan, *A difficult difference*, 116.

63 Ibid., 117.

64 Bonnett, *Anti-racism*, 7.

65 Martin Luther King Jr, 'Letter from Birmingham Jail' (1963), 3, www.uscrossier.org/pullias/wp-content/uploads/2012/06/king.pdf (accessed 1 September 2016).

66 Ibid.

67 The declaration is available online at www.archives.gov/exhibits/charters/declaration_transcript.html (accessed 1 September 2016).

68 Stephanie McCurry, 'The two faces of Republicanism: gender and proslavery politics in antebellum South Carolina', *Journal of American History* 78.4 (1992): 1245–1264.

69 Karl Marx, *Wage labour and capital*, 9.

70 Ibid.

71 C. L. R. James, *The Black Jacobins: Toussaint L'Ouverture and the San Domingo revolution* (New York: Vintage, 1963).

72 Smyth, *The men of no property*.

73 Bonnett, *Anti-racism*, 4–5.

74 Ibid., 5.

75 Karl Marx and Frederick Engels, *Manifesto of the Communist Party*, 16.

76 Ellen Meiksins Wood, *The origin of capitalism: a longer view* (London: Verso, 2002), 179.

77 Paul Mason, *Meltdown: the end of the age of greed* (London: Verso, 2009), vii.

78 Gianluca De Fazio, 'Civil rights mobilization and repression in Northern Ireland: a comparison with the US Deep South', *The Sixties* 2.2 (2009): 177.

79 John Holloway and Sol Picciotto, 'Introduction: towards a materialist theory of the state', in *State and capital: a Marxist debate* (London: Edward Arnold, 1978), 19.

80 Moore, 'Race relations in the Six Counties', 38.

81 Bonnett, *Anti-racism*, 6.

82 UNESCO, Declaration on Race and Racial Prejudice, Article 1, clause 2.

83 Bonnett, *Anti-racism*, 6.

84 Charles Taylor, 'The politics of recognition', in *Multiculturalism*, ed. Amy Gutmann (Princeton, NJ: Princeton University Press, 1994), 25.

85 Ibid.

86 Wendy Brown, *Regulating aversion: tolerance in the age of identity and empire* (Princeton, NJ: Princeton University Press, 2006), 43.

87 Malik, 'Making a difference', 370.

88 Macpherson, *The Stephen Lawrence Inquiry*, sec. 6.17.

89 Alana Lentin, 'Replacing "race", historicizing "culture" in multiculturalism', *Patterns of Prejudice* 39.4 (2005): 379–396; Malik, 'Making a difference'; Cillian McBride, 'Toleration, respect and recognition in Northern Ireland', in *Tolerance and diversity in Ireland, north and south*, ed. Iseult Honohan and Nathalie Rougier (Manchester: Manchester University Press, 2016), 249–265.

90 King, 'Letter from Birmingham Jail', 2.

5

Rethinking anti-racism

We have highlighted some inconsistencies within the Race Relations approach. In the chapter on racism and sectarianism, for example, we noted the failure to extend the UK's Race Relations Acts to Northern Ireland in the 1960s, 1970s and 1980s. We also pointed out the inconsistent approach to the place of religion in Race Relations theory and policy – treating anti-Semitism and Islamophobia as forms of racism, but excluding sectarianism in Northern Ireland. In the previous chapter we noted that the development of Race Relations policy happened in parallel with disavowed racist policies on the part of nation-states. The detention of Frank Kakopa and the other Black Africans who were apprehended at the same time as him provides an example of this inconsistency. Their detention draws our attention to institutional racism in UK immigration policy. This institutional racism, however, exists alongside a state commitment to anti-racism. How are we to interpret this inconsistency?

One way of doing so is to suggest that there is nothing wrong with Race Relations theory, but that the problem lies with the implementation of the theory. One reason why Frank Kakopa may have settled out of court for a fairly small amount of money (£7,500) is that there is a chance that he would have lost his case had it gone to court. Immigration is one of the areas, along with national security and Parliament, which enjoys exemptions under UK Race Relations legislation. As a report by the Northern Ireland Human Rights Commission puts it, a UK immigration official, 'acting on the instruction of a Minister, may discriminate on grounds of nationality, or ethnic or national origin. In this way, the practice of racial profiling, condemned by international standards is not categorically outlawed in the UK.'[1] In other words, knowingly discriminating against someone on grounds of nationality, ethnicity or national origin (such as, for example, only stopping Black Africans) is permitted in UK law if the discrimination is done by an immigration officer instructed to do so by a government minister. If the BIA were able to demonstrate in court that its officers had been acting on the instruction of a minister then Frank Kakopa would have lost his case. Jenny Bourne points to the double standard that operates in UK Race Relations policy when she notes that the UK state outlaws institutional racism in public bodies, while at the same time sneaking it in through the back door with racist immigration and asylum laws, its caveats re freedom of information, restrictions on jury trials, proscription of specific refugee organisations in legislation against terrorism – all of which affect black people and refugees in particular.[2]

One possible conclusion that could be drawn from the double standard that operates in UK Race Relations policy is that tackling 'institutional racism' is an effective way to eradicate racism and is a sound policy approach; it just needs to be applied consistently. The Stephen Lawrence Inquiry, which introduced the concept of 'institutional racism' into UK Race Relations policy, was not established because of the murder of a single Black man (Stephen Lawrence). It was established because significant sections of the UK state acknowledged that the unsuccessful Metropolitan Police Service investigation into Lawrence's murder was symptomatic of a wider problem of racism in the MPS. Moreover, and even more importantly from the point of view of state authority, this problem of police racism was undermining the legitimacy of the criminal justice system.[3] It could be argued that the logic of the 'institutional racism' framework dictates that in order to both maintain the legitimacy of immigration controls and take a consistent approach to anti-racism, the UK state should extend the Race Relations (Amendment) Act of 2000 to also cover immigration policy.

Another way of interpreting the inconsistencies in the Race Relations approach might be to argue that policy-making and implementation is a messy business in which a lot of conflicting interests are involved. Inconsistency, in this view, could be interpreted as an unfortunate outcome of the political process. Advocates of this view might argue that human error is an inevitable feature of human society and that is why we need lots of different mechanisms – such as anti-racist legislation, or bodies such as the Equality Commission Northern Ireland and the Northern Ireland Human Rights Commission – to act as checks and balances against attempts to subvert or circumvent anti-racist policy. In this view it is impossible to completely eradicate racism because of the imperfect nature of human beings. Since humans are imperfect, the logic goes, it is impossible to create a perfect anti-racist policy. We can manage or minimise racism, but not eradicate it. In the words of Banton, previously cited in Chapter 3: 'racial discrimination [is] a normal characteristic of social relations … Official action could reduce it … but it would not eliminate discrimination.'[4]

These two ways of interpreting the inconsistencies in the Race Relations approach both treat Race Relations *theory* as unproblematic. The inconsistencies, in these interpretations, arise when it comes to translating theory into policy. In this chapter we challenge the idea that Race Relations theory is unproblematic. We argue that Race Relations theory in-and-of-itself is complicit in the perpetuation of racisms. We challenge any interpretation that presents Race Relations theory as relatively unproblematic. Race Relations theory is not innocent; through the confusions that they have perpetuated, Race Relations theorists have played an important role in the crisis of anti-racism.

In the first part of this chapter we examine the conventional social science approach that underpins Race Relations theory and contrast this with the Hegelian-inspired approach that underpins the work of Karl Marx and the emancipatory strands of post-Marx Marxism. The purpose of this examination is not to provide an exhaustive explanation of either approach, but rather to highlight the essentially elitist nature of Race Relations theory. This elitism is not an incidental feature, or a problem of the subjective outlook or prejudices of individual theorists – it is hard-wired into Race Relations theory. In the second part we highlight the tendency, in Race Relations theory, to treat social phenomena as if they are static things rather than dynamic processes. This tendency is a product of the methodology of Race Relations theory, which treats the subjective outlook of human beings as inherently problematic, rather than as something that enables us to transcend the limitations imposed on us by nature. We go on to argue that the concept of 'racialisation' is an advance on the concept of 'race relations' because it draws attention to the processes through which 'race' is made to appear real and avoids the problem of reifying 'race'. In the third section we draw attention to the limitations of the social constructionist conception of 'race' and racism and argue that its one-sided emphasis on human subjectivity ignores the objective conditions, inherent in capitalism as a social system, that give rise to the idea of 'race' and practices of racisms. In the final section we sketch out some of the key principles of an emancipatory anti-racism, one that holds out the possibility of transcending racisms and consigning them to the dustbin of history.

Conventional social science versus Marx

Immanuel Kant, the Enlightenment philosopher, has had a profound influence on the development of social science as an approach to understanding the social world. Kant aimed to reconcile empiricist and rationalist approaches in philosophy. According to the empiricist view of the world, all knowledge comes through experience. We know the things that we know because we have experienced them with our senses – taste, touch, sight, hearing, smell. Rationalists take a different view, arguing that reason and innate ideas are prior to experience. Our senses, they point out, can deceive us. By the use of rational principles such as logic, mathematics, ethics and metaphysics we can contemplate and come to understand the world. Rationalists and empiricists have fundamentally different conceptions of how we, as human beings, know what we know. In the empiricist view, we know racism because we have experienced or witnessed it in action. In the rationalist view, we have a concept of racism and this is what enables us to recognise it when we experience it with our senses.

Kant attempted to reconcile these two different approaches to understanding the relationship between thinking and being. He argued, against the empiricists, that experience is purely subjective – it is raw, unfiltered being. We need reason, he argued, in order to process our experiences. Our experiences must be filtered through ideas and concepts (the tools of reason) in order for our minds to make sense of these experiences. Without reason, experience is, literally, meaningless. The use of reason imposes meaning on our sensory experiences. It organises the raw data of experience and makes sense of it.[5] The use of reason without application to experience, on the other hand, only leads to theoretical illusions. Unless we gather data from the real world and filter this through our ideas and concepts, our capacity for reason cannot develop beyond solipsistic self-indulgence. Reason, says Kant, 'must approach nature in order to be taught by it … not in the character of a pupil who listens to everything the teacher has to say, but of an appointed judge who compels the witnesses to answer the questions which he himself has formulated'.[6] We can apply this to the concept of racism.

From a rationalist perspective, the concept of racism exists independently of any experience. We can discuss racism in the abstract, outside of any empirical examples in the real world, because we have a concept of racism. From an empiricist perspective this rationalist approach ignores the real world of empirical sensuous human experience. From an empiricist perspective, racism is not something abstract, it is something that people experience in the real world – we can observe it, describe it and measure it. Conventional social science brings those two perspectives together. In doing so, it allots a special role to social scientists as 'appointed judges' who interrogate the world of sensuous experience in order to generate knowledge about the nature of the social world. Against the empiricists they say that we cannot observe racism unless we have a concept of racism. The rationalists are correct in saying that we need abstract concepts in order to understand experience. Against the rationalists they say that we cannot know if these concepts make any sense out of our experience of the social world if we do not test them against the social world. The social scientist is someone who stands at the interface of reason and experience – he or she brings reason and experience into contact with each other. The concept of racism is judged by whether it makes sense of experience, not simply by whether it makes sense in the abstract. The evidence from the real world (i.e. empirical data) can only be judged if we have criteria against which we are judging it. That is why we require concepts. The evidence and the concepts can only be tested through the social scientists interrogating them in relation to each other.

The aim of social science, in this view, is to interrogate the social world in order to better understand the phenomena that the social scientist is investigating. As part of this investigation the social scientist devises tools (such as concepts, definitions, surveys, experiments) that enable her or him to ask penetrating questions of reality. The use of these tools enable the researcher to stand above their own individual subjective experience of the world and obtain an objective understanding of the particular social phenomena under examination. The more comprehensive and appropriate the tools employed, according to this view, the better the understanding will be. Banton describes this approach to understanding the social world in the following terms:

> Orthodox social scientists seek sharp definitions that enable the research worker to make systematic observations which, because they are related to theories, permit an accumulation of knowledge. For them, objectivity resides in the use of techniques which permit individual observers to transcend the subjectivity of their perceptions and agree that certain of their observations are matters of fact.[7]

This summary of conventional social science methodology is based on the idea that the social world has an objective existence, but human comprehension of this objective reality is necessarily filtered through a subjective mind. We lessen this subjectivity by using a range of social science techniques in an attempt to minimise our individual subjective biases. One of these techniques is the honing of sharp definitions. These help to minimise subjective bias by, for example, providing a means by which different researchers can check that they are examining and talking about the same phenomena. Social scientists have also developed a range of methods (such as questionnaires, structured observation in a controlled environment, content analysis of the written or spoken word, ethnography and participant observation, interviews, or focus groups) that enable systematic analysis.[8]

This idea of an objective social science which stands above the subjective viewpoints of members of society was challenged by G. W. F. Hegel and Karl Marx. For Hegel and Marx, a key problem with Kant's conception is that he mechanically separates subjective thought and objective reality. We can illustrate the difference through examining the distinction that Banton makes between an observer's model of the social world (the viewpoint of the social scientist) and an actor's model of the social world (the common-sense, folk or everyday viewpoint). An actor's model is one that is used to steer a course through everyday life. Ordinary people, Banton says, rarely use terms such as 'race' or 'ethnicity'. They use practical language. In Malaysia, for example, they use terms such as Malay, Chinese, Indian, Muslim, Buddhist, Christian. Ordinary people, he says, know

> that persons assigned to these categories vary in their cultural distinctiveness. In the languages they use, the costume they wear, the use they make of leisure time etc., some are more culturally distinctive, and in this sense, more 'ethnic', than many of the adolescents who listen to the same pop music, eat similar foods, and mix more readily.[9]

The observer's model is one that attempts to abstract from this complexity and discern underlying patterns and causal mechanisms. As Banton puts it, they 'look for regularities of which the actors are unaware or about which the actors have insufficient information'.[10] Social scientists use sharply defined abstract concepts like 'ethnic group', 'race', 'social stratification', 'social closure' and 'race relations'. They attempt to isolate out the key elements that account for phenomena, such as racism, and discern the relative importance of each of these elements.

One way in which social scientists do this is through the use of a comparative method. They examine a particular phenomenon, such as racial intolerance, in different settings and in doing so they can discern the incidental and essential features of the phenomenon that they are investigating, and the causal mechanisms through which they operate. Banton talks, for example, about comparing a setting in Malaysia with one in Bosnia 'to distinguish ethnic, national and religious attributes in order to compare [ethnic/national/religious] relations ... and in this way learn about the causes of tolerance and intolerance'.[11]

Hegel and Marx criticised approaches that differentiate between the external world of objective reality and the internal world of subjective understanding. Hegel and Marx talk about the *unity* of the objective (external reality) and subjective (internal thought). Just as you cannot have a magnet with only a north or south pole, you cannot have external reality without internal thought. When you break a magnet in half, you do not end up with one magnet that has a north pole and another with a south pole. Both magnets have north and south poles, because the poles are an expression of a relationship between all the electrons in the magnet, not a property of either end of a magnet. External presupposes, and therefore cannot exist without, internal, and vice versa. Marx and Hegel concur on this conception of the essential unity of opposites (objective and subjective, reality and thought, practice and ideas, etc.). They talk about a unity between seemingly opposed things, not a separation between them. In the Kantian perspective, separate things have their own independent existence; any relationship between them is incidental to their existence, rather than constitutive of it. Franz Jakubowski helps to clarify further what Marx means by unity when he distinguishes it from identity: '*identity* of thought with being can only be asserted by eliminating one of the two elements ... it prevents a real, dialectical *unity* between the two'.[12] Unity involves a relationship in which change in one pole of the opposition brings about a reciprocal change in the other pole. Identity between two things collapses the distinction between them. Unity involves a dynamic interaction. It involves processes of change and development, growth and decay, conscious human agency and impersonal structural constraints.

Marx, however, criticises Hegel for one-sidedly conceiving this unity in the realm of ideas. In Europe in the eighteenth century, there were two main philosophical camps: materialists and idealists. 'Those who asserted the primacy of mind over nature,' as Engels puts it, 'formed the camp of idealism. The others, who regarded nature as primary, belonged to the various schools of materialism.'[13] Marx criticised Hegel from a materialist perspective. To comprehend how Hegel could develop his understanding of the unity of objective and subjective, Marx argued, we need to locate the development of his philosophy in the material conditions of Europe at that time. A revolution in the real world, the French Revolution of 1789, provided the material conditions for Hegel's revolution in thought. His conception of thought as a process of constant movement did not appear magically from within the confines of his skull, but was rooted in the disruption that was the French Revolution. In critiquing Hegel, Marx draws on Hegel's own method. He argues that all thought, Hegel's included, needs to be understood in its relationship to actual human activity. As Raya Dunayevskaya puts it, Hegel's revolution in thought 'can be fully understood only in the light of the revolutions in action, particularly the development of the great French Revolution. There is nothing in thought – not even in the thought of a genius – that has not previously been in the activity of the common man.'[14]

Marx critiqued Hegel from a materialist perspective. It is, however, too one-sided to see Marx as a materialist; he was also an idealist, not in the sense of being optimistic about the prospects for a better world, but in the sense that he did not believe that materialism was superior to idealism. The two exist in unity with each other; each on its own is too one-sided. The chief defect of materialism, as Marx puts it,

> is that the thing, reality, sensuousness, is conceived only in the *form of the object or of contemplation*, but not as *sensuous human activity, practice*, not subjectively. Hence, in contradistinction to materialism, the *active* side was developed abstractly by idealism – which, of course, does not know real, sensuous activity as such.[15]

Marx fused idealism and materialism through pointing to the key role of active human practice as mediating between objective reality and subjective perception. 'The question whether objective truth can be attributed to human thinking is not a question of theory,' Marx says, 'but is a practical question. Man must prove the truth – i.e. the reality and power, the this-sidedness of his thinking in practice. The dispute over the reality or non-reality of thinking that is isolated from practice is a purely *scholastic* question.'[16] Marx referred to this new approach, which merged idealism and materialism, variously as historical materialism, dialectical materialism or scientific socialism.[17]

From a Marxist perspective, the approach of conventional social science, of attempting to minimise the subjective viewpoint of the observer in order to better grasp objective reality, ruptures the unity of the objective and the subjective. Banton's observer is essentially passive in relation to social change. The observer is only active in testing and recording theories about society. The observer's aim is to achieve an approximation of objective reality, not to alter that reality. In this conventional view, there is an essential division of labour between those who think (social science researchers) and those who act (states, political parties, pressure groups, charities, etc.). Researchers can advise government or charities or other kinds of organisations, but it is these organisations that should act on the world, not the researcher. From the perspective of conventional social science, social actors – whether these are states, pressure groups or political parties – cannot be trusted to act as objective observers because they are working to a preconceived agenda. Social scientists, on the other hand, should aim for objectivity – even though, in practice, this is impossible to attain. This conception of a division of labour is shared by many of those, particularly in academia, who describe themselves as Marxists. Both these self-styled Marxists and conventional social scientists believe that they stand above society and observe its inner workings. The academic Marxist believes that he or she is observing society from the perspective of the objective interests of the working class. The conventional social scientist believes that she or he is observing society from the objective perspective of humanity as a whole.

From the perspective of conventional social science, this division between mental and manual labour is simply a matter of specialisation in the workforce. Social scientists are white-collar workers who have been trained to operate as objective observers of society. Marx views it differently. He located the division between mental and manual labour in the historical development of class societies. Rather than viewing social scientists as arising from the need to have specialist thinkers who can aim for an objective understanding of society, Marx viewed the idea that it was possible to take a view outside of society as itself a product of the division between mental and manual labour. As Marx and Engels put it in *The German Ideology*:

> [A social d]ivision of labour only becomes truly such from the moment when a division of material and mental labour appears. (The first form of ideologists, priests, is concurrent.) From this moment onwards consciousness can really flatter itself that it is something other than consciousness of existing practice, that it really represents something without representing something real; from now on consciousness is in a position to emancipate itself from the world and to proceed to the formation of 'pure' theory, theology, philosophy, ethics, etc.[18]

Here we see, once again, Marx arguing against the separation of subjective outlook and objective reality (subjective consciousness flatters itself that it is something other than consciousness of existing practice).

From the perspective of conventional social science, including academic Marxism, human actors need to be educated. The objective observer is able to see the underlying patterns in society that the ordinary subjective actor cannot see. Consequently, the social scientist is in a unique position to educate social actors about society. For the Race Relations theorist, this involves explaining racism so that a scientifically robust anti-racist policy can be developed. For the academic Marxist, this involves explaining the connection between capitalist society and features of this society, such as racism, because the working class can only ever spontaneously develop trade union consciousness (e.g. that wages should more fairly reflect the work that has been done). From the perspective of Marx, the division between mental and manual labour is a feature of all class societies. The emancipation of humanity from class oppression goes hand-in-hand with the eradication of this distinction.[19] From the perspective of Marx's theory of human liberation, the point is not to deny the division between mental and manual labour; this division is real and has material roots in class society. The point is to recognise that this division artificially separates thought and practice. Achieving the goal of human emancipation involves overcoming this distinction in both thought and practice.

From the perspective of Marx, the self-appointed role as educator is essentially elitist because this view of society 'forgets that circumstances are changed by men and that it is essential to educate the educator himself. This doctrine must, therefore, divide society into two parts, one of which is superior to society.'[20] For Marx, human self-consciousness develops through the unity of theory and practice. This means not only educating the working class through teaching them about Marx's theory, but also that theorists themselves have to be educated by the working class and others who suffer from the oppression and indignities that are generated by capitalist society. The oppressed, not intellectuals, understand at a more fundamental, organic level how capitalism dehumanises. Their understanding of society develops as they struggle against dehumanisation. The artificial separation between theory and practice is overcome in theory through the recognition, by intellectuals, that the struggle against oppression is a form of knowledge itself and, by the oppressed, through their recognition that practice without theory (i.e. without understanding the social laws that underpin the operation of capitalist society) is insufficient to overcome their oppression. The artificial separation between theory and practice is overcome through the transformation of the social conditions through which humanity is reproduced (i.e. through the revolutionary transformation of the social relations of production).

Static things and dynamic processes

In conventional social science there is a tendency to approach the study of the social world as if it can be investigated using the same methods as can be used to study the natural world. In the Kantian view, the scientific method involves observing the social world – the social scientist experiences and investigates the social world with his or her senses, and the tools (such as questionnaires) that augment their senses – and the social scientist processes those experiences through the use of reason (using theories and concepts). In doing so the social scientist aims for objectivity. The aim is to take an objective stance external to the world that the social scientist is examining. Examining the social world in the same way as the natural world is, however, problematic. As Kenan Malik notes:

> At the heart of the scientific methodology is its view of nature, and of natural organisms, as machines: not because ants or apes work like computers or TVs, but because, like all machines, they lack agency and will … To study nature scientifically requires us to make a distinction between a humanity that is a thinking subject and a nature that presents itself to thought but is itself incapable of thought. When studying 'external' nature the distinction between the thinking subject and the object of study is easy to make. But with the study of humans, such a neat division becomes impossible: human beings are simultaneously the subject that thinks and the object of that thought.[21]

Human beings, unlike anything else in nature, have agency and will. Non-human animals do act in the world. They eat, they procreate, they even, in more highly evolved forms, use tools and have rudimentary language skills. They do not, however, have agency and will. They are unable to imagine a different world and to try to bring this different world into being. The social world is fundamentally different to the natural world. It is dynamic, evolving and changing – but at a pace set by human invention and intervention, not at a pace set by nature.

In conventional social science there is strong tendency to rupture the unity of subject and object and treat the social world as an object. This method works well in the study of the natural world, where living things can be treated as things – as inanimate material objects, as distinct from beings with consciousness – but it dehumanises the social world by treating humans as if they are the same as the rest of nature. In Race Relations theory this 'scientific' approach to understanding society tends to treat social phenomena as static objects, rather than as dynamic processes. In this section we will illustrate this tendency in two ways: first, through the use of definitions that attempt to fix the phenomena of racism in order to study it, and secondly, through the reification of 'race'.

Definitions

Banton, as we previously noted, says that mainstream 'social scientists seek sharp definitions that enable the research worker to make systematic observations which, because they are related to theories, permit an accumulation of knowledge'.[22] Banton, in one of the earliest attempts to define racism within UK Race Relations theory, defined it as 'the doctrine that a man's behaviour is determined by stable inherited characteristics deriving from separate racial stock having distinctive attributes and usually considered to stand to one another in relations of superiority and inferiority'.[23] Banton is saying that racism is a body of ideas with three essential features: humanity is understood to be composed of different races; the behaviour of individuals from these races is understood to be genetically determined; and these different racial groups relate to each other as superiors and inferiors. This definition, Robert Miles and Malcolm Brown point out, refers 'exclusively to nineteenth-century scientific arguments about "race".

As a result, given that those ideas had been largely discredited by science, Banton concluded that racism was dead.'[24]

Miles and Brown argue that Banton's rejection of the concept of racism shows the limitations of his definition. He took a 'concept of racism [that] was shaped by the particular historical context, and political strategies, of the 1930s and 1940s' and examined it in the different historical and political context of the 1960s.[25] Miles and Brown cite a number of different authors who point out that between the 1930s and the 1960s racism changed in form, from an ideology based on biologically rooted 'racial' inferiority/superiority (scientific or inegalitarian racism) to an ideology based on cultural 'racial' incompatibility (new or differentialist racism). The definition that was developed in the context of the 1930s, and used by Banton, was unable to account for this change in form. (The difficulty that conventional social science has in grasping changing forms underpins the confusions over the distinction between 'race' and 'ethnic group' explored in Chapter 2.) When a definition rooted in one particular historical and political context was uprooted and transported to a different context and then exposed to the judgement of history, it withered and died. In Miles and Brown's view it was Banton's definition that died, not racism.

Banton, however, takes a different view. When he rejected the concept of racism he was doing so because he acknowledged that something changed between the 1930s and 1960s. He asks, if the rationale for denying 'equal treatment to members of ethnic minorities now appeal[s] primarily to cultural instead of biological variation, should we describe their views as racist?'[26] Banton thinks not. If we describe this new rationale as racism, he says, 'We may get an emotional satisfaction from doing so but there is a danger that such usage may conceal the changing nature of the tendency we wish to combat.'[27] Instead of using the concept of racism, Banton argues that 'these new arguments and sentiments are more accurately classified as forms of ethnocentrism'.[28]

Banton's argument is logical and it is consistent with conventional social science approaches to understanding the social world. He uses a precise definition of racism. This provides stable and consistent criteria against which he can measure a range of different things in order to ascertain their nature, and these criteria are independently verifiable. This definition allows him to show that something has changed. Defining racism in reference to biological criteria enables him to say that racism existed in the UK in the 1930s but not to any significant extent in the 1960s. His definition also allows us to see that there is some continuity between the two points in time. Other observations show that ethnic minorities are being discriminated against, and consequently they stand in a relation of inferiority to UK citizens. Banton can see that there is continuity in terms of the kinds of people being treated as inferior, but the rationale that is provided for doing so has changed. The criterion for discrimination in the 1960s was cultural difference, not biologically inherited characteristics, and therefore a more precise definition for this phenomenon would be ethnocentrism.

Hegel and Marx took a different approach to understanding the social world. They emphasised processes, movement, change, interactions, the becoming and unbecoming of things. As Frederick Engels, Marx's closest collaborator, puts it, for Hegel, the social world

> is to be comprehended not as a complex of ready-made *things*, but as a complex of *processes*, in which apparently stable things no less than the concepts, their mental reflections in our heads, go through an uninterrupted change of coming into being and passing away, in which, through all the seeming contingency and in spite of all temporary retrogression, a progressive development finally asserts itself.[29]

In Marx and Hegel's view, Kant treated the things which make up the social world as stable entities. This appearance, that the social world is made up of many apparently stable things that interact with each other, is derived in part from the method of analysing the world adopted by Kant. The meanings of things is fixed, not because that is in the nature of the things named, but because the 'sharp definitions' and the 'techniques which permit individual observers to transcend the subjectivity of their perceptions' attempt to pin down reality in order to examine and understand it. This sense of phenomena that are always in a process of change is highlighted by Ambalavaner Sivanandan when he pointed to the category 'Black' as one that undergoes change, rather than having a fixed nature. In his discussion about the decline of radical anti-racism in the UK during the 1980s, he argues that the concept of 'ethnicity' was used as an ideological

> tool to blunt the edge of black struggle, return 'black' to its constituent parts of African Caribbean, Asian, African, Irish … separating the West Indian from the Asian, the working-class black from the middle-class black … Black, as a political colour, was finally broken down when government moneys were used to fund community projects, destroying thereby the self-reliance and community cohesion that we built up in the 1960s.[30]

Here the concept of 'Black' does not have a fixed meaning, but is given meaning by the political context in which it is articulated. The new, depoliticised sense of 'Black' was tied up with a declining collective sense of common oppression and the rise of sectionalised claims. Community self-organisation was eroded as 'representatives' of different racialised categories of people sought to lay claim to a share of the resources made available as part of the UK state's institutionalising of race relations.

Rather than providing fixed definitions, Marx was interesting in specifying the conditions under which things come into being and are modified and change through their continual interaction with the wider world. Kenan Malik takes this approach when he says that

Capitalism destroyed the parochialism of feudal society, but it created divisions anew ... The conviction grew that inequality, whether within Western society or between the West and the non-Western world, was in the natural order of things. The tendency to view social differences as natural became rationalised through the discourse of race. The concept of race emerged, therefore, as a means of reconciling the conflict between the ideology of equality and the reality of the persistence of inequality. Race accounted for social inequalities by attributing them to nature.[31]

Malik does not specify the forms that the idea of 'race' takes in the abstract. Instead he specifies the conditions for its existence. In very broad terms, Malik suggests, a condition for the existence of racism is the contradiction between the commitment to equality and the reality of inequality. This approach treats the idea of 'race' as historically specific to the world that has been shaped around the ideals of the French and American revolutions and the reality of the inability of capitalism to deliver prosperity to all of humanity. Malik can acknowledge that a distinction between civilised and barbarian was made at the frontier of the ancient Roman Empire (one of Rex's 'race relations situations'), but argue that the social context in which this distinction arose is fundamentally different to the emergence and development of capitalism. He explores ways in which the particular forms that racism is manifested in racisms are shaped by social and historical forces. He examines changing forms of the idea of 'race' from the Enlightenment to the end of the Cold War. Malik's open-ended approach means that he can be alert to changing forms of the idea of 'race'. Banton's definition tied him to saying that racism was dead when a new form emerged.

Racialisation and reification

Advocates of the Race Relations approach deny the existence of 'race'. Paul Connolly, for example, in his influential summary of the literature on 'race' and racism in Northern Ireland, warns that terms such as 'race' and 'racial group' are problematic as 'they often carry with them biological connotations. There is a danger therefore that the continued and unquestioning use of these terms can encourage an understanding of the social and cultural differences that exist between groups as being something that is biological or innate.'[32] So, it is dangerous, inaccurate and confusing to use terms like 'race' and 'racial' because this perpetuates the key racist idea that humanity is composed of many differ- ent races, and that these racial differences are innate. Race Relations advocates, however, also continually talk in terms of 'race' and 'racial'. Connolly raises his warning about the terms 'race' and 'racial group' immediately after noting that the term 'racial group' is central to the Race Relations (NI) Order (and welcom- ing this extension of Race Relations law to Northern Ireland). This contradiction regarding the existence of 'race' is continually reproduced in the Race Relations approach. We can see it in the use of the term Race Relations. We can also see it in the use of the concepts of 'ethnic', 'ethnicity' and 'ethnic group' and in the rejection of the hierarchical ordering of humanity into superior and inferior races, ethnic groups, nations or peoples alongside the upholding of the right to have one's racial or ethnic difference recognised.

The Race Relations approach continually reifies 'race'. In other words, it treats 'races' as if they really exist as things in the world. The reification of 'race' is a form of what Rogers Brubaker calls groupism, which he describes as 'the tendency to take discrete, sharply differentiated, internally homogeneous and externally bounded groups as basic constituents of social life, chief protagonists of social conflicts, and fundamental units of social analysis'.[33] Groupism, in other words, involves a way of thinking which views groups (e.g. 'Irish', 'British', 'Chinese', 'Africans', 'Irish Travellers', 'Protestants', 'Catholics') as clearly differentiated from each other. It also involves the idea that all members of these groups share common characteristics (are internally homogeneous). In addition, it involves the idea these groups are active agents which are in conflict with others (protagonists) over issues such as the distribution of society's resources.

In the context of Northern Ireland, 'groupist' thinking is not just applied to immigrants, it is central to the idea that the 'problem' in Northern Ireland is one of fundamental conflict between two communities. This conception of the conflict can be seen in official documents such as the Anglo-Irish Agreement (1985) and the Peace Agreement (1998). This conception of the conflict is central to community relations policy.[34] The idea is accepted well beyond the walls of institutions such as the Northern Ireland Community Relations Council. The idea that the conflict is, fundamentally, a matter of inter-group relations is so widely and routinely accepted among academics and policy-makers that it is often presented as if it were a self-evident fact. In John Whyte's review of the literature on the Northern Ireland conflict, he argues 'that there is a widespread consensus on the heart of the problem being an internal conflict between two communities in Northern Ireland'.[35] Authors who Whyte characterises as taking an internal conflict approach vary in the binary terms they use to name these two communities: Catholic and Protestant; Nationalist and Unionist; Irish Nationalist and Ulster Unionist; northern Nationalist and Ulster loyalist; or Catholic/Nationalist and Protestant/Unionist. They vary in their characterisation of the nature of the distinction between the two groups – the divide is variously characterised as ethnic, nationalist, ethno-nationalist, religious, sectarian, ethno-sectarian. And they also vary in the importance they attach to factors external to Northern Ireland, such as Anglo-Irish relations, as part of the explanation for the conflict. They all agree, however, that at the core of the conflict are two opposed groups.

A key problem with this inter-group conflict understanding is its treatment of categories – such as Catholic or Nationalist or Irish or Protestant or Unionist or British – as if they are groups. Scholars and policy-makers routinely treat Catholics and Protestants (or Nationalists and Unionists) in Northern Ireland as if they are distinct from each other, are internally homogeneous populations and act as a collective. They are not, however, internally homogeneous populations. Within the 'groups' who self-identify, or are identified by others, as Catholic and Protestant there are class differences, gender differences, differences in levels of religiosity (and, among Protestants, a range of different denominational affiliations) and there have been persistent disagreements about the political future of Northern Ireland. A large majority of Protestants have consistently wanted Northern Ireland to remain part of the UK, but a small minority have consistently supported a united Ireland. Catholics have been much more divided over their attitude towards the constitutional future of Northern Ireland. A significant minority have consistently shown a preference for remaining part of the UK and, in recent years, opinion polls have occasionally indicated that a majority of Catholics support the Union. On a whole range of issues, from whether Northern Ireland should have a Truth Commission to the flying of contentious flags in public places, Catholics disagree with each other, and so do Protestants. Opinions on a whole range of issues cut across confessional lines. In some respects, some Catholics have more in common with some Protestants than they do with other Catholics, and vice versa.[36]

Banton acknowledges that calling policy aimed at tackling racial discrimination 'race relations' policy is problematic.[37] He argues, however, that in 'penalizing action "on racial grounds" the law does not "reflect back" or legitimate false ideas. To the contrary, it stigmatises them' and is serving to change people's personal behaviour for the better.[38] Robert Miles and Malcolm Brown argue against this view. They say that although it is 'possible to use the idea of "race" to generate anti-racist mobilisation or legislation against indirect racism', this does not alter the fact that 'the concept of "race" represents human beings and social relations in a distorted manner'.[39] The Race Relations approach, they argue, does not challenge the perception that 'races' exist, but institutionalises this perception. We can illustrate what they mean through the example of the Good Relations Indicators, which are used to measure the extent of the problem of racisms in Northern Ireland. The indicators draw on public opinion surveys to measure prejudiced attitudes towards racialised minorities, immigrants and the other 'community' (Catholic/Protestant; Nationalist/Unionist; Irish/British), crime statistics to measure anti-social incidents with a racial or sectarian motivation, and employment tribunal data to measure discrimination.[40] All of these sources require people to think in terms of 'racial groups' and to self-categorise (or be categorised by others) as a member of a 'racial group'. The data generated from these sources can tell us what proportion of those surveyed self-categorise (or are categorised by others) according to one of the predetermined categories provided. They do not tell us that 'races' exist. They assume that 'races' exist and they require us to allocate ourselves to a 'racial group'. The indicators and other forms of ethnic monitoring are tools that have been fashioned to help tackle 'racial' discrimination, but they also continually reinforce the idea that humanity is composed of different 'racial groups'.[41] The Race Relations approach suffers from an inherent contradiction – it sets out to tackle racism, but the approach that it takes to doing so continually reinforces the key racist idea, that humanity is composed of different 'racial groups'.

Brubaker warns against treating 'groups' as if they are homogeneous collective actors. He notes that the attempt to treat ethnic groups as if they have a unified view and purpose 'is central to the *practice* of politicized ethnicity'.[42] Ethnopolitical actors attempt to stir, mobilise and energise ethnic 'groups' and bring them into being as collectives. He warns that analysts should not mistake this rhetoric of groupness for the reality. He points out that it is *organisations*, not ethnic groups, which are the protagonists in 'ethnic' conflicts. These include states, paramilitary organisations, political parties, ethnic associations, churches, newspapers and a whole range of other kinds of organisation. It is a mistake, however, to equate these organisations with ethnic groups. Or, in other words, in situations which are characterised as ethnic conflicts, a range of organisations claim to be representing particular ethnic groups, or claim that the conflict is a problem created by ethnic groups. People who are categorised as belonging to these ethnic 'groups', however, do not necessarily agree with what is done in their name. Sinn Féin, for example, claims to represent Irish Nationalists in Northern Ireland, but so does the Social and Democratic Labour Party and dissident Republican organisations. Each of these organisations, however, have different conceptions of the nature of the problem in Northern Ireland and disagree with each other over how to tackle sectarianism. They also enjoy different levels of support from the 'group' that they claim to represent.[43] People who self-consciously belong to the 'group' that these organisations claim to represent do not necessarily accept any, and certainly not all, of these organisations as representing their 'group'. The same applies to organisations that claim to speak for, or act on behalf of, 'racial' groups.

When Irish Nationalist politicians talk about the 'Irish people', when Ulster Unionist politicians talk about the 'Protestant community', or when someone claims to be a spokesperson for the 'Poles' (or the 'Africans', 'Chinese', 'Lithuanians', 'Portuguese' etc.), they are treating these categories of people as if they are 'discrete, sharply differentiated, internally homogeneous' groups. Categories of practice, Brubaker says, are categories 'for doing – designed to stir, summon, justify, mobilize, kindle and energize'.[44] Because terms such as the 'Irish people', 'Protestant community' or 'Poles' are used in racial thought, we should not ignore them in social analysis. In attempting to understand the social world we need to engage with that world, but we also need to remind ourselves that these are concepts (mental reflections in our head, as Engels puts it) not things-in-themselves.

One means that some social scientists have suggested to help avoid the reification of 'race' is to examine the *processes* through which 'races' are *made to appear to* exist. Racialisation is a concept developed by social scientists to draw our attention to the active process of making, or constructing, 'race'.[45] The concept does not treat 'race' as something given by nature, but instead as something that is *socially created*. Thinking in terms of racialisation is radically different to thinking in terms of 'race'. Instead of thinking of 'races' as different groups that exist in society, we need to think of 'races' as things that are brought into existence through ways of thinking about, and acting in, the world. That requires us to focus on the social actors who bring 'races' into existence in particular social situations, and the ways in which they do so. The concept of racialisation, as Steve Garner notes, 'draws attention to the process, of making "race" relevant to a particular situation or context, and thus requires an examination of the precise context in which this occurs: who the "agents" are, who the actors are. In other words, who does what and how?'[46] Thinking in terms of racialisation helps us to understand why racisms are complex, changing and contextual – because racisms are always in a process of formation and adaptation and because racisms are created through ongoing processes of interaction between different social actors in specific social contexts.

Thinking in terms of racialisation also allows us to appreciate that 'races' are categories, ways of classifying people together under a common heading, not actual groups of people who have a collective sense of belonging and purpose. The concept of racialisation allows us to keep in mind the distinction, made by Brubaker, between groups and categories. Racial thought involves talking about different categories of people as if they are actual 'races' of people – Black, White, Chinese, Irish, Irish Catholic, Ulster Protestant, Irish Traveller, etc. The concept of racialisation allows us to understand that these terms – Black, White, etc. – are categories that people use to describe or engage with the world. When we think of them as categories we are acknowledging that the terms, and what they seek to describe or conjure up, are human creations, not products of nature. In other words, the Irish (or any other racialised category of people) do not exist. The category 'Irish' exists and people self-identify, or are identified by others, as fitting into the category, but there are a number of different ways of defining the 'Irish' and consequently an individual could be considered 'Irish' by one definition and not by another. The 'Irish' are, in this sense, an artefact of the way in which they are defined, not an objective entity.

We have argued against the reification of races on the grounds that, as Brubaker puts it, this reification involves 'the tendency to take discrete, sharply differentiated, internally homogeneous and externally bounded groups as basic constituents of social life, chief protagonists of social conflicts, and fundamental units of social analysis'.[47] We argued that the concept of 'racialisation' is useful because it captures the sense that 'race' is something that is made and unmade. It draws attention to 'race' as a *process*, rather than something that is given by nature.

Those scholars who argue against the reification of 'race' acknowledge that it is a social construct. These scholars argue that 'race' is a subjective invention of our minds, not an objective reality. They point out that thinking in terms of Black, White, Chinese, Irish, etc. is a subjective state of mind. In the words of Banton, quoted in Chapter 3, the

> racial classifications of everyday life are social constructions based in the popular consciousness. Racial relations are therefore to be identified by shared subjective definitions ... Even if an individual realized that there was no objective basis for the distinction, and that appearances were socially generated, he or she was [or can be] regarded as still trapped by others' perceptions.[48]

Banton appears to agree with his critics that 'race' is a social construct. He argues against those who accuse him of reifying 'race' by talking about 'race relations'. Banton, in his defence, says that Race Relations theory is not the study of relations between different 'races', but rather involves 'analysis of interaction between racialised categories'.[49] It is possible to study 'race' relations, he argues, because people are racialised (i.e. have adopted a racial category by choice, or are categorised as a member of a 'racial' group by others), and interact with others based on an understanding that humanity is composed of different 'racial' groups.

Banton's self-defence is based on a logical argument that makes sense from the perspective of conventional social science. From a Marxist perspective, however, Banton's argument involves the artificial separation of subject and object. It is true that Black, White, Chinese, Irish etc. are racial categories. They are symbolic representations of humanity as divided into different racial groups. They are shared subjective definitions. They can also, however, have an objective existence outside the minds of those who share these subjective definitions. Banton implicitly acknowledges this when he says that the study of Race Relations is the study of interactions between racialised categories of people. These interactions are real, objective interactions between living, breathing human beings. We can illustrate this point using the example of the category 'Irish'.

You do not have to consider yourself Irish to have a conception of who the Irish are and what makes them Irish (i.e. what constitutes the nature of Irishness). Stereotypes about the Irish are examples of shared subjective definitions. If they were not shared they would not be stereotypes. Stereotypes are also abstractions. They involve stripping away the rich diversity of dimensions of those objective, actually existing human beings who are categorised and self-categorise as Irish and making simplified generalisations about this category of people. In this sense of the concept, the Irish do not have an objective existence, but are an artefact of our minds, a way of thinking about the social world. The Irish are also, however, an objective entity with a subjective sense of themselves, in as far as there is a collective form of social organisation that thinks of itself and acts (i.e. that self-racialises or self-identifies) as the Irish people. In other words, there are no Irish people in the abstract, there are only real, living, breathing, acting human beings. At various moments in history a significant number of human beings have come together as the Irish, in a self-conscious collective attempt to make history by achieving national self-determination as a people. For most of the twentieth century, however, people who have self-identified as Irish have had a much more passive sense of themselves as a collective body. They have, for example, come together in large numbers to celebrate sporting achievements or historical commemorations. In these ways they are consumers of Irishness, rather than producers of historical change. In both the active and passive sense of the Irish as a people, the Irish exist subjectively (as a category) in the minds of many people. They also, simultaneously, exist objectively as real, living human beings who self-consciously act in the world as Irish people. Banton's approach to analysing society, with its emphasis on the intersubjective constitution of 'race', artificially separates the subjective and objective aspects of 'race'.

Racisms as an expression of capitalist contradictions

The social constructionist conception of society, as intersubjectively constituted, prioritises the subjective factor in the making of the social world. Logically, however, these ideas must come from somewhere. If they are purely subjective – if, in other words, they are created in our minds without any reference to external objective reality – how do they come into being? If, in the case that we are examining in this book, 'race' is a social construct, where does the idea of 'race' come from? If the idea of 'race' arises without any external reference point then, logically, it is either hard-wired into our minds or arises arbitrarily as a random mutation. From a Marxist perspective, things look different. Racialisation is not a purely subjective process. It involves dynamic interaction between objective reality and subjective interpretation. As Marx and Engels put it in *The German Ideology*:

> we do not set out from what men say, imagine, conceive, nor from men as narrated, thought of, imagined, conceived, in order to arrive at men in the flesh. We set out from real, active men, and on the basis of their real life-process we demonstrate the development of the ideological reflexes and echoes of this life-process … Life is not determined by consciousness, but consciousness by life.[50]

Biologists, geneticists, anthropologists, sociologists and other natural and social scientists have demonstrated that 'races' do not exist, that they are social constructs. The idea of 'race', however, persists. This persistence is not (as Banton suggests) because humanity is trapped by the shared subjective definition of 'race' that a majority of society still believes. The idea of 'race' persists (or put another way, humanity is still trapped by the shared subjective definition of 'race') because the material conditions for its existence persist. The idea of 'race' came into being, as Marx and Engels might have put it, as an ideological reflex of real life-processes.

Those real life-processes were, in the first instance, the conquest and domination of peoples in Africa, Asia and the Americas and the creation of plantation slavery in the Americas. It was these real life-processes that both laid the basis for the development of capitalism (through the accumulation of huge funds for investment in economic production, what Marx refers to as primitive accumulation), and created the conditions for the idea of 'race'. As Marx wryly notes in volume one of *Capital*:

> The discovery of gold and silver in America, the extirpation, enslavement and entombment in mines of the aboriginal population, the beginning of the conquest and looting of the East Indies, the turning of Africa into a warren for the commercial hunting of black-skins, signalised the rosy dawn of the era of capitalist production. These idyllic proceedings are the chief momenta of primitive accumulation. On their heels treads the commercial war of the European nations, with the globe for a theatre. It begins with the revolt of the Netherlands from Spain, assumes giant dimensions in England's Anti-Jacobin War, and is still going on in the opium wars against China, &c ... These methods depend in part on brute force, *e.g.,* the colonial system. But, they all employ the power of the State, the concentrated and organised force of society, to hasten, hot-house fashion, the process of transformation of the feudal mode of production into the capitalist mode, and to shorten the transition.[51]

The uprooting, enslavement and setting to work of the peoples of the Americas and of Africa did not happen because these peoples were Black. It happened because the European colonial powers desired the gold, silver and other resources of Africa and the Americas and because the European powers had superior technology – principally weaponry and ships – that allowed them to coerce people who looked phenotypically different to Europeans.[52] The peoples of the Americas, Asia and Africa were not dominated because they were Black, but because they were dominated they became Black. Or, looked at from another angle, there was no pre-existing idea of the superiority of the White 'race'; the idea of the superiority of the White 'race' arose out of real life-processes. The case of Ireland, England's first colony, indicates that it was not biologically innate differences or ideas of racial superiority that drove colonisation, but that these ideas of superiority arose as an ideological reflection of real relations of domination in the material world.

Once the idea of 'race' has been established in the minds of many human beings, once it is a shared subjective definition, racism as the conscious, willed subjection of peoples *because* they are viewed as inferior becomes an objective phenomenon. Ideas do matter, they do have consequences. They only, however, matter to the extent that they correspond to objective reality. Ideas also compete with other, contradictory ideas. Those ideas which dominate in any given situation depend on the social context they inhabit. This context can involve the triumph of the subjective will over objective social structures, but this only happens (on anything more than a sporadic basis) when human wills combine to create collective movements (i.e. independent collective organisations that concentrate and augment the power of many wills). Most of the time contradictory ideas coexist alongside each other, and it is the organisational context that dictates the outcome. We can illustrate this point with the example of racialised immigration controls.

It is the nation-state as an institution, rather than the subjective outlook of immigration officers, that explains why Black people are disproportionately detained and deported. This can be seen in the testimony of one of the immigration officials interviewed by the Northern Ireland Human Rights Commission (NIHRC), who stated that 'Removing economic migrants who are here illegally is the hardest. You always have some sympathy; they work hard trying to support their families, but the law is the same for them and you just have to do it.'[53] This immigration official is directly responsible for the deportation of hard-working people, not because he or she is 'trapped by others' perceptions', but because it is a requirement of the job. The officers deport people despite their own subjective sympathies, not because of them. The immigration official's rationalisation, 'you just have to do it', points to a common feature of contemporary forms of racism; a fatalistic sense that the world just is the way it is and there is very little we can do about it. This can be seen in the testimony of another official interviewed by NIHRC, who said that 'it's an accident of birth that we are from the UK, [a] pretty affluent society ... and you'd understand why people want to come here. But, at the same time we need to have control over that.'[54] In doing so, he or she acknowledges some social conditions, the uneven economic development of the world, that drive migration. He or she, however, ends up concluding that that's just the way things are. This sense of resignation to blind fate, 'that's just the way things are', involves a refusal to ask too many searching questions. We might expect this from an immigration official who is grappling with their own conscience in a situation where their actions have dramatic consequences for racialised others. Treating human actions, the detention and deportation of human beings in this case, as natural is not something that we would expect from social scientists, especially ones who argue that 'racial' distinctions are not natural, but are socially constructed. The Race Relations approach, however, in not questioning the nation-state itself as a form of social organisation, is complicit in naturalising it. Nation-states, uneven development and racial discrimination, Banton appears to suggest, are natural features of the world.

The idea of 'race', and the racist practices that are justified by the idea of 'race', arise from conditions inherent to capitalism. Paradoxically, both racism and anti-racism are spontaneously generated by capitalism as a system of production.

This paradox is fundamental to the crisis of anti-racism. It is, possibly, the greatest confusion of all the confusions that afflict anti-racist thought and practice.

The development of capitalism revolutionised the production of human needs and desires. The Enlightenment, the ideological reflection of the emergence of capitalism, revolutionised human thought. Enlightenment humanism championed individual human autonomy, human reason, the development and application of scientific methods to understanding the natural and social world, and human progress. Enlightenment ideals are summed up in the battle cry of the French Revolution – liberty, equality, fraternity. Marx recognised, however, that the way in which human needs and desires were produced in a capitalist society acted as a barrier to the realisation of Enlightenment ideals in practice. The promise of these ideals and their denial in practice provide the fertile soil in which both racism and anti-racism can coexist as contradictory tendencies in capitalist society. The commitment to liberty, equality and fraternity in a capitalist society is not merely rhetorical. Capitalism as a social system does require liberty and equality and does connect up the whole of humanity. As Marx himself noted in *Capital*, the market (or more precisely, the sphere of circulation of commodities)

> is in fact a very Eden of the innate rights of man. There alone rule Freedom, Equality, Property and Bentham.[55] Freedom, because both buyer and seller of a commodity, say of labour-power, are constrained only by their own free will. They contract as free agents, and the agreement they come to, is but the form in which they give legal expression to their common will. Equality, because each enters into relation with the other, as with a simple owner of commodities, and they exchange equivalent for equivalent. Property, because each disposes only of what is his own. And Bentham, because each looks only to himself. The only force that brings them together and puts them in relation with each other, is the selfishness, the gain and the private interests of each. Each looks to himself only, and no one troubles himself about the rest, and just because they do so, do they all, in accordance with the pre-established harmony of things, or under the auspices of an all-shrewd providence, work together to their mutual advantage, for the common weal and in the interest of all.[56]

In the realm of the market all buyers and sellers, regardless of class, colour or creed, are free and equal. They are free agents who choose when, and to whom, they sell their property. They are equal because they exchange equivalents – property is not worth more, or less, because of the class, colour or creed of the property owner. It is impersonal market forces that dictate the price of property, not the qualities of the buyer or seller. Each individual enters the marketplace as a free individual with their own selfish interests, but through the mechanism of the market their mutual interests are satisfied. In this respect, through realising the common weal and the interests of all, the market provides the basis for a common humanity (fraternity).

This freedom, equality and fraternity, however, is limited. It is *capitalist* free-dom, equality and fraternity. The freedom, equality and fraternity that reigns in the sphere of circulation disguises the unfreedom, inequality and alienation that is fundamental to the sphere of capitalist production. The development of capi-talism has been manifested in the vast expansion of market choices with the ever more extensive creation of commodities. The conditions for the production of these commodities, however, were created by freeing peasants from their means of living in agriculture and forcing them into the factory as wage-labourers who rely on capitalists to buy their labour-power in order for them to acquire their means of living. From the origins of capitalism up to the present day all wage-labourers are free to sell their labour-power to whomsoever they choose, and they are free to starve. Underlying the apparent freedom of the market is the constant threat of compulsion. In the labour market the capitalist buys labour-power at the price which it costs to procure. In the realm of production, however, the capitalist compels workers to produce more than the value of their labour-power. It is this surplus, unpaid labour that is the source of capitalist wealth and the source of the vast inequalities of capitalist society.

Labour is one of the qualities that distinguishes humans from the rest of the animal kingdom.[57] Creating the means of subsistence for humanity as a whole – which is exchanged through the market – is something that should be a crea-tive, life-fulfilling act which connects us to the rest of humanity. The market, the exchange of equivalents, is, however, not a mechanism through which wage-labourers directly engage with other human beings. It is their labour-power, not the products of their labour, that wage-labourers bring to the marketplace. It is capitalists, the owners of the products of human labour, who bring all other commodities to the marketplace. The capitalist purchases human labour-power in exchange for a wage. The commodities that are produced by the labourer do not belong to the labourer, they belong to the capitalist. The act of labour, then, is not experienced as acting to help fulfil the needs and desires of humanity as a whole (the interests of all). It is not experienced as a means of realising the common weal. It is, rather, experienced as fulfilling the interests of the capitalist employer.

The alienation of human labour, which is fundamental to capitalist produc-tion, provides the material conditions for human unfreedom, for inequality and for the alienation of individual human beings from humanity as a whole. It is these conditions which provide the material basis for racisms in a capitalist soci-ety. The particular forms in which racisms are manifested are mediated through myriad mechanisms. The particular forms of racisms are generated through processes of racialisation that evolve and arise anew over time. In the nineteenth century and the first half of the twentieth century, for example, the British Empire was central to processes of racialisation that contributed to the subjec-tive conception of 'race' that most people in Britain shared. After the Second

World War immigration from the New Commonwealth became more central to processes of racialisation. From the 1960s onwards the process of racialisation was further mediated by the institutionalising of Race Relations policy. In the twenty-first century there were further significant shifts which impacted the process of racialisation. These factors include the growth of significant numbers of immigrants from eastern Europe, the increasing integration of the descendants of New Commonwealth immigrants into UK society, the rise of jihadist Islam, and even more recently, the vote by UK citizens to leave the EU. In all of these cases changes in the real world have given rise to changes in consciousness.

Race Relations theory is unable to point to a way in which racisms can be eradicated because it does not investigate, or often even acknowledge, the connection between capitalism as a system founded on alienated labour and racism as a manifestation of alienation rooted in capitalist production. Race Relations theory and practice occasionally acknowledges the mutual coexistence of racism and anti-racism in capitalist society. In the UN International Convention on the Elimination of All Forms of Racial Discrimination, the idea that racisms can be eradicated is articulated in the preamble (the part that provides the rationale for it), as well as in its title. The main body of the convention (the part that contains the obligations that signatory states agree to when ratifying it), however, provides a different view of racisms. The main body of the convention articulates the view that racial discrimination is normal in situations where people differentiate *themselves* in terms of 'race, colour, descent, or national or ethnic origin'. If we look more closely at the ICERD, we can see two ways in which the signatories are, as nation-states, intimately associated with creating the conditions for racism. All anti-discrimination legislation defines a protected class of people who it is illegal to discriminate against. The ICERD's 'article 1.1 creates such a class [i.e. racial] divided into five subclasses: race, colour, descent, national origin, and ethnic origin'.[58] In doing so the UN, and the nation-states that are signatories to the ICERD, are involved in the process of racialising the world's population. People are not differentiating themselves in this process; they are being differentiated by nation-states. The ICERD is an anti-racist document; it protects the 'human rights and fundamental freedoms, including equality before the law, the right to security, political and civil rights, and economic, social, and cultural rights' of racialised people.[59] It also, however, a racist document. It provides a significant exemption for nation-states when it explicitly permits the 'right of states to distinguish between citizens and noncitizens'.[60] This right to distinguish between citizens and non-citizens underpins immigration controls. Frank Kakopa was questioned more vigorously and then detained because he was a non-citizen. Immigration officials questioned and detained the other Black Africans that Kakopa encountered because they suspected that they were not EU citizens. As we noted in Chapter 3, the UK Border and Immigration Agency's chief inspector denied the charge of racial discrimination and said that 'inevitably EU citizens can quickly satisfy us. It is not terribly surprising to find it is people who are black or of other ethnicities who are detained.'[61]

The development and institutionalising of official anti-racism has, in parallel with the decay of grassroots anti-racism, precipitated the crisis of anti-racism. The Race Relations approach holds out the promise of eliminating racisms, but is itself intimately involved in perpetuating racisms. This contradiction is an expression of a contradictory capitalist society, which spontaneously produces and reproduces both racism and anti-racism. Humanity can only eradicate racisms through transcending the conditions that give rise to both racism and anti-racism.

Emancipatory anti-racism and the limits of capitalist society

In the late 1990s Banton complained that the concept of racism suffered from being too subjectively loaded. As he put it:

> Debates about the definition of racism ought to be resolved by considering the utility of alternative definitions in the development of more powerful explanations, but they are often confounded because the word is used for rhetorical purposes. It has been employed so often to condemn certain kinds of action that it has acquired a heavy emotional loading ... In ethnic and racial studies writers have too often been allowed to propagate personal values in the guise of social science.[62]

In this view, the morally and politically loaded nature of the concept is considered to be a problem for social science. It would be much easier for the theorist if the concept was not so burdened with subjective human outlooks, as this would make the task of understanding 'ethnic and racial relations' more straightforward. Banton acknowledges 'the rhetorical value of the word [racism] in mobilizing political action and in empowering social criticism, especially criticism originating from the victims of racial discrimination', but he thinks that the fight against racism is better served by clearly distinguishing between the social scientific and the political uses of the word.

We think that it is worth turning this idea on its head. The concept of 'racism' is so morally, emotionally and politically charged because it is a category through which we, as human beings, discuss and define what it means to be human, and what kind of society we want to live in. The emotional loading of the concept is an index of its importance to our humanity at the beginning of the twenty-first century. We need to fuse the subjective (the emotional, moral and political) and the objective (scientific) as part of the struggle to transform and transcend the conditions in which racisms are formed and perpetuated. The term racism is so charged because we, as human beings, have a powerful aversion to oppression. We recognise, at some level, that the dehumanisation of any section of humanity necessarily dehumanises us all. Capitalism has massively extended human freedoms and more extensively connected human beings around the globe. It has also, however, brutalised humanity. War, famine, terror, torture, homelessness, unemployment, depression and alienation are as much a part of capitalism as mobile phones, skyscrapers, cancer research and the Internet. The majority of human beings, all over the planet, have an interest in overcoming the limitations of capitalism and moving to a society that operates in the interests of all. The struggle against racisms is an integral part of that struggle for a better society.

The enduring appeal of the ideals of liberty, equality and fraternity is an indication of how they are integral to what it means to be human. Freedom, as Marx put it, is so much the essence of humanity that no one fights against freedom as such. At most, they fight against the freedom of others.[63] The ideal of equality does not appeal because we think that all people are the same. It appeals because we think that people should not be treated as less human because of what nature has randomly allocated us – such as testes or a uterus, physique, or the colour of our skin. The ideal of fraternity appeals because we recognise that human beings are essentially social creatures. The nature of this sociality is qualitatively different to that of any other animal. We are born with the capacity for language and self-awareness, but it is through interaction with other human beings that we become individuals. As Kenan Malik puts it:

> Feelings and thoughts may be internal, but meanings are external. Meanings arise through social intercourse … If my mind were truly private, then, I could neither know my own mind nor communicate its contents to anyone else … The contents of my inner world mean something to me, in part at least, in so far as I live in, and relate to, a community of thinking, feeling, talking beings. I can make sense of my mind, in other words, to the extent that I can make sense of yours. Paradoxically, humans become aware of themselves as individual selves only insofar as they are social beings.[64]

Capitalism as a system for the production of human needs and desires does not allow us to fully realise liberty, equality and fraternity. It does not allow us to be fully human. Capitalism treats liberty as something that needs to be qualified – the free movement of some, for example, not all. Capitalist societies continually uphold the principle of equality of opportunity, and simultaneously undermine this principle by demanding the right of inheritance of wealth. Capitalism continually sets boundaries on human sociality. We are told that people have a natural desire to be with their 'own' kind. We are told that the borders of the nation-state must be defended. We are told that 'they' are a threat to 'our' freedoms.

Those who genuinely want to eradicate racism need to develop an emancipatory form of anti-racism that connects with the human aspiration for liberty, equality and fraternity, identifies the barriers to these being realised for the whole of humanity and smashes through those barriers. This means recognising that it is ordinary working people who are the agents of change. We should not look to states, government or political parties (of whatever kind) to lead the way because this will always be on their terms and will always lead to a destination they aspire to. This means that emancipatory anti-racism needs to oppose not just racisms, but also those forms of anti-racism that accept the parameters of capitalism as a social system. This means recognising that the struggle for the eradication of racisms and the emancipation of the working class are complementary struggles. The working class cannot hope to emancipate themselves from the domination of capital if they do not oppose racisms. Emancipatory anti-racism means acknowledging that our common humanity is an aspiration that needs to be achieved, not a living reality. As long as any section of society does not enjoy liberty then there is no fraternity. It is only when we live in a society 'in which the free development of each is the condition for the free development of all' that we will have a genuinely human-centred world.[65]

Conclusion

In the previous chapter we highlighted the inconsistency between the development of anti-racist policies by nation-states, including the UK, and the pursuit of racist policies. In this chapter we have examined various ways in which Race Relations theory parallels this inconsistency on the part of nation-states. The aim of providing an objective understanding of the world, through conventional social science methodology, is upheld by Race Relations theorists as the standard by which good research should be judged. Research that deviates from this is commonly accused of bias. We have argued that human subjectivity is not a problem to be overcome in order to achieve an objective understanding of the world. The problem to be overcome is the separation of the subjective and objective, which can only be done through uniting theory and practice. Anti-racism will not emancipate humanity from racisms unless it engages the mass of society in transforming the conditions that nurture racisms.

We have argued that the conventional social science methodology that underpins Race Relations theory is limited because it is elitist and involves a very limited conception of social change and allocates a relatively passive role to the mass of society. This research can often provide interesting insights, or provide data that enables policy-makers and activists to effect change, but it does so within limited parameters. Race Relations theory does not interrogate the nature of capitalist society. It takes capitalism for granted. Consequently, racisms are understood as an inherent feature of humanity and anti-racism as necessary in order to manage relations between people in nation-states where two or more 'races' inhabit the same polity. Race Relations theory conceptualises the nation-state as a neutral institution. In this view states can be racist or anti-racist; the extent to which they are one or the other depends on the subjective outlooks of those who control them as institutions. The nation-state, however, is a historical creation of the capitalist era. It is a historically specific way of organising human relations. It is integral to the process of racialising humanity. The nation-state has also, since the 1960s increasingly so, been the principal institution through which anti-racism has been promoted.

Race Relations theory counterposes racism and anti-racism as opposites. We have taken a different approach. We have asked why it is that racism and anti-racism so readily coexist within the same nation-state? What are the social conditions that permit both racisms and anti-racism to coexist? At their most basic level, racism and anti-racism have their roots in capitalism as a social system. Both are integral to, and arise out of, the contradiction between the ideals of liberty, equality and fraternity and a system of production that limits the realisation of these ideals in practice. When we look at the issue of racism and anti-racism in this way – as arising out of contradictions inherent to capitalism – it suggests that emancipatory anti-racism needs to be directed at overcoming these contradictions.

Notes

1 Latif and Martynowicz, *Our hidden borders*, 37.
2 Bourne, 'The life and times of institutional racism', 20.
3 See, for example, David Rose, *In the name of the law* (London: Vintage, 1996).
4 Banton, *International action against racial discrimination*, 60.
5 Immanuel Kant, *Critique of pure reason* (London: Henry G. Bohn, 1855).
6 Kant, *Critique of pure reason*, quoted in Michael Banton, 'Epistemological assumptions in the study of racial differentiation', in *Theories of race and ethnic relations*, ed. John Rex and David Mason (Cambridge: Cambridge University Press, 1986), 45.
7 Ibid., 47–48.
8 The list is not exhaustive, and is derived from the chapter headings of the UK's best-selling undergraduate textbook on research methods: Alan Bryman, *Social research methods* (Oxford: Oxford University Press, 4th edn, 2012).
9 Michael Banton, 'Modelling ethnic and national relations', *Ethnic and Racial Studies* 17.1 (1994): 6.
10 Ibid.
11 Ibid.
12 Franz Jakubowski, *Ideology and superstructure in historical materialism* (London: Pluto Press, 1990), 16.
13 Frederick Engels, *Ludwig Feuerbach and the end of classical German philosophy* (Moscow: Progress Publishers, 2000), 17.
14 Raya Dunayevskaya, *Marxism and freedom* (Amherst, NY: Humanity Books, 3rd edn, 2000), 28.
15 Karl Marx, 'Theses on Feuerbach', I; emphasis in the original.
16 Ibid.; emphasis in the original.
17 Engels, *Ludwig Feuerbach*; Karl Marx and Fredrick Engels, *The German ideology*,

Marxist Internet Archive; Karl Korsch, *Marxism and philosophy* (London: New Left Books, 1970); Jakubowski, *Ideology and superstructure*; Fredrick Engels, *Socialism: utopian and scientific.*

18 Marx and Engels, *The German ideology*, 8.

19 As Marx puts it in *The critique of the Gotha Program*, 5. 'In a higher phase of communist society, after the enslaving subordination of the individual to the division of labor, and therewith also the antithesis between mental and physical labor, has vanished; after labor has become not only a means of life but life's prime want; after the productive forces have also increased with the all-around development of the individual, and all the springs of co-operative wealth flow more abundantly – only then can the narrow horizon of bourgeois right be crossed in its entirety and society inscribe on its banners: From each according to his ability, to each according to his needs!'

20 Marx, 'Theses on Feuerbach', III.

21 Kenan Malik, 'What is it to be human?', in *What is it to be human? What science can and cannot tell us*, ed. Tony Gilland (London: Institute of Ideas, 2001), 14.

22 Banton, 'Epistemological assumptions in the study of racial differentiation', 47–48.

23 Michael Banton, 'The concept of racism', in *Race and racialism*, ed. Sami Zubaida (London: Tavistock Publications, 1970), 18.

24 Miles and Brown, *Racism*, 60.

25 Ibid., 80.

26 Banton, 'The concept of racism', 31.

27 Ibid.

28 Ibid.

29 Engels, *Ludwig Feuerbach*, 41.

30 Ambalavaner Sivanandan, *Communities of resistance: writings on black struggles for socialism* (London: Verso, 1990), 67.

31 Malik, *The meaning of race*, 6.

32 Connolly, *'Race' and racism in Northern Ireland*, 6.

33 Rogers Brubaker, 'Ethnicity without groups', *Archives Europeennes de Sociologie* 43.2 (2002): 164.

34 Community Relations Council, *A good relations framework: an approach to the development of good relations* (Belfast: Community Relations Council, 2004); Frazer and Fitzduff, *Improving community relations*. For critical perspectives on 'community relations', see Bill Rolston, 'What's wrong with multiculturalism? Liberalism and the Irish conflict', in *Rethinking Northern Ireland: culture, ideology and colonialism*, ed. David Miller (Harlow: Longman, 1998), 253–274; Jennifer Todd and Joseph Ruane, *From 'A shared future' to 'Cohesion, sharing and integration': an analysis of Northern Ireland's policy framework documents* (York: Joseph Rowntree Foundation, 2010).

35 Whyte, *Interpreting Northern Ireland*, 209–210.

36 See the annual Northern Ireland Life and Times survey for details of public attitudes in Northern Ireland. Available online at www.ark.ac.uk/nilt (accessed 10 January 2017).

37 Banton, 'The race relations problematic', 115.

38 Ibid., 129.

39 Miles and Brown, *Racism*, 7.

40 OFMDFM, *A shared future and racial equality strategy: good relations indicators base-line report.*

41 Simpson, '"Race" statistics: theirs and ours'; Ann Morning, 'Toward a sociology of racial conceptualization for the 21st century', *Social Forces* 87.3 (2009): 1167–1192.

42 Brubaker, 'Ethnicity without groups', 166.

43 See, for example, Bean, '"New dissidents are but old Provisionals writ large"?'; Gerard Murray and Jonathan Tonge, *Sinn Féin and the SDLP: from alienation to participation* (London: C. Hurst, 2005); Sinn Féin, *The Sinn Féin/SDLP talks: January–September 1988* (Dublin: Sinn Féin, 1998); Tonge, '"No-one likes us; we don't care"'; Jocelyn Evans and Jonathan Tonge, 'Social class and party choice in Northern Ireland's ethnic blocs', *West European Politics* 32.5 (2009): 1012–1030; McGlynn, Tonge and McAuley, 'The party politics of post-devolution identity in Northern Ireland'.

44 Brubaker, 'Ethnicity without groups', 166.

45 See, for example, Karim Murji and John Solomos (eds), *Racialization: studies in theory and practice* (Oxford: Oxford University Press, 2005); Miles and Brown, *Racism*; Robert Miles, 'The racialization of British politics', *Political Studies* 38.2 (1990): 277–285; Bonnett, 'How the British working class became white'; J. E. Fox, L. Morosanu and E. Szilassy, 'The racialization of the new European migration to the UK', *Sociology* 46.4 (2012): 680–695.

46 Garner, *Racisms*, 21; emphasis in the original.

47 Brubaker, 'Ethnicity without groups', 164.

48 Banton, 'The race relations problematic', 116. Banton attributes the origins of this idea to Robert E. Park and E. W. Burgess of the Chicago School of sociology.

49 Ibid., 117.

50 Marx and Engels, *The German ideology*, Part 1, B, page 6.

51 Marx, *Capital: volume 1*, 533–534.

52 Colonialism predates, and helped to bring into existence, capitalism as a social system. Once capitalism in its industrial form became established, the significance of the colonies as centres for the extraction of wealth diminished relative to wage-labour as a means of extracting a surplus. As Marx puts it in *Capital*: 'Today industrial supremacy implies commercial supremacy. In the period of manufacture properly so called, it is, on the other hand, the commercial supremacy that gives industrial predominance. Hence the preponderant rôle that the colonial system plays at that time. It was "the strange God" who perched himself on the altar cheek by jowl with the old Gods of Europe, and one fine day with a shove and a kick chucked them all of a heap. It proclaimed surplus-value making as the sole end and aim of humanity' (vol. I, 535).

53 Latif and Martynowicz, *Our hidden borders*, 50.

54 Ibid.

55 Jeremy Bentham was a nineteenth-century liberal philosopher and social reformer, who is commonly viewed as the founder of utilitarianism. Marx is scathing about Bentham's contribution to human thought. At one point in *Capital* Marx pours scorn on 'the arch-Philistine, Jeremy Bentham, that insipid, pedantic, leather-tongued oracle of the ordinary bourgeois intelligence of the 19th century' (vol. I, 426).

56 Marx, *Capital: volume I*, 123.

57 'Men can be distinguished from animals by consciousness, by religion or anything else you like. They themselves begin to distinguish themselves from animals as soon as they begin to produce their means of subsistence, a step which is conditioned by their physical organisation. By producing their means of subsistence men are indirectly producing their actual material life' (Marx and Engels, *The German ideology*, Part 1, A, 3).

58 Banton, *International action against racial discrimination*, 64.

59 Ibid.

60 Ibid.

61 McKay, '"They were chaining people up like animals"'.

62 Michael Banton, 'Racism today: a perspective from international politics', *Ethnic and Racial Studies* 22.3 (1999): 613–614.

63 Cited in Dunayevskaya, *Marxism and freedom*, 53.

64 Malik, 'What is it to be human?', 18–19.

65 The quote is from Marx and Engels, *The Communist Manifesto*, 27.

6

From civil rights to multiculturalism

We humans, uniquely among the animal kingdom, have the ability to step outside our immediate experiences and imagine a different world. We have the capacity to look at the world from a different perspective, whether the perspective of other people, or of a future society that does not yet exist. Not only can we imagine a world that does not yet exist, we can also act to try to bring the world of our imaginations into being in the real world. Bees can build beehives, large complex structures, but they only build beehives. Humans have built a vast array of different kinds of structures – cottages and mansions, factories and beach huts, statues and airports, pyramids and orbiting space stations. As humans we can, as Kenan Malik puts it,

> climb out of our individual minds, as it were, and view the world from a more external viewpoint. To go beyond the view afforded by a particular culture ... This process of climbing out of our immediate circumstances to achieve a more inclusive view is precisely the process of transcendence. Without such a process neither history nor science would be possible. To understand how we are human, therefore, we need to understand not so much whether we are creatures of nature or nurture, but how we are simultaneously object and subject, how we are at the self-same time a psychically determined being and a social being and moral agent.[1]

Humans make history. Humans imagine new ways of doing things and new ways of living. We set goals for ourselves, and for society more broadly, and we try to achieve these. Most of the time these goals are relatively modest. As Perry Anderson puts it: 'Throughout history ... the overwhelming majority of people for the overwhelmingly major part of their lives have pursued "private" goals: cultivation of a plot, choice of a marriage, exercise of a skill, maintenance of a home.'[2] These actions are part of the flow of human history. We often have to adapt to what life throws in our path, whether the actions of other people or unexpected events. These private goals, as Anderson puts it, 'are inscribed within existing social relations and typically reproduce them'.[3] There are also, however, moments in history when people act collectively to try to shape the world around them. Instead of going with the flow of history, a collective mass of people push against the constraints that shape the path of history. In Northern Ireland, a collective movement for social change erupted into history at the end of the 1960s. In the space of less than three years, from August 1969 to March 1972, Northern Irish society and politics were transformed through the mobilisation of a newly politicised mass of people. It was a time of intense collective political activity, in opposition to the sectarian state and institutionalised oppression. The idea that excited so much activity was the idea of civil rights.

The civil rights movement transformed the political landscape of Northern Ireland. Between early 1970 and late 1972 four of the five current main political parties were born, and the other (the Ulster Unionist Party (UUP), which had been the party of government for almost fifty years) was torn apart over how to respond to the demands for civil rights. The Nationalist Party, which had been the main political party representing Northern Irish Catholics, was swept aside by the civil rights mobilisations. The Social Democratic and Labour Party (SDLP) was formed by an alliance of former Nationalist Party members, moderate civil rights activists and trade unionist Irish Nationalists. The Irish Republican Army (IRA), which had recently given up its weapons and shifted to political campaigning, split over whether or not to resume its military strategy. The militarists broke away and formed the Provisional IRA and its political wing, Provisional Sinn Féin. Unionism was in turmoil. Liberal, reform-minded Unionists formed the Alliance Party of Northern Ireland (APNI), which managed to attract Catholic and Protestant middle-class professionals and business people. Other Unionists, vehemently opposed to what they saw as Unionist government concessions to Catholics, formed the Democratic Unionist Party (DUP).

The civil rights movement was an anti-racist movement. It was opposed to the entrenched sectarian privilege that was the Stormont state. Protestors, inspired in part by the Civil Rights movement in the USA, mobilised against injustice and sectarian inequality. The universalist and egalitarian demands of the civil rights movement polarised society. The demand that Catholics in Northern Ireland should have the same rights as any other citizen of the UK threatened both entrenched interests and institutionalised state practice. Large sections of the Unionist population mobilised in defence of Protestant privilege. They attempted to block the flow of historical change. The civil rights movement, with some partial exceptions, proved unable to realise its ambition to unite Catholic and Protestant. Instead, Northern Ireland settled into one of the longest running guerrilla wars of the twentieth century.

In the 1990s Northern Ireland's political landscape, once again, altered dramatically. A peace process emerged, initially through secret talks between the UK government and Sinn Féin and the Provisional IRA. After the declaration of a unilateral ceasefire by the IRA the peace process developed through a mix of public political wrangling and private negotiation. This time the population of Northern Ireland were largely passive observers, who were occasionally marshalled from the sidelines to provide a democratic veneer to decisions that were often deliberately designed to be insulated from public scrutiny and accountability. The peace agreement that was signed in 1998 created a new institutional framework for the governing of the region. A multicultural form of anti-racism is central to this new framework.

In Chapter 4 we noted that there are various forms of anti-racism and that these differ in their conception of the nature of the problem and the suggested solution. In the form in which we presented them – sectarian, egalitarian and social justice, social cohesion, multicultural – they are defined by their underlying premises. In this chapter we examine anti-racisms as they actually existed in the process of historical change and development. Our concern is not to test our definitions of the different forms of anti-racism identified in a previous chapter, but to understand their relationship to the specific historical context in which they are situated and their role within the processes of social change. The phenomenon that we are examining, to paraphrase Engels, is not a complex of ready-made things, but a complex of processes. The civil rights movement in Northern Ireland was underpinned and guided by an egalitarian and social justice conception of anti-racism, but it was a *movement*, not a coherent *thing*. The civil rights movement contained many different social actors who were picked up and swept along in its current. In the process, the conditions for the existence of these social actors changed and some became radicalised and intensified their opposition to the sectarian state. Others revealed themselves to be more concerned with social cohesion than social transformation and accommodated to the sectarian state. Ideas and interests played crucial roles in guiding the actions of social actors in this process of change.

All of these changes took place against the backdrop of broader social changes in the world. The changes in Northern Ireland also partly fed into and informed these broader changes. The Northern Ireland civil rights movement was part of the 1960s revolt against imperialism, authoritarian regimes and the statist left. In this sense, the civil rights movement was part of the New Left. The civil rights movement, and the backlash against it, was also a product of the end of the postwar economic boom and the beginnings of the global shift of industrial production from the West to the East. The Northern Ireland peace process of the 1990s was just one of a number of parallel peace processes that emerged and developed at the end of the Cold War. It was also, as we argue in this chapter, built on the defeat of left-wing movements for social change. Racisms and anti-racisms emerge and develop in the process of broader social change. Human consciousness plays a crucial role in this process.

The sectarian state unsettled

From its foundation in 1921 until the suspension of the Stormont parliament by the UK government in 1972, Northern Ireland was a Unionist-dominated society in which the prevailing Unionist ideological consensus was that Catholics were a treasonous minority who wanted to destroy Northern Ireland and politically reunify the island of Ireland. There was some basis to this perception. The political party that enjoyed the most electoral support from Catholics, the Nationalist Party, supported a united Ireland. The IRA was a minor but real threat. It was living proof that many Catholics not only viewed Northern Ireland as an illegitimate political entity, but that some of them were willing to use guerrilla tactics to undermine Unionist power. Unionist insecurities were further fuelled by the irredentist claim to jurisdiction over the whole of the island of Ireland, a claim that became enshrined in the constitution of the Republic of Ireland. Unionist fears were given further weight by the fact that they viewed this neighbouring country, with considerable justification, as a priest-ridden theocracy in which Catholic morality dominated both state and society.[4]

Unionist perceptions of the Catholic minority, however, ignored the Unionists' own role in creating a seditious racialised minority in their midst. Anti-Catholic discrimination was institutionalised in employment recruitment to state positions, and in job promotion and the allocation of public resources. Discrimination against Catholics was also rife in the private sector, most notoriously in Belfast's shipyards.[5] Anti-Catholicism was embodied in the key role that was given to the Orange Order (or the Grand Orange Lodge of Ireland, as it was officially named), a fraternal society that acted as a crucial civil society organisation which mediated different class interests as a means to maintain Protestant supremacy. Suspicion of the Catholic population was institutionalised in special powers that allowed the Northern Ireland government to suspend *habeas corpus* and arrest and indefinitely detain without trial anyone suspected of sedition.[6] The enforcers of this law, the Royal Ulster Constabulary (RUC), were almost entirely Protestant, and their power was supplemented by a part-time reserve force, the Ulster Special Constabulary (colloquially known as the B-Specials), whose membership was entirely Protestant and who were notoriously anti-Catholic. Protestant supremacy was endorsed at the highest level of government. It was perhaps most explicitly articulated by Northern Ireland's first Prime Minister, James Craig, in 1933 when he declared in a parliamentary speech: 'I am an Orangeman first and a politician afterwards ... All I boast is that we are a Protestant parliament [Stormont] and a Protestant state.'[7]

In the 1960s cracks began to appear in the anti-Catholic sectarian edifice that was the Northern Ireland state. The global shift of traditional manufacturing away from Western industrialised economies took a heavy toll on two key sectors of the Northern Ireland economy, linen manufacturing and shipbuilding. Protestant workers, who were over-represented in these sectors, were particularly affected by the decline of these industries. The Northern Ireland government sought to compensate for these losses by attempting to attract new investment from overseas. Liberal Unionists suggested reforms, such as normalising relations with the Republic of Ireland, in an effort to make Northern Ireland a more attractive place to invest. This strategy created tensions within Unionism.

Other changes were taking place. Increasing numbers of Catholics had benefited from UK-wide educational reforms that had been introduced after the Second World War. Many had gained academic qualifications through compulsory post-primary education and some had gone on to university. The Catholic middle class was growing, but sectarian employment practices meant that employment opportunities and career advancement was severely limited for them. The Nationalist Party, encouraged by the emergence of liberal Unionism, changed policy and adopted the role of official opposition in Stormont.

The attempts of liberal Unionists to modernise the state created space for an egalitarian anti-racism to emerge. This anti-racism took the form of a civil rights movement, a diverse coalition of different elements of Northern Irish society. It included liberal Protestant Unionists, conservative Catholic businessmen, various types of socialists and trade unionists, communists aligned to the Soviet Union, anarchist and Trotskyist students and veteran Irish Republicans. The only thing that united this disparate collection of groups and individuals was their desire to reform Northern Ireland by removing the illiberal aspects of the state. They did not agree on why this discrimination was a problem, or what should be done about it. Liberal Unionists, for example, wanted to reform Northern Ireland so that it looked like a liberal democracy. Others, influenced by various strands of Marxism, saw equal rights as an issue that could expose the contradictions of capitalist society as a precursor to anti-capitalist revolution. One of the key civil rights organisations, the Northern Ireland Civil Rights Association (NICRA), agreed on six demands that they would campaign around: an equal vote for every individual; an end to the gerrymandering of electoral wards; an end to discrimination in state employment; an end to discrimination in the allocation of public housing; the removal of the Special Powers Act; and the disbanding of the B-Specials.[8]

The same process that created space for the liberal anti-racism of the civil rights movement alarmed sections of Unionism who had their power-base in traditional anti-Catholic practices. This split within Unionism went to the heart of government. The Prime Minister (Terence O'Neill) was in favour of reforms, but the Minister for Home Affairs (William Craig) was opposed. O'Neill was, at least initially, able to claim the electoral support of the majority in Northern Ireland. Among active politically orientated civil society organisations, however, opposition to reform dominated. Long-established organisations, most notably the influential Orange Order, opposed concessions to Catholics. A range of new organisations – such as the loyalist paramilitary Ulster Volunteer Force, various Paisleyite bodies such as Ulster Protestant Action and the Ulster Protestant Volunteers – grew up in active opposition to O'Neill's attempts at reform.[9]

The reform process might have slowly unfurled over the next few decades if the attempts to gain civil rights demands had stayed at the level of lobbying. But they didn't. The civil rights movement, influenced in part by the Civil Rights movement in the USA, and later by the May '68 global protest movements, organised protest marches in an attempt to draw public attention to sectarian discrimination and the restrictions on civil liberties.[10] Craig responded by restricting and then banning civil rights protests. Counter demonstrations were organised by radical Unionists, such as the Revd Ian Paisley. RUC policing of civil rights protests was heavy handed. A key turning point was a civil rights march in Northern Ireland's second city, Derry/Londonderry, in October 1968 organised by NICRA and a local civil rights organisation, the Derry Housing Action Committee. The Catholic population of Derry/Londonderry was smaller than that of Belfast. Unlike Belfast, however, Catholics were a majority of the city's population.[11]

Derry/Londonderry was a prime example of the sectarian state in practice. In a city where Catholics were the majority, the local council (Londonderry Corporation) enjoyed a Unionist majority, thanks to the gerrymandering of the electoral boundaries. The corporation practised discrimination in the allocation of public housing, funding and employment. Catholics were unhappy with this situation, but until the advent of the civil rights movement they were quiescent in their oppression. The October protest was banned by Craig, but the organisers and a few hundred supporters defied the ban and attempted to march. They were attacked by the RUC who bludgeoned protestors. This repressive response provoked rioting from Catholics in the working-class Bogside district of the city. The RUC and the B-Specials attempted to put down the riots, but their actions only served to escalate the violence. The repressive response to the civil rights march shifted action from specialist lobbying to a mass movement as the Catholic working class in Derry/Londonderry, who had previously been quiescent, now took to the streets in open defiance of the Stormont government, the local corporation and the despised police force. By the end of November 1968, state control of the city was proving ineffective as the ban on marches was persistently defied. When civil rights became a mass movement with the mobilisation of the Catholic working class in Derry/Londonderry, the pace of change altered significantly. Liberal Unionists and more conservative elements within the Catholic population, such as small businessmen, tried to contain the growing radicalism of the movement and channel it into formal pressure-group politics. Their scope to do so, however, was limited by the institutionalised sectarianism of Northern Irish society on the one hand and the hopes and aspirations of civil rights protestors on the other.

Tensions came to a head on the occasion of the annual Apprentice Boys of Derry parade in Derry/Londonderry in August 1969. The Apprentice Boys are the local Orange organisation in the city. The annual parade was normally a provocative display of Protestant supremacy. There were calls for the parade to

be included in the blanket ban on civil rights marches. The Minister for Home
Affairs refused to ban the parade and drafted in extra police, an estimated third
of the entire force, to ensure that it went ahead. Predictably, the city erupted
in violence. There were running street battles between Catholic youths from
the Bogside and the police. Barricades were erected in the Bogside and a 'no go
area' was declared by protestors. The police were attacked with petrol bombs.
This time rioting also broke out in Belfast. After four days of intense street
fighting, ten people had been killed and hundreds of others injured, millions
of pounds worth of damage had been caused and more than a thousand people
had been permanently displaced from their homes. The fighting died down, not
because the protestors had been crushed, but because the police were exhausted.
It was only then, when part of the UK had become ungovernable, that British
troops were deployed on the streets of Belfast and Derry/Londonderry. These
troops were deployed 'in aid of the civil power' – in other words, to support the
Unionist government.[12]

The civil rights movement, in the words of Richard Rose, confronted the
Northern Ireland government 'with new types of protestors, employing methods that are illegal but technically non-violent, to express in extreme form their
rejection of the regime'.[13] The civil rights movement created a crisis of state
authority. The attempt to reassert authority through coercion not only failed,
but served to further undermine the authority of Stormont. The intervention of
the Westminster government was a tacit acknowledgement that state rule could
no longer continue in the form of the local sectarian state. Westminster, however, did not want to sweep aside the Stormont government. Discussion about
establishing direct rule, Rose notes, was 'opposed at Westminster on the ground
that it would pollute British politics by introducing an alien part of the United
Kingdom into the mainstream of British politics'.[14] The UK government wanted
to maintain Northern Ireland as a place apart, but some changes were required.
Westminster demanded reforms, including some control from Whitehall (the
UK's administrative centre). The British Army's General Officer Commanding
was charged with responsibility over the security forces in Northern Ireland,
including the RUC and B-Specials in their role of policing disorder (but not
in their 'normal' policing roles).[15] Security *policy*, however, remained in the
hands of the Minister for Home Affairs at Stormont. An inquiry, under the
direction of Lord Scarman, was established to investigate 'the acts of violence
and civil disturbance which occurred' between March and August 1969.[16] The
Hunt Committee was established to 'examine the recruitment, organisation,
structure and composition' of the RUC and B-Specials.[17] A centralised housing authority, with responsibility for all public sector housing, was created.
Local government was restructured and some Race Relations measures were
introduced. Westminster did not, however, extend the 1968 Race Relations Act
to the region. Instead, it passed the Prevention of Incitement to Hatred (NI)

Act, insisted on the creation of a post of Minister for Community Relations at Stormont and created a quasi-autonomous state body, the Northern Ireland Community Relations Commission (NICRC).[18] (The latter was modelled on the one created under the terms of the 1968 Race Relations Act.)

Liberty, equality, instability

The Community Relations Commission, whose remit covered the rest of the UK, was charged with promoting harmonious 'relations between people of different racial origins'.[19] The NICRC was established to promote good relations between Catholics and Protestants in Northern Ireland. Community relations policy, like the Race Relations approach which underpins it, was from its inception centrally concerned with social cohesion. The chair of the NICRC, Maurice Hayes, made this clear when he said that the leaders of the organisation interpreted the NICRC's role as 'stabilising society by encouraging people to seek solutions to their problems through institutional channels ... and to identify with others in the society in search of common goals of peace, prosperity, justice and happiness ... without violence'.[20] The NICRC was conceived as an intuitional means through which to channel Catholic discontent and a mechanism through which Catholic grievances could be accommodated and the crisis of state authority ameliorated. The NICRC took a capacity-building approach to Race Relations. Hayes had spent time in the United States and had been impressed by the Community Action Programs that had been introduced during Lyndon Johnston's presidency, as part of the post-Civil Rights War on Poverty initiative. Hayes sought to develop something similar in Northern Ireland. The NICRC subsequently appointed Hywel Griffiths as its director. Griffiths was appointed because of his experience working for the UK Colonial Office as a Community Development Officer in Zambia. Community development policy was one of the Colonial Office's initiatives established after the Second World War as part of the attempt, as Suke Wolton puts it 'to enhance their legitimacy in the practical business of economic development and welfare provision to the poor ... at a time when Britain's position in the world was being threatened by the United States'.[21] Community development policy was conceived as a means to establish links between local communities and the central state and to shift the rationale for colonial rule from White supremacy to development and poverty reduction.[22]

The UK government's reforms sought to stabilise Northern Ireland. Their effect, however, was sometimes the opposite. Some sections of the Protestant population viewed the reforms as a lack of resolve in the face of Catholic insurgency, or outright treachery on the part of the UK government. When, for example, plans to disband the B-Specials and disarm the RUC were announced in October 1969 there were violent clashes on the Shankill Road in Belfast between the British Army and Protestant protestors, which resulted in three deaths and 66 injuries. As trust in government deteriorated, pro-state vigilante groups sprang up in Protestant areas. The UK government's desire to work through the devolved government at Stormont also meant that many aspects of the sectarian state remained intact. Justice policy was still in the hands of the Minister for Home Affairs at Stormont. Sectarian practices continued. Civil rights protestors, for example, were prosecuted for actions related to the disturbances in August 1969, but no members of the RUC or B-Specials faced prosecution. When Bernadette Devlin, a leading civil rights protestor who had been elected to Westminster, was jailed for her role in the clashes with the security forces in June 1970, rioting broke out in Belfast and Derry/Londonderry.[23]

Other changes were also going on. The opposition to the sectarian state was taking shape in response to the actions of the security forces and government reforms. Contrary to popular myth, the IRA did not start the conflict in Northern Ireland; it was transformed by it. In the mid-1960s the IRA had given up on the use of military means as a way to end British rule in Ireland. Its new strategy was based on the Stalinist two-stage theory of national independence. The first stage involved democratising the state; only when this was completed could the second stage of gaining independence be attempted. In the late 1960s the IRA was in disarray. Many IRA members were unhappy with this policy. The repressive response of the state in 1969 led to an internal debate. Some members, particularly those based in Northern Ireland, argued for a return to armed struggle. The debate led to a split in the organisation and the formation of the Provisional IRA (which from this point onwards we will simply refer to as the IRA).[24] By mid-1970 the IRA had regrouped and rearmed and, with some level of support from local Catholic communities, began to attack the British Army and bomb commercial premises in urban areas.[25]

For some opponents of the sectarian state, the IRA's military actions appeared to be a rational response to an increasingly militarised situation; for others it was a worrying development. The civil rights movement began to diverge on the issue of whether the state was reformable within the UK, or if being a region of the UK was part of the problem itself. Sections of the civil rights movement were involved in forming the SDLP in 1970, as a means to push for reform through parliamentary channels within the UK state.[26] Those who formed, and joined, the SDLP were encouraged by the reforms promoted by Westminster, and were concerned about social stability in Northern Ireland. These, mainly middle-class Catholics, with a few liberal Protestants and some statist leftists, argued in favour of reforms and looked to the Westminster government and pro-reform Unionists to dismantle the sectarian state. The IRA argued that British rule was colonial rule, that the UK state was incapable of treating Catholics and Protestants equally and that national self-determination was the only route to uniting Catholics, Protestants and dissenters. This argument, which only a few years earlier had seemed out of date, now appealed to many Catholics and a tiny minority of left-leaning Protestants who had been radicalised by the civil rights protests. The issue of whether the state was reformable or not tended to coalesce around the issue of armed struggle. For many of those who viewed the state as irreformable, the use of military means to end British rule appeared to be the only viable option. For those who viewed the state as reformable, the IRA's military strategy only encouraged sectarian violence from Protestant pro-state vigilantes and strengthened the arguments of the sectarian strands of Unionism against the reformers.

Violence was a polarising issue, but it could swing waverers either way, depending on the nature of the violence. The SDLP withdrew from Stormont in July 1971 when its demands for an inquiry into the killing of two Catholics by British soldiers in Derry/Londonderry were refused. The following month the Unionist government introduced internment without trial in an attempt to quash the IRA, which only served to escalate violence even further. Many people, Protestant and Catholic, were drawn to join, respectively, pro- and anti-state paramilitary organisations. The SDLP's advocacy of reform appeared inadequate. It announced a campaign of civil disobedience in protest at the introduction of internment. It supported rent strikes and resigned from public bodies. It established a Nationalist Assembly of the Northern Irish People as an alternative government in October 1971. The repression of the security forces both helped to contain and inflame violence. Given that the role of the security forces was to maintain social stability, their actions were always going to be disproportionately directed at the 'disloyal' Catholic population. The demands of maintaining stability on the security front meant that the British Army had to act in a sectarian manner. In January 1972 (in an event colloquially known as Bloody Sunday), British soldiers from the parachute regiment shot dead 13 unarmed civilians taking part in a mass protest against internment. After Bloody Sunday the attempt to reform the Northern Ireland state appeared to be futile. The UK government withdrew its support for Stormont when the Unionist Prime Minister refused to completely relinquish control over law and order. In March 1972, the Stormont parliament was suspended and direct rule from Westminster was imposed on Northern Ireland.

The limits of egalitarian anti-racism

The suspension of the Stormont parliament both vindicated the egalitarian anti-racism of the civil rights movement and exposed its limits. It vindicated the civil rights movement because the collapse of Stormont was a clear demonstration that Protestant supremacy was an unviable form of government. It demonstrated that the subjective desire for freedom from sectarian domination had become such a powerful objective force in society that it had toppled the institution that had most embodied that sectarian domination. The anti-sectarianism of the civil rights movement, which had once appeared to be a utopian and unrealistic ideal, had proven its rationality in practice. The collapse of Stormont also, however, exposed the limits of the emancipatory anti-racism of the civil rights movement. The political form of sectarian domination had been abolished, but the substance of Catholic inequality, and the reality of the sectarian divide, had not. The anti-racisms of the dominant strands of the civil rights movement were all limited by the, implicit or explicit, assumption of the nation-state as the medium through which sectarian ideas and practices could be overcome.

The SDLP was formed as a coalition, which was mainly composed of 'red' socialists and 'green' (i.e. Irish) nationalists. The party was formed from the top down by 'non-Unionist' candidates who had been elected to Stormont in the February 1969 election.[27] There was a tension between the red and green sections of the party regarding the emphasis that should be given to their socialism and their nationalism. The red wing was either ambivalent towards an all-Ireland dimension or was openly hostile to it. This socialist section of the party was universalist in the sense that they wanted to transcend the sectarian nature of politics in Northern Ireland and move on to the ground of social issues contested on a left–right spectrum, as was the case in the rest of the UK. They were particularist in the sense that they did not challenge the nation-state as an institution that divides human beings into different 'groups' by nationality. The nationalist wing of the party was more conservative. They were particularist in that they viewed Irish nationalists as culturally different to Unionists and wanted this difference to be given institutional recognition. Two factors modified the form of the 'Irish dimension'. The acknowledgement that the majority of Protestants were hostile to a united Ireland meant that the party emphasised that 'reunification could only come about by the consent of the majority in Northern Ireland'.[28] The unlikeliness of Protestants consenting to this in the foreseeable future, combined with the reluctance of the government in the Republic of Ireland to insist on an Irish dimension, meant that this idea was 'aspirational'.[29] It was something to uphold as a guiding ideal, but there was no practical means of achieving it. Consequently the focus of the practical activity of both the red and green wings of the party was on reform within the UK. The party was held together by a combination of this reformist focus, its opposition to the sectarian privilege of the Stormont regime and its opposition to the violent methods of the IRA. Within the SDLP, there was an uneasy relationship between egalitarian anti-racism and a concern with social cohesion. In the turbulent years of the early 1970s it was often willing to prioritise equality and social justice over social cohesion, particularly when civil rights protestors became radicalised by state repression and threatened to bypass the party. Its opposition to the state, however, was conditional. Its overall trajectory, of steering protest in the direction of looking to the UK state to tackle the sectarianism of Unionists, continually reasserted itself.

The Provisional IRA emerged in 1970 as the organisation that was best able to give expression to the anger that had been unleashed by civil rights protests. As the veteran civil rights campaigner, Eamonn McCann, put it:

> people in the Bogside were just raging mad at what was being done to their community, the civil rights militants and left wingers generally had no prepared channels to divert that anger into, and no structure of organisation to try to recruit people into, and no commonly accepted and clear political ideas that we were trying to impose on the situation. The one group which emerged from that situation, and which had absolutely clear ideas about what was happening – Britain oppressing Ireland – and had the organisation to give it expression, was the Republican movement.[30]

The IRA prioritised egalitarian anti-racism over social cohesion. Irish Republicans claim an anti-racist tradition that goes back to the United Irishmen's attempt, in the 1790s, to unite Catholic, Protestant and dissenter in an independent sovereign Ireland. Republicans were heavily involved in the civil rights movement. The IRA, however, has always been a broad grouping that contains many different strands. Some of these strands are not egalitarian. Some conservative Catholics, for example, opposed the anti-Catholicism of Stormont, but wanted an all-Ireland Catholic state. Cultural nationalists, who draw on the tradition of the Gaelic League, view Catholics and Protestants as different 'races' (defined by their cultural traditions, rather than biology). For these 'racial' Republicans, anti-racism was a source of moral authority with which to beat Protestant suprematists, rather than a means towards achieving a universal humanity. In this regard, they expressed a form of sectarian anti-racism, not an egalitarian one.[31]

Neither of these 'racial' strands, however, was dominant in the IRA. The dominant strand was a socialist one that looked to the tradition of James Connolly, and argued that sectarianism was used by British imperialists to divide and rule the working class. In the early days of the Provisional IRA, the different strands were held together by their shared opposition to what they saw as the British colonial occupation of Ireland, and the sectarian form that they argued this necessarily took. The Provisional IRA was organisationally strong, but politically weak. In some respects, it is misleading to talk about different theoretical outlooks within the IRA, as the organisation was focused on action, and there was significant suspicion of theory as armchair activity. There was hostility from different sections of the IRA to what was interpreted as the 'political turn' that led to the organisation giving up the armed struggle in the 1960s. This experience of the 'political turn', combined with the clandestine nature of a guerrilla army and the pressing practical needs of training personnel and securing weapons, meant that the organisational aspect of the IRA developed at the expense of theory. The IRA did not have to work hard to convince recruits to join – the British Army, the RUC and the Stormont government were doing that job for them. The IRA established a strong, but fairly exclusive, organisational base among working-class Catholics in urban centres and border areas. It made no attempt, however, to appeal to working-class Protestants and little attempt to appeal to workers in the Republic of Ireland. In effect, it had a two-stage strategy for tackling sectarianism: unite Ireland first, then unite Catholic and Protestant. The realisation of egalitarian anti-racism was, thus, postponed until after British withdrawal from the north-east corner of Ireland. A nation-state framework imposed a severe limit on the radicalness of their anti-racism.[32]

The radical activist elements of the civil rights movement played a key role in turning it from a genteel lobbying platform into a mass movement. Their tactics paralleled those of the Civil Rights movement in the USA. They focused on the contradiction between the promise of equality, which was being offered by liberal unionism, and the reality of inequality, which other Unionists sought to defend. The moderate middle-class leadership of NICRA wanted to avoid direct confrontation with the defenders of the status quo, particular the RUC and the Paisleyites. The radical activists, however, often welcomed confrontation. They wanted to provoke an overreaction as a way of intensifying the contradiction between liberal and reactionary Unionism. This radical element took shape as People's Democracy. Although small and lacking in financial resources, People's Democracy made an impact well beyond its size. Their tactics of disruption and provocation were based on a broader New Left political understanding, which they applied to explaining the situation in Northern Ireland. They argued for a class analysis of the situation and argued that the issue of civil rights should not be seen in religious terms, but in class terms. The middle-class leadership of NICRA and many of its local affiliates, they argued, would settle for reforms that provided them with access to power and social mobility. They appreciated the need to win Protestant working-class support for civil rights and argued that the underlying issues were social issues. They argued, for example, that 'Those who want to confine the civil rights demands to "equal rights" for all ignore the fact that fair allocation of jobs and houses within the existing system ... would simply mean equal shares of unemployment and bad housing for all.'[33] They were, in many ways, the intellectual and activist powerhouse of the civil rights movement.[34]

As the civil rights movement grew, People's Democracy became frustrated with the conservativism of NICRA. At a NICRA rally in Strabane in July 1969, for example, Devlin condemned the local NICRA notables as sectarian and argued that if civil rights meant 'fighting for nothing more than equality for Catholics, the middle class would be equal and the working class would "all be equal – at the bottom"'.[35] People's Democracy broke from NICRA. Outside NICRA, however, their organisational weakness was exposed. In the words of Paul Arthur, they subsequently 'floundered around seeking a role, reacting to events and government policy rather than initiating radical alternatives', and in the process began to fragment and decline as an organisation.[36] As a result of their unwillingness to confront their organisational decline and fragmentation, People's Democracy ended up becoming politically isolated and started to play the role of critical friend to Irish Republicanism. As they put it themselves in a pamphlet published in 1972:

> the Northern crisis will be only one stage of a long struggle and when it is temporarily resolved and emphasis shifts to the struggle against the ruling class, North and South, then more and more people will turn to the socialists for advice and leadership, Meanwhile P.D. [People's Democracy] of course should co-operate with the Republicans, knowing that the vast majority of their volunteers want to go the full road to the Workers Republic. Our current path though isolated, is in honourable tradition.[37]

People's Democracy recognised the limits of egalitarian anti-racism in a society based on class division. They took the most consistently anti-sectarian stands during the civil rights period. Their organisational weakness, however, meant that they were unable to establish any significant influence among either the Protestant or Catholic working class.

Another strand of the civil rights movement developed into the Alliance Party of Northern Ireland (APNI). This strand, which represented the outlook of liberal Unionism, was the least engaged with civil rights as a movement. Some liberal Unionists were involved with NICRA, but they were the first to balk at any whiff of social disorder. This strand did, however, give rise to what has been the only significant 'cross-community' political party in Northern Ireland. Its embryonic beginnings were as the New Ulster Movement (NUM), a ginger group within the UUP, which was set up to help further the process of change initiated by O'Neill when he took over as UUP leader. The NUM thought that Northern Irish society needed to modernise. For them this meant ending sectarian discrimination and promoting employment based on merit, attracting foreign capital to the region and opening up the UUP to Catholic members. When O'Neill was ousted as leader of the UUP by sectarian hardliners, NUM members broke with the UUP and formed the APNI.[38] The party was established as an explicitly bi-confessional party. It succeeded, where every other party failed, in attracting both Catholics and Protestants in good proportion.[39] It attracted Catholics who had formerly been members of the Northern Ireland Labour Party and others who had no previous involvement in any political party. The membership of the party was predominantly middle class and well educated. It gained 13.7 per cent of the vote in the first election it stood in, the 1973 district council elections. Since then its vote has only once risen above 10 per cent, in the 1979 Westminster general election. The APNI self-consciously casts itself as playing a mediating role between the two ethnic blocs.[40] It tends to hold a technocratic view of society, placing a lot of store on education (particularly non-denominational integrated education), and viewing sectarian allegiances as irrational attachments to the past, or as manifestations of an inability to come to terms with the changes that capitalist modernity produces. Its outlook is one in which the affluent and educated middle classes are the model for the rest of society. Sectarianism is viewed as a hangover from the past, which will be eradicated through market forces with the assistance of technocratic intervention from the state to stifle atavistic urges that interfere with the 'natural' process of change. While the APNI has succeeded in bridging the sectarian divide, it has, unsurprisingly, failed to bridge the class divide. It has very little appeal outside of its middle-class base. To many working-class people, Catholic and Protestant, the APNI are condescending toffs. The APNI most readily prioritises social cohesion over egalitarianism, and its conception of egalitarian anti-racism is one that views the issue in terms of equal opportunities law, rather than transforming social relations of inequality.

From civil rights to containment

After the collapse of Stormont and the imposition of direct rule from Westminster, the dynamic of the civil rights movement was arrested. In part, the decline in popular engagement was due to the success of the movement. Many of the demands that NICRA campaigned around were achieved. The property qualification that provided disproportionate votes to the wealthy and disenfranchised the poor was abolished. Local government was reorganised, and in the process, gerrymandering was removed. The Northern Ireland Housing Executive was created to tackle discrimination in the allocation of public housing. The achievement of these egalitarian demands, however, went alongside the prioritising of social stability over equality and social justice. The UK government wanted to contain the conflict in Northern Ireland, both in the sense of achieving 'acceptable levels of violence' (as the Home Secretary Reginald Maudling put it in early 1971), and in the sense of not letting an alien element pollute the British body of UK politics. The UK government attempted to return power to Stormont, in the form of a power-sharing executive that operated for the first five months of 1974. This devolved government, colloquially known as Sunningdale, fell when the majority of Unionist members withdrew in protest at both the power-sharing element and the minor 'Irish dimension'. With the fall of Sunningdale, the UK government shifted away from attempting a political solution and focused its efforts on the security front.[41]

The collapse of Stormont only changed the form of the sectarian state. The sectarian nature of state rule continued, most obviously in the development and enforcement of security policy.[42] Security measures were, necessarily, directed against those who were perceived as being a threat to security. Consequently, as Brewer notes, Catholics were 'subject to intimidation from a source which Protestants do not experience; namely, the security forces, whose presence in working-class Catholic areas in many of the large towns approaches saturation'.[43]

Security policy disproportionately affected Catholics in other ways. Kevin Boyle, Tom Hadden and Paddy Hillyard, for example, note that there were significant 'differences in sentences imposed on Protestant and Catholic defendants' in prosecutions for possession of unauthorised firearms or explosives.[44] Catholics, they found, tended to be assumed to be guilty and were likely to be charged with the most serious offence of possession with intent to endanger life. Membership of 'the UDA [Ulster Defence Association], on the other hand, was not generally regarded as an aggravating factor' and membership of the Ulster Defence Regiment (UDR) 'was often taken as a ground for the mitigation of sentence'.[45] There was also collusion between pro-state loyalist paramilitary groups and state security forces. A classified military intelligence report, drawn up in 1973, estimated that up to 15 per cent of UDR soldiers had links to loyalist groups. The report also stated that the 'best single source of weapons, and only significant source of modern weapons for Protestant groups, has been the UDR'.[46]

The collapse of Stormont removed the executive and legislative power of Ulster Unionism, but it did not remove Unionism as a social force in Northern Irish society. The failure of the civil rights movement to make any connection with the Protestant working class meant that class politics retained a sectarian character. The flight of liberal Unionism from the UUP to the APNI only served to strengthen the dominance of sectarian strands within the UUP. The APNI's condescending attitude towards the working classes meant that it was unable to provide an effective counterweight to sectarian ideas in Northern Irish society. The IRA's prioritising of British withdrawal, and its use of violent military means to achieve this, meant that it alienated many Protestants from the idea of equality. Civil rights increasingly appeared to mean rights for Catholics rather than social equality. When the Protestant working class organised, it was not on the basis of equality, but of preventing what they saw as a potential take-over of the state by Catholics. The largest demonstration of the power of Protestant workers came with the Ulster Workers Council strike of 1974. This was not, however, a protest against social conditions, growing unemployment or conditions in the workplace. It was a protest against the Sunningdale power-sharing government. Their actions were instrumental in bringing down the government.[47]

Once direct rule had been introduced, the limitations of IRA strategy began to be exposed. Their actions had played a key role in bringing down the Stormont government, but now there was direct rule from Westminster and more British troops on the ground. They had helped to bring about the end of the sectarian state, but sectarian killings at the hands of loyalist paramilitaries were striking terror into the hearts of Catholics, and UK government security policy continued to enforce sectarian domination over working-class Catholics. Their failure to gain any significant support outside the Catholic working class in Northern Ireland left them isolated. This isolation, however, was also a source of strength. As Mark Ryan notes,

The narrowness of the IRA's support base was the source of both its strengths and weaknesses. It helped the organisation in the sense that they now had a very coherent and, for a nationalist movement, extremely homogeneous, social base … [but this also] obscured the real problem; the failure to connect with the rest of Irish society … although they espoused national ideals, they never developed from being a community-based movement … Hence the claim to being a national movement was undermined from the beginning.[48]

The realisation of the IRA's aspiration to unite Catholic, Protestant and dissenter relied on first achieving a united Ireland. Their failure to broaden their base of support, however, meant that their espoused egalitarian anti-racism would only remain an aspiration. The narrow social base of the IRA made the organisation extremely resilient to the counter-insurgency efforts of the security forces. After the collapse of the Sunningdale government, the IRA settled into a 'long war' of attrition.[49] Westminster's strategy of containment and the IRA's 'long war' strategy were mirror images of each other. Neither could win, but both were determined that they would not lose.

Against a backdrop of increasing sectarian division, and an overall emphasis on security, there were some attempts by Westminster to promote egalitarian anti-racism. In parallel with the 1976 Race Relations Act, the UK government passed the 1976 Fair Employment Act which established the Fair Employment Agency (FEA) as a statutory body to tackle discrimination in employment.[50] Bob Cooper, one of the founding members of the APNI, left the party to head up the FEA.[51] In this role, he battled with entrenched sectarianism and a lack of political will. Against the backdrop of the decline of manufacturing, the UK government concentrated on job creation, rather than equal opportunities.[52] The FEA was underfunded and the Northern Ireland Civil Service (NICS), which in the 1970s was still Protestant dominated and heavily Unionist orientated, paid no attention to its guidelines and 'resisted an investigation by the FEA into its practices'.[53] Throughout the 1970s and 1980s social cohesion and egalitarian anti-racism were in conflict, and social cohesion remained the dominant priority for the UK government.

The rise of multicultural anti-racism

After the collapse of the power-sharing government, the UK government sought to increase the isolation of the IRA. It attempted to undermine the legitimacy of the IRA's campaign by a range of measures designed to present the conflict as a local issue of criminality. It revoked the Special Category status of 'terrorist' prisoners. It withdrew the British Army from its frontline role and pushed the RUC to the fore. It localised the military dimension by giving a greater role to the UDR. These aspects of security policy, which became known as Ulsterisation, had the effect of further racialising the conflict by making it appear to be a conflict between a Catholic IRA and Protestant security forces and paramilitaries.[54] The IRA attempted to overcome its isolation. It was, however, people outside the ranks of the IRA, People's Democracy and the relatives of IRA prisoners, who played a key role in kick-starting a movement that would broaden support for egalitarian anti-racism. Campaigners focused on issues of civil liberties. They argued that jailed Republicans were not common criminals, but were politically motivated. They were prisoners of conscience of an authoritarian regime. They drew attention to humanitarian and civil liberties issues, such as RUC brutality against IRA and INLA suspects in detention and the use of emergency law such as the jury-free Diplock courts.

These campaigns against state repression provided an organisational mechanism through which people could become engaged with opposition to British rule without having to be part of a clandestine military organisation. This new movement engaged people who had been involved in civil rights, but who had disengaged when the military campaign had taken precedence over the political one. The movement gained significant momentum when it launched a campaign in support of Irish Republican hunger-strikers. Opponents of the IRA were being put in a position where they either had to justify support for state repression or support the IRA's claim to be a politically motivated movement. The movement campaigned beyond the borders of Northern Ireland. In the rest of the UK it gained some support among trade unionists and some on the left of the Labour Party (including the then backbench Labour MP, Jeremy Corbyn). In the Republic of Ireland, pro-hunger-strike candidates were elected to the national parliament. In the USA, Noraid, the main support organisation for the IRA, was transformed by a new influx of supporters.[55] The campaign, however, with its focus on opposition to repression, was unable to connect with the Protestant working class. In the eyes of many Protestants, the IRA were terrorists who were devoted to destroying their way of life. This viewpoint was given a fillip by the UK government's racialised security policy.

The Fine Gael government in the Republic of Ireland worried that the SDLP might be eclipsed by Sinn Féin. It established the New Ireland Forum to examine new approaches to tackling the conflict.[56] The forum helped to pave the way for the Anglo-Irish Agreement (AIA), an intergovernmental agreement signed by the governments of the UK and Republic of Ireland in 1985. The AIA marked the beginning of the institutionalising of official multicultural anti-racism. It shifted the understanding of the conflict from one of national sovereignty, to present it in cultural and psychological terms.[57] Instead of the universalist language of equality *regardless of* race, religion or ethnicity, the AIA talked about taking 'measures to recognise and accommodate the rights and identities of the two traditions … [which will] include measures to foster the cultural heritage of both traditions'.[58] This conception of the conflict, as one between two groups differentiated by their cultural traditions, is the kind of understanding that underpins the racialised conception of society articulated by Douglas Hyde and other cultural nationalists. Irish revisionists and other scholars who favour an 'internal conflict' interpretation of Northern Ireland have, with various different emphases depending on the scholarly background of the individual, developed the idea of the conflict as one between two 'racial' groups.[59]

The policy area of community relations was revived following the signing of the AIA. This time, however, the community development dimension was to be more tightly controlled by the UK government. This community development dimension was subordinated within the multicultural framework of recognising the rights and identities of the two 'groups' in Northern Ireland. In 1987 the UK government established a Central Community Relations Unit at the heart of the NICS. The same NICS that had rendered the FEA virtually impotent in the late 1970s now helped to institutionalise a community relations approach to governing Northern Ireland. By the late 1980s there had been almost two decades of direct rule from Westminster. The UK government had made some progress in pushing the recruitment and promotion of Catholics in the NICS and there was growing recognition that Unionist dominance would never return.[60] An egalitarian dimension to regional governance was given a jolt with the revamping of the FEA, now armed with greater powers, in 1989.[61] A community relations industry was developed, in parallel to the Race Relations one in the rest of the UK.[62]

Sinn Féin and the IRA were initially hostile to the attempt to develop this multicultural agenda. They recognised that this shift was part of an attempt to undermine them. A significant part of the AIA was concerned with security matters, including more cross-border cooperation between the judiciary, police and military in the UK and the Republic of Ireland. Moreover, alongside the promotion of community relations in the community and voluntary sector, the UK government also undertook a policy of denying funding to groups that, in the opinion of the Secretary of State for Northern Ireland, had some association with paramilitarism.[63] This appeared to be a deliberate attempt to challenge Sinn Féin's strategy of setting up advice centres and playing key roles in neighbourhood-based community activity.[64] Sinn Féin responded by continuing to uphold the principle of national self-determination. They argued that the SDLP proposal that a united Ireland must be conditional on the consent of Unionists effectively handed a veto on the self-determination of the people to a minority on the island.[65] Significantly, they did not challenge the multicultural perspective that underpinned the new racialised approach being taken by the UK government.

Unionists also opposed the AIA. UUP and DUP politicians resigned their seats at Westminster in protest. Huge demonstrations were held across Northern Ireland in protest at the AIA. Loyalists attacked the homes of hundreds of RUC members. These attacks were an indication of the depth of alienation and anger that Protestants felt. In Unionist political culture there has always been distrust of Westminster. It was, after all, the UK government that had passed

Irish Home Rule legislation in the first decade of the twentieth century. The British Army was sometimes viewed as an extension of Westminster. The RUC, however, was viewed as a Unionist institution. These attacks expressed a sense of betrayal by 'our own' people. The AIA, in the words of Christopher Farringdon, 'provided arguably the greatest challenge to Unionists since the Third Home Rule crisis'.[66] The AIA, however, had been deliberately designed to circumvent Unionist protest. In the words of Brendan O'Leary, the AIA was designed to coerce Unionists into sharing power with Irish nationalists or risk more unaccountable (to Unionists) involvement from the irredentist Republic of Ireland in the affairs of Northern Ireland. This measure was necessary, O'Leary argues, because political parties in the region were 'highly democratic, in the sense of being representative of and responsive to their members … [which] leaves political leaders constantly looking over their shoulders, both to their electorate and to potential rival elites in their party'.[67] The AIA circumvented this democratic will by making the representative role in Northern Ireland government dependent on 'cross-community' power-sharing. A pluralist politics of recognition implicit in the AIA was being used to try to displace the majoritarian politics of democratic representation.

The rise of multiculturalism in Northern Ireland happened under the premiership of Margaret Thatcher. For many on the left, multiculturalism is viewed as a project of the left, which the political right is hostile to. As Arun Kundnani puts it: 'Ever since Margaret Thatcher's comment in 1978, that the British people were worried that "this country might be rather swamped by people with a different culture", those on the right of British politics have seen cultural diversity as a threat to national cohesion and security.'[68] The case of Northern Ireland suggests something different. Multicultural policy was not an outcome of the civil rights movement, it was part of an attempt to enforce cohesion and security. Official multicultural anti-racism was part of the broader attack on what were viewed as barriers to the proper operation of free market forces. In Northern Ireland these barriers were understood to be entrenched sectarianism and the IRA's campaign against the sectarian state. In the rest of the UK, it was the trade unions and state socialism. In lots of ways, the Conservative government eroded the democratic accountability of state institutions. The rise of multicultural anti-racism in Northern Ireland was part of this process of eroding democratic accountability.

The peace process and the consolidation of multiculturalism

Sinn Féin's position on the official multicultural anti-racism of community relations policy changed at the beginning of the 1990s, as the organisation began to accommodate to the idea that Northern Ireland was reformable. It conceded to the SDLP argument that the British government could be a neutral arbiter between Irish Nationalists and Ulster Unionists, and it looked to an elite pan-Nationalist alliance, rather than its support base among the Catholic working class, as the key agent for enabling it to achieve its goals.[69] The logic behind this shift was signalled in an internal policy document drawn up in the months leading up to the declaration of the IRA ceasefire in September 1994. The goal of a united 32-county democratic socialist republic had not changed, the document stated, but 'republicans at this time and on their own do not have the strength to achieve the end goal. The struggle needs strengthened; most obviously from other nationalist constituencies led by SDLP, Dublin government and the emerging I.A. [Irish-American] lobby.'[70]

The new strategy marked an acceptance of the community relations interpretation of the Northern Ireland conflict. Instead of the UK government being viewed as an occupying power, it was now conceived as a potential persuader of Unionists. Instead of Unionists as stooges of an occupying government, they were presented as a barrier to a peaceful settlement. Instead of talking about uniting Protestants, Catholics and dissenters in an independent Ireland, Sinn Féin started to talk about the diversity of different traditions on the island of Ireland. The embracing of a pan-Nationalist alliance against an intransigent Unionism was the Republican version of a demand for recognition of an Irish identity and tradition in a new, reformed Northern Ireland.[71] Recognition was conferred on Republicans as legitimate representatives of their 'community' through the peace process. The more Republicans lowered the scale of their ambitions, the more recognition they were given. As Ryan puts it, 'Republicans found themselves in a paradoxical position. If they asserted their claim to be the centre of Irish politics, the more isolated and marginalised they found themselves, while the more they accepted their marginal role, the more they were accepted in the mainstream.'[72]

The Northern Ireland peace process involved all of the parties accepting a marginal role. Unionists had to accept that there could be no return to majority rule, and that the government of the Republic of Ireland would have an institutionalised role in the governance of the region. The APNI had long accepted that it had a marginal role, and positioned itself as a mediator between the two ethnic blocs. The peace process advanced through political deception and obfuscation, rather than honesty and clarity. It took place largely away from public view. Aspiration was presented as leading to conflict. Inclusion and dialogue were presented as both a means and a mode for different 'traditions' to live together. All of this was considered necessary in order to demobilise the population of Northern Ireland and shift them from a conflict orientation, and 're-educate' them as consumers of politics rather than active makers in the future of society.[73] The peace process of the 1990s culminated in the 1998 Agreement. The Agreement institutionalised multicultural government in Northern Ireland. This multiculturalism suffuses the region, from the Executive at the core of the Assembly, through virtually every aspect of government policy, from criminal justice to education to housing, and from policing to sport.[74]

The Agreement has been criticised on the grounds that it is racist because it institutionalises sectarian division at the heart of government.[75] John McGarry and Brendan O'Leary disagree. They argue that the aim of this form of government is

> to achieve equality and proportionality between divided communities, i.e. to erode discrimination and untrammelled majority control, and to permit cultural autonomy … They are not meant to, and need not, institutionalize hatred for other communities, or indeed hierarchical relations between them. They are intended to foster tolerance, mutual recognition, and respect for differences.[76]

McGarry and O'Leary are correct. These are the aims. The new Northern Ireland now has a raft of policies intended to foster tolerance, mutual recognition and respect for differences.

The critics of consociationalism, however, do not argue that the Agreement will institutionalise hierarchical relations between ethnic communities. The revival of Stormont as the seat of government has not led to a return to Unionist supremacy; instead it has been achieved by tipping Stormont on its side so that the political system is horizontally, not vertically, segmented. McGarry and O'Leary's defence misses the point. Critics were arguing that cultural diversity measures provide structural incentives to reify ethnic differences and to invoke these differences as a means of maintaining electoral support.[77] O'Leary implicitly accepts that his critics were correct in an article co-written with Paul Mitchell and Geoffrey Evans and published in 2009. O'Leary and his co-authors point out that both Sinn Féin and the DUP have moderated their stances and when in government have been pragmatic, rather than extremist. They argue that Sinn Féin and the DUP can best be characterised as ethnic tribune parties that 'seek to maximise the group's share of resources extractable from participation in the power-sharing institutions. The ethnic tribune party can be simultaneously pragmatic over resources and intransigent about identity.'[78] The consequence of this new political system, however, has been the disengagement of large swathes of the population from politics.

Conclusion

The successes of the civil rights movement demonstrate the power that anti-racist ideas can have when they inspire masses of people into action. For ideas to be translated into practice, however, they require an organisation that can give them expression as a movement in society. The sections of the civil rights movement that had a more radical, class-based understanding of liberty and equality failed to give those ideas organisational expression. Through their involvement in NICRA, they transformed the organisation from a lobby group to a movement with a mass base in the Catholic working class. They failed, however, to broaden that social base to also engage sections of the Protestant working class. They also failed to win leadership in the movement that they were instrumental in creating. Instead, they remained as subordinate elements within an organisation whose leadership was dominated by more conservative elements. The IRA was organisationally stronger, and was able to attract radicals who wanted to overthrow the state, but it did so within a nation-state framework that aimed to create a new, Irish nation-state. When the main body of radicals, People's Democracy, broke with NICRA its organisational weakness was exposed. In part, this organisational weakness had its roots in theory. As an organisation, People's Democracy was content to allow lots of competing ideas to coexist. They did not struggle for clarity; instead they provided a space for every shade of radical opinion. As a consequence, they ended up becoming critical friends to organisations that they thought contained like-minded radicals.

The attempt of the civil rights movement to transform Northern Irish society succeeded in fundamentally altering the political landscape, but it was also contained in the process. It was contained by the British state's 'arm's-length' approach to governing the region. It was contained by legal and military repression. It was contained by large sections of the Protestant working class who thought that they had more to gain from tying their fortunes to the Union than organising on the basis of class interests. And it was contained by sections of the civil rights movement itself. Liberal Unionists were the first to abandon the fight for equality. They chose the route of official anti-racism instead. Middle-class Catholics supported the civil rights movement when it was a challenge to the sectarian state. For these Irish nationalists, equality was a worthy cause when it was equality for Catholics; when it went beyond equal opportunities, however, they were more equivocal.

The emergence and consolidation of multicultural anti-racism is widely viewed as the maturing of Northern Ireland as a pluralist liberal democratic society. The arrival of immigrants in significant numbers in the twenty-first century has been welcomed as signalling the emergence of a cosmopolitan society. In contemporary Northern Ireland, cultural diversity is celebrated. The new Northern Ireland has the outward appearance of being a vibrant society. The conflict has been converted into heritage and is being sold as a tourist attraction. Northern Ireland is a society in which aspirations to consciously, collectively transform the conditions of our existence have been shelved. The vast majority of people's actions are directed towards private goals. The lives of people in Northern Ireland are, as Anderson puts it, 'inscribed within existing social relations and typically reproduce them'. Existing social relations are not, however, very engaging. Many people are indifferent to the political parties that were forged in the heat of the civil rights era. Many people, particularly in working-class areas, feel alienated from the changes that have taken place. Behind the pleasant facade, discontent rumbles.

Notes

1 Malik, 'What is it to be human?', 17.
2 Perry Anderson, *Arguments within English Marxism* (London: Verso, 1980), 19.
3 Ibid.
4 Much of the material in this section is drawn from standard histories of Northern Ireland. See, for example, Paul Bew, Peter Gibbon and Henry Patterson, *Northern Ireland, 1921–1996: political forces and social classes* (London: Serif, 2nd edn, 2002); Brendan O'Leary and John McGarry, *The politics of antagonism: understanding Northern Ireland* (London: Athlone Press, 1993); Farrell, *Northern Ireland: the Orange state*; Jonathan Bardon, *A history of Ulster* (Belfast: Blackstaff Press, 1992).
5 Whyte, 'How much discrimination was there?'
6 Laura K. Donohue, 'Regulating Northern Ireland: the Special Powers Acts, 1922–1972', *The Historical Journal* 41.4 (1998): 1089–1120.
7 Niall Meehan, '"A Protestant parliament for a Protestant people"?', *History Ireland*, 2008, www.historyireland.com/20th-century-contemporary-history/a-protestant-parliament-for-a-protestant-people-2/ (accessed 10 January 2017).
8 On the civil rights movement, see Purdie, *Politics in the streets*; Paul Arthur, *The People's Democracy, 1968–1973* (Belfast: Blackstaff Press, 1974); O'Dochartaigh, *From civil rights to Armalites*.
9 Sarah Nelson, *Ulster's uncertain defenders: Protestant political, paramilitary and community groups and the Northern Ireland conflict* (Belfast: Appletree, 1984); Steve Bruce, *God save Ulster: the religion and politics of Paisleyism* (Oxford: Oxford University Press, 1989); Eric Kaufmann, *The Orange Order: a contemporary Northern Irish history* (Oxford: Oxford University Press, 2007).
10 Simon Prince, 'The global revolt of 1968 and Northern Ireland', *The Historical Journal* 49.3 (2006): 851; Michael Farrell (ed.), *Twenty years on* (Dingle: Brandon, 1988); Brian Dooley, *Black and green: the fight for civil rights in Northern Ireland and black America* (London: Pluto Press, 1998).
11 On civil rights in Derry/Londonderry, see O'Dochartaigh, *From civil rights to Armalites*; Eamonn McCann, *War and an Irish town* (London: Pluto Press, 2nd edn, 1980).
12 See Chris Gilligan, 'Community responses to disaster: Northern Ireland 1969 as a case study', in *Handbook of community movements and local organizations*, ed. Ram A. Cnaan and Carl Milofsky (New York: Springer, 2007), 311–328; O'Dochartaigh, *From civil rights to Armalites*.
13 Richard Rose, *Governing without consensus: an Irish perspective* (London: Faber and Faber, 1971), 18.
14 Ibid., 394.
15 The GOC NI was responsible to the Minister of Defence in Whitehall, not to the Stormont government.
16 Lord Scarman, *Violence and civil disturbances in Northern Ireland in 1969: report of tribunal of inquiry, Cmd.566* (Belfast: HMSO, 1972), http://cain.ulst.ac.uk/hmso/scarman.htm (accessed 10 January 2017).

17 Baron Hunt, *Report of the Advisory Committee on Police in Northern Ireland* (Belfast, 1969), doi:SBN 337 10535 9.
18 Cunningham, *British government policy in Northern Ireland*, 4–10.
19 See the 1968 Race Relations Act, available online at www.legislation.gov.uk/ukpga/1968/71/contents/enacted (accessed 10 January 2017).
20 Hayes, 'Community relations', 10.
21 Wolton, *Lord Hailey*, 24.
22 On community relations policy and the NICRC, see Rolston, 'Community politics'; Hywel Griffiths, 'Community reaction and voluntary involvement', in *Violence and the social services in Northern Ireland*, ed. John Darby and Arthur Williamson (London: Heinemann Educational, 1978), 165–194; Hayes, 'Community relations'; Hywel Griffiths, *Community development in Northern Ireland: a case study in agency conflict* (Coleraine: University of Ulster, 1974); Terry Robson, *The state and community action* (London: Pluto Press, 2000).
23 For useful accounts of the early years of the Northern Ireland conflict, see Liam O'Dowd, Bill Rolston and Mike Tomlinson, *Northern Ireland: between civil rights and civil war* (London: CSE Books, 1980); Paul Bew and Henry Patterson, *The British state and the Ulster crisis: from Wilson to Thatcher* (London: Verso, 1985); Sunday Times Insight Team, *Ulster* (Harmondsworth: Penguin, 1972).
24 For more detailed histories of the Provisional IRA (and the Official IRA), see J. Bowyer Bell, *The secret army: the IRA 1916–1979* (Dublin: Academy Press, 3rd edn, 1979); Kevin Kelley, *The longest war: Northern Ireland and the IRA* (London: Zed Books, 1982); Ed Moloney, *A secret history of the IRA* (London: Allen Lane, 2002); Tommy McKearney, *The Provisional IRA: from insurrection to parliament* (London: Pluto Press, 2011).
25 IRA actions that local communities viewed as defensive were generally supported by the Catholic population. There was, however, less support for 'offensive' military actions such as the bombing of commercial premises or other non-combatant targets. See Jeffrey A. Sluka, *Hearts and minds, water and fish: support for the IRA and INLA in a Northern Irish ghetto* (Greenwich, CT, and London: JAI Press, 1989); Frank Burton, *The politics of legitimacy: struggles in a Belfast community* (London: Routledge and Kegan Paul, 1978).
26 Murray and Tonge, *Sinn Féin and the SDLP*; Gerard Murray, *John Hume and the SDLP: impact and survival in Northern Ireland* (Dublin: Irish Academic Press, 1998).
27 Ian McAllister, *The Northern Ireland Social Democratic and Labour Party: political opposition in a divided society* (London: Macmillan, 1977), 25–35.
28 Ibid., 34.
29 Murray, *John Hume and the SDLP*, 12–15.
30 Cited in Greg Martin and Graham Ellison, 'Policing, collective action and social movement theory: the case of the Northern Ireland civil rights campaign', *British Journal of Sociology* 51.4 (2000): 689–690.
31 See, for example, McKearney, *The Provisional IRA*; McGarry and O'Leary, *Explaining Northern Ireland*, 13–91.
32 Robert W. White, 'From peaceful protest to guerrilla war: micromobilization of the Provisional Irish Republican Army', *American Journal of Sociology* 94.6 (1989): 1277;

Mark Ryan, 'From the centre to the margins: the slow death of Irish Republicanism', in *Peace or war? Understanding the peace process in Northern Ireland*, ed. Chris Gilligan and Jon Tonge (Aldershot: Ashgate, 1997), vol. 1, 72–84.

33 Cited in Purdie, *Politics in the streets*, 241.

34 Gerry Adams, who went on to become president of Sinn Féin, acknowledges the key role of People's Democracy as a radical force in NICRA. Gerry Adams, 'A republican in the civil rights campaign', in *Twenty years on*, ed. Michael Farrell (Dingle: Brandon, 1988), 39–53.

35 Purdie, *Politics in the streets*, 241.

36 Arthur, *The People's Democracy, 1968–1973*.

37 People's Democracy, *People's Democracy: what it stands for, its attitudes* (Dublin: People's Democracy, 1972), 18.

38 Marc Mulholland, '"Modernising conservatism": the Northern Ireland Young Unionist Movement in the 1960s', *Irish Political Studies* 25 (2010): 67–94.

39 Explicitly anti-Catholic parties (such as the DUP) did not attract members from across the sectarian divide. The other parties had their social base in one of the 'ethnic blocs'. The UUP has only ever been able to attract a small number of Catholics. The SDLP and the IRA (and its political wing, Sinn Féin) only ever attracted a small number of members from Protestant backgrounds.

40 Ian McAllister and Brian Wilson, 'Bi-confessionalism in a confessional party system: the Northern Ireland Alliance Party', *Economic and Social Review* 9.3 (1978): 207–225.

41 O'Dowd, Rolston and Tomlinson, *Northern Ireland*; Bew and Patterson, *The British state and the Ulster crisis*; Sunday Times Insight Team, *Ulster*.

42 For a detailed analysis of the changing forms of sectarian rule in the 1970s, see O'Dowd, Rolston and Tomlinson, *Northern Ireland*.

43 Brewer, 'Sectarianism and racism', 363.

44 Kevin Boyle, Tom Hadden and Paddy Hillyard, *Law and state: the case of Northern Ireland* (London: Robertson, 1975), 112.

45 Ibid.

46 Cited in 'What is collusion?', *BBC News Online*, 22 January 2007.

47 Nelson, *Ulster's uncertain defenders*; Don Anderson, *Fourteen May days: the inside story of the Loyalist strike of 1974* (Dublin: Gill and Macmillan, 1994).

48 Ryan, 'From the centre to the margins', 76–77.

49 Kevin Bean, *The new politics of Sinn Féin* (Liverpool: Liverpool University Press, 2007); McKearney, *The Provisional IRA*; Kelley, *The longest war*.

50 Osborne, 'Equality of opportunity and discrimination'.

51 'Obituary: Sir Robert (Bob) Cooper', *Belfast Telegraph*, 17 November 2004.

52 Robert D. Osborne and R. J. Cormack, 'Fair employment: towards reform in Northern Ireland', *Policy & Politics* 17.4 (1989): 287–294.

53 Cunningham, *British government policy in Northern Ireland*, 39.

54 See, for example, the debate between White and Bruce on whether the IRA was sectarian: Robert W. White, 'The Irish Republican Army and sectarianism: moving beyond the anecdote', *Terrorism and Political Violence* 9.2 (1997): 120–131; Steve Bruce, 'Victim selection in ethnic conflict: motives and attitudes in Irish Republicanism',

Terrorism and Political Violence 9.1 (1997): 56–71; Robert W. White, 'Don't confuse me with the facts: more on the Irish Republican Army and sectarianism', *Terrorism and Political Violence* 10.4 (1998): 164–189.

55 F. Stuart Ross, 'Between party and movement: Sinn Féin and the popular movement against criminalisation, 1976–1982', *Irish Political Studies* 21.3 (2006): 337–354; Liam Clarke, *Broadening the battlefield: the H-Blocks and the rise of Sinn Féin* (Dublin: Gill and Macmillan, 1987); Brian Hanley, 'The politics of Noraid', *Irish Political Studies* 19.1 (2004): 1–17; Martin O'Donnell, 'The impact of the 1981 H Block hunger strikes on the British Labour Party', *Irish Political Studies* 14.1 (1999): 64–83; Martin Collins (ed.), *Ireland after Britain* (London: Pluto Press, 1985).

56 Garret FitzGerald, *All in a life: Garret FitzGerald, an autobiography* (Dublin: Gill and Macmillan, 1991).

57 Gilligan, 'The Irish Question and the concept "identity"'.

58 Government of Ireland and the Government of the United Kingdom, *Anglo-Irish Agreement, 1985, Pl.3634* (Dublin/London: Stationery Office/HMSO, 1985), Article 5, clause (a).

59 On revisionism, see, for example, David George Boyce and Alan O'Day (eds), *The making of modern Irish history: revisionism and the revisionist controversy* (London: Routledge, 1996); Andrew Finlay, 'Cultural pluralism and the peace process', *Irish Studies Review* 15.3 (2007): 333–345; Daltun O'Ceallaigh (ed.), *Reconsiderations of Irish history and culture* (Dublin: Leirmheas, 1994).

60 Robert D. Osborne, 'Policy dilemmas in Belfast', *Journal of Social Policy* 25.2 (1996): 181.

61 See Robert D. Osborne, '"Evidence" and equality in Northern Ireland', *Evidence & Policy* 3.1 (2007): 79–97; Jennifer Todd and Joseph Ruane, 'Beyond inequality? Assessing the impact of fair employment, affirmative action and equality measures on conflict in Northern Ireland', in *Affirmative Action in plural societies*, ed. Graham Brown, Arnim Langer and Frances Stewart (Basingstoke: Palgrave, 2012), 182–208.

62 On Northern Ireland's community relations industry, see Knox and Hughes, 'Local government and community relations'; Anthony M. Gallagher, 'The approach of government: community relations and equity', in *Facets of the conflict in Northern Ireland*, ed. Seamus Dunn (Basingstoke: Macmillan, 1995), 27–42; Nic Craith, *Culture and identity politics in Northern Ireland*; Mari Fitzduff, 'Public policy in a divided society', in *Intercultural Europe: diversity and social policy*, ed. Jagdish Gundara and Sidney Jacobs (Aldershot: Ashgate, 2000); Rolston, 'What's wrong with multiculturalism?'; Robbie McVeigh, 'Between reconciliation and pacification: the British state and community relations in the North of Ireland', *Community Development Journal* 37.1 (2002): 47–59. On the UK race relations industry, see, for example, Paul Gilroy, 'The end of anti-racism', in *Race and local politics*, ed. Wendy Ball and John Solomos (Basingstoke: Macmillan, 1990), 191–209; Ambalavaner Sivanandan, 'RAT and the degradation of black struggle', *Race & Class* 26.4 (1985): 1–33.

63 Feilim O'hAdhmaill and Philip Watt, *Political vetting of community work in Northern Ireland* (Belfast: Political Vetting of Community Work Group, 1990).

64 Bean, *The new politics of Sinn Féin*.

65 Sinn Féin, *The Sinn Féin/SDLP talks: January–September 1988*.

66 Christopher Farrington, *Ulster Unionism and the peace process in Northern Ireland* (Basingstoke: Palgrave Macmillan, 2006), 48.
67 Brendan O'Leary, 'The limits to coercive consociationalism in Northern Ireland', *Political Studies* 37.4 (1989): 577.
68 Arun Kundnani, *The end of tolerance: racism in 21st century Britain* (London: Pluto Press, 2007), 6.
69 See Chris Gilligan, 'Peace or pacification process? A brief critique of the peace process', in *Peace or war? Understanding the peace process in Northern Ireland*, ed. Chris Gilligan and Jon Tonge (Aldershot: Ashgate, 1997), 19–34; Bean, *The new politics of Sinn Féin*; Ryan, 'From the centre to the margins'.
70 This TUAS document is reproduced in the appendices of Moloney, *A secret history of the IRA*, 498–501.
71 See Bean, *The new politics of Sinn Féin*; Ryan, 'From the centre to the margins'; McKearney, *The Provisional IRA*.
72 Ryan, 'From the centre to the margins', 82–83.
73 Gilligan, 'Peace or pacification process?'; Paul Dixon, 'Political skills or lying and manipulation? The choreography of the Northern Ireland peace process', *Political Studies* 50.4 (2002): 725–741; David Mitchell, 'Cooking the fudge: constructive ambiguity and the implementation of the Northern Ireland Agreement, 1998–2007', *Irish Political Studies* 24.3 (2009): 321–336.
74 For more on the Agreement, see *Aspects of the Belfast Agreement*, ed. Rick Wilford (Oxford: Oxford University Press, 2001); *After the Good Friday Agreement: analysing political change in Northern Ireland*, ed. Joseph Ruane and Jennifer Todd (Dublin: UCD Press, 1999); O'Leary, 'Nature of the British-Irish Agreement'.
75 Rupert Taylor, 'The Belfast Agreement and the limits of consociationalism', in *Global change, civil society and the Northern Ireland peace process*, ed. Christopher Farrington (Basingstoke: Palgrave Macmillan, 2008), 183–198; Wilford and Wilson, *The trouble with Northern Ireland: the Belfast Agreement and democratic governance*.
76 McGarry and O'Leary, *Explaining Northern Ireland*, 135.
77 Taylor, 'The Belfast Agreement and the limits of consociationalism'; Peter Shirlow and Brendan Murtagh, *Belfast: segregation, violence and the city* (London: Pluto Press, 2006); Todd and Ruane, *From 'A shared future' to 'Cohesion, sharing and integration'*; Gilligan, 'The Irish Question and the concept "identity"'.
78 Mitchell, Evans and O'Leary, 'Extremist outbidding in ethnic party systems is not inevitable', 403.

7

Hate crime

In early January 2004 the London-based *Guardian* newspaper announced that

> Northern Ireland ... is fast becoming the race-hate capital of Europe. It holds the UK's record for the highest rate of racist attacks: spitting and stoning in the street, human excrement on doorsteps, swastikas on walls, pipe bombs, arson, the ransacking of houses with baseball bats and crow bars, and white supremacist leaflets nailed to front doors.[1]

Two days after the *Guardian* article, the Dublin-based *Irish Independent* repeated the claim that Northern Ireland was the 'race-hate capital', in an article about discrimination against Fijian rugby players who were visiting the region.[2] Four days after the *Guardian* article, the *BBC Northern Ireland News* website noted that 'With a racist attack in Northern Ireland almost every day, it has been dubbed the race-hate capital of Europe in some quarters.'[3] In February 2005, as Robbie McVeigh and Ronit Lentin note, 'the influential German magazine *Der Spiegel* announced that Belfast was "the most racist city in the world"'.[4] By February 2006, Duncan Morrow was describing Northern Ireland as a 'criminally hating society'.[5]

In our attempts to understand sectarianism and other forms of racism, we have argued that it is important to place racisms into a broader social and historical context. In the process, however, have we been guilty of downplaying the brutal reality of the lived experience of the racialised? Paul Connolly and Michaela Keenan draw our attention to the impact of racist harassment on the everyday lives of racialised minorities (like the Awoyelu family or James Turley who we mentioned in the opening chapter of this book) when they say that

> racist harassment is a particularly pernicious and evil part of society ... it is embedded in the routine behaviour and processes within Northern Ireland society. It takes on many different forms from overt acts of verbal and physical abuse to more subconscious and often unintentional actions and behaviour ... The combined effects of racist harassment are to violate minority ethnic people's sense of dignity in society and to create an environment for them that is intimidating, hostile, degrading, humiliating and/or offensive. It ensures that many live in a constant state of low level anxiety while some live in fear.[6]

Our analysis up to this point could be open to the accusation, which Michael Banton makes regarding the work of Robert Miles, that we have neglected the significance of interpersonal relations in our focus on structures and social processes. Surely, defenders of Race Relations (or community relations or good relations) might say, we should acknowledge that harassment is the most brutal and dehumanising manifestation of racism and it should be front and centre of any analysis of racisms. The Race Relations approach, Banton argues, offers the best way to tackle racisms. Through Race Relations policy, and the law in particular, racial prejudices and actions have been stigmatised and racist ideas and behaviours in society have been changed as a consequence.[7]

We agree that racisms are demeaning. We agree that many people live in a constant state of low-level anxiety, and some live in fear. If we focus on harassment as the problem, however, we are only focusing on symptoms, not on underlying causes. The criminal justice system plays the lead role in tackling harassment and its agents concentrate on maintaining social order. Harassment is a crime and the harasser a criminal. The criminal justice system holds the individual harasser, or harassers, responsible for their crime(s) and attempts to identify and prosecute them. Consequently, a focus on harassment can only ever point to ways to manage racisms, not ways to overcome them. Treating racisms as crimes, rather than as manifestations of social contradictions, also involves identifying individuals in society as the perpetrators of racisms and the state as the upholder of anti-racism.

In this chapter, we explore the limitations of a Race Relations approach to harassment through a critical examination of the most recent innovation in official anti-racism, hate crime policy, which formally came into operation in Northern Ireland in September 2004.[8] In the first part of this chapter, we briefly introduce the topic of hate crime. We outline some of the key features of hate crime policy and we examine the political context and discussions which shaped the introduction of hate crimes law to the region. Hate crime laws present racist and sectarian harassment as manifestations of prejudice. One prominent strand of this discussion around hate crime in Northern Ireland identifies Protestants as being particularly prejudiced and prone to racist and sectarian behaviour. In the second part of the chapter, we critically examine this idea. In the third part of the chapter, we critically examine the idea that a 'hate' motivation is key to 'hate crime' through looking at studies that have examined the topic from the perspective of perpetrators of racist and sectarian crime. These studies suggest that the state of mind or psychological motivation of the perpetrator provides a very limited insight into understanding racisms. We argue that 'race hate' becomes more comprehensible when examined in the social contexts that create the conditions in which racist or sectarian acts are enabled. In the main part of the chapter, we shift the focus from the crimes and the motivation to examine hate crime policy as a form of multicultural crime fighting. We argue that hate crime policy is built on, and extends in new directions, the official multicultural approach that underpins the Agreement and the political institutions that have been built on the Agreement. We locate the rise of hate crime policy in the wider context of the decline of the anti-racist movements of the 1960s and the rise of authoritarian state responses to social problems.

Hate crime policy

Hate crime policy involved amending existing laws to increase the severity of punishments for those found guilty of offences – including various forms of assault, criminal damage and intimidation – where these criminal actions were motivated by hostility towards victims who are (or who the offender presumes to be) members of a racial, religious, sexual orientation or disability group.[9] Hate crime policy thus has a broader scope than Race Relations policy. In the rest of the UK, as Derek McGhee puts it, the policy is 'targeted at identified vulnerable minority communities … ethnic minority communities, religious minority communities and some sexual minority communities'.[10] Hate crime policy aims to protect vulnerable groups in society, not just racialised minorities. Hate crime is viewed as particularly despicable because any attack on an individual victim is also viewed as an attack on a wider community. The Northern Ireland Council for Ethnic Minorities (NICEM) argued along these lines in its submission to the 2002 consultation on hate crimes. NICEM argued that the victim of a racist incident is chosen 'simply because she or he is Chinese, Pakistani, black, Traveller or asylum seeker', and consequently, 'the impact is not merely on the victim but on his or her community as a whole – leading to widespread fear, intimidation and alienation'.[11] Advocates of hate crime laws believe that the perpetrators of 'race' hate or sectarian hate crimes racialise their victims. The Northern Ireland Council for Voluntary Action suggests this when it says that 'victims of crime who have been targeted because of their perceived race or community are victims twice over … the attack goes beyond the individual as it is "a message" sent out to all others from that community'.[12] Hate crime laws are designed as a response to this message from racists and other bigots. In the words of the Police Service of Northern Ireland, hate crime laws aim to send 'out a very clear message that crime is unacceptable, but crime that is motivated by prejudice is particularly unacceptable'.[13]

The very idea of *hate* crime focuses attention on the state of mind of the offender. Hate crime laws involve a view of racism, sectarianism, homophobia and disablism as manifestations of prejudice, intolerance and bigotry. The Public Prosecution Service of Northern Ireland, for example, describes hate crimes as 'violent manifestations of intolerance'.[14] The UK government's official submission to the 2004/05 Inquiry into Hate Crimes in Northern Ireland stated that these crimes are 'motivated by … hatred and prejudice'.[15] All of the criminal acts covered in the new hate crime law were already criminal offences – the new law has not criminalised the offences, it is the *intention or motivation* of the offender (their 'hate') that has been criminalised.

It was the Westminster-based Northern Ireland Office (NIO), not the regional Northern Ireland Assembly (NIA), which steered the legislation on to the statute books. Part of the reason why the NIO took the lead was because at that time responsibility for policing and justice matters had not been devolved to the NIA. The policy area of criminal justice was deemed too sensitive to place in the hands of politicians in Northern Ireland.[16] The NIA may not have had the power to pass legislation on hate crime, but MLAs at Stormont had been calling for hate crime laws prior to their introduction. In May 2001, for example, the SDLP MLA Danny O'Connor raised the issue. In expressing the need for hate crime laws, he drew on his own experience of sectarian attacks on his family home. David Trimble, the UUP leader and Northern Ireland's First Minister, deplored the attacks, but also pointed out that responsibility for criminal justice was a reserved matter for Westminster. Trimble went on to say, however, that two junior ministers at Stormont had met with the Secretary of State for Northern Ireland 'to discuss the scope for strengthening legislation in this area'.[17] A year later, there had been no apparent progress. The Alliance Party raised the issue again. It accused the UK government of 'stalling over bringing forward proposals for hate crime legislation' and claimed that these proposals had 'been in the pipeline' since the end of the previous year.[18]

Hate crime policy is not unique to Northern Ireland. Despite the presentation of Northern Ireland as a particularly violent place, as a criminally hating society, it was not the first part of the UK to introduce hate crime laws. They were introduced into the rest of the UK in 1998, before they were introduced in Northern Ireland.[19] The UK government claimed that it did not extend hate crime laws to Northern Ireland in 1998 because sectarian crime was not recognised in UK law at that time. Consequently, the inclusion of 'offences with a sectarian motivation … would have required more careful consideration of the issues than was possible at the time'.[20] In addition, the government considered that 'it would be anomalous to introduce higher sentencing tariffs for racially motivated offences than would have been available for offences with a sectarian motivation'.[21] This lack of a definition of sectarianism, as we noted in Chapter 3, was highlighted as a problem by the official inquiry into hate crime, which concluded that 'Nothing could illustrate the dysfunction of Northern Ireland society better than the absence, until recently, of an agreed, official definition of sectarian hate crime.'[22]

The UK government could have treated sectarianism as a form of racism, but instead it batted the issue back to Northern Ireland. In November 2002 the NIO produced a consultation paper *Race Crime and Sectarian Crime Legislation in Northern Ireland*.[23] The consultation paper was sent out to a wide range of organisations, including faith groups, local councils, charities, minority ethnic community associations, women's groups, disability support groups and organisations concerned with criminal justice policy (representing relevant professions and civil liberties groups). These consultees were asked to consider whether legislation was required, and if so whether it was required for both racist and sectarian offences. The NIO noted that, in the Northern Ireland context, it was difficult to formulate definitions of aggravated crime 'which would effectively differentiate racial offences from sectarian offences' and it noted that the definition of a racial group in UK Race Relations law, 'if used in Northern Ireland, might apply to sectarian offences'.[24]

The consultation found little support for extending hate crime laws from England and Wales to Northern Ireland. This was not, however, because the organisations that responded to the consultation rejected hate crime laws outright. There was widespread agreement that the courts should have the power to impose harsher penalties as a way of sending out a message that attacks on vulnerable minorities are particularly despicable. There was also a 'widespread feeling that legislation could play only a small part' in tackling the issue, and that 'training, education and raised awareness' to change attitudes was 'key to good relations'.[25] The consultees dodged the issue of treating sectarianism as a form of racism. They did, however, argue that sectarian hate crime should be pursued with as much vigour as racist hate crime. They also argued that hate crime policy should be extended to include homophobic hate crime.[26]

The Committee for the Administration of Justice explains the lukewarm response to extending UK law when it argues that

> it is better to separate out the alleged crime – murder, assault, etc. – from the alleged motivation of the criminal act … in England, the merger of two concepts 'offence' and a 'racially aggravated' offence, has proved quite difficult to operationalise. In practice, the fusion of two quite different notions has meant that people clearly guilty of an offence escaped any punishment at all, since the racial aggravation element of the charge could not be sufficiently proven.[27]

In other words, the law in England and Wales was viewed as ineffective, which undermined the intention of sending out a clear message that prejudice-motivated crime is particularly odious and will be punished more severely. Northern Ireland opted to impose a statutory duty on the courts to take motivation into account when sentencing. If a suspect is found guilty of a crime (such as assault or criminal damage) then they will be charged, regardless of whether a hate motivation can be proven or not. The court, however, is duty bound to consider hate motivation if this has been raised as relevant, and if the court is persuaded that a hate motivation was involved, then a harsher penalty will be imposed. There are thus two key elements to a hate crime from a criminal justice perspective: the motivation of the offender, and the identification of the victim as belonging to one of the categories named in law.

Protestant prejudice

The idea of Protestants as particularly prejudiced or supportive of the negative treatment of immigrants, ethnic minorities and Catholics is a prominent feature of media and academic discussions. Angelique Chrisafis, writing as the Ireland correspondent for the *Guardian* newspaper, painted the following frightening picture of 'race hate' in Belfast in early 2004. 'Protestant working-class neighbourhoods,' she said,

> are showing a pattern of orchestrated house attacks aimed at 'ethnically cleansing' minority groups. It is happening in streets run by loyalist paramilitaries, where every Chinese takeaway owner already pays protection money and racists have plentiful access to guns. The spectre of Catholics being systematically burnt out of similar areas during the Troubles hangs in the air.[28]

Many others also draw a link between the treatment of Catholics in Northern Ireland's past and of immigrants and ethnic minorities in the present. Protestants are said to be particularly prejudiced. A number of different factors are cited to explain their bigoted nature. They are considered, like other colonial settlers, to suffer from a siege mentality. They feel threatened, on the one hand by the natives who they believe want to overthrow them, and on the other by their metropolitan rulers (at Westminster) who they fear are willing to abandon them.[29] Others locate the hostility towards immigrants in the context of post-Agreement Northern Ireland. They argue that many Protestants believe that they are losing out to Catholics, and more recently to immigrants.[30] Some authors further substantiate the evidence of Protestant bigotry by pointing to links between loyalist paramilitary groups and the racist far right in the rest of the UK and argue that there is an ideological affinity between loyalism and fascism.[31]

There is ample evidence to support the idea that Protestants are particularly bigoted and support or perpetuate racist and sectarian attacks. Evidence from attitude surveys consistently shows that Protestants are more prejudiced against ethnic minorities and immigrants than Catholics.[32] Studies of racist attacks show that a significant majority of these take place in areas that are predominantly Protestant, and that loyalist paramilitaries are closely associated with attacks on immigrants and other ethnic minorities.[33] These data, however, need to be interpreted carefully. The attitudinal data, for example, could be interpreted as indicating that Protestants are more honest about their prejudices than Catholics.

Fionnuala Meredith points to the irony of this presentation of Protestants when she says, 'wait a minute. Condemning an entire community or ethnic group on the basis of the actions of a few people? Doesn't that, itself, sound a bit like ... racism?'[34] Meredith points to cases where Protestants have helped or supported immigrants or other ethnic minorities. The anti-deportation campaign in support of 'Nigerian woman Comfort Adefowoju and her children', Meredith notes, involved significant input 'from her church congregation right in the middle of working-class east Belfast'.[35] When the home of Polish woman Anna Bloch was attacked in a staunchly Protestant area of east Belfast in January 2014, she was inundated with flowers 'sent by local well-wishers, keen to offer care and support and to distance themselves from the perpetrators of this cruel, cowardly attempt to drive a family from their home'.[36] Bill Rolston points to an important case in which leaders of the loyalist paramilitary Ulster Volunteer Force (UVF) intervened and forced one of its local commanders, who had supported racist attacks in the Village area of South Belfast, to stand down.[37] Henry McDonald points to an anti-racist campaign by the Ulster Defence Association, the other main loyalist paramilitary group, in support of Poles in Lisburn.[38] The late Revd Ian Paisley, renowned for his anti-Popery, is less well known for the support that he has given to Black Africans, such as the Kazadi family from the Democratic Republic of Congo, threatened with deportation by UK immigration authorities.[39]

The idea that Protestants are particularly prejudiced, like hate crimes policy, focuses on psychological disposition rather than structural factors. A number of authors, however, note that as a result of a combination of sectarian residential segregation and the greater geographical mobility of Protestants historically there is more vacant housing stock available in 'Protestant' areas of Belfast. Consequently, most immigrants to Northern Ireland reside in Protestant areas.[40] Given that many 'race hate' incidents happen at or near the victim's residence, we would expect that more attacks would take place in Protestant areas.

Robbie McVeigh also points out that the issue of loyalist violence has been politically sensitive in the context of post-Agreement Northern Ireland. He notes that the Independent Monitoring Commission (IMC), which was established in 2003 to monitor and evaluate the activities of paramilitary organisations in Northern Ireland, and the PSNI took a softly-softly approach to the issue of 'race hate' by loyalist paramilitaries. The first mention of this by the IMC was in its third report, published in 2004. It noted that members of the UVF had been 'responsible for a series of violent racial attacks in Belfast' and qualified this by saying that 'we believe these were not sanctioned by the leadership'.[41] In its eighth report, published in 2006, the IMC noted

> no significant change to the broad pattern of the UVF's involvement in organised and other crime but we believe that elements within the leadership are making efforts to reduce criminality … One important step would be for loyalist paramilitaries, including the UVF and RHC, to stop targeting nationalists and ethnic minorities.[42]

McVeigh notes that it was 'odd that the IMC launched into this instruction to stop targeting members of ethnic minorities, given that it had never previously recognised that they had started this targeting'.[43] Regarding the PSNI, McVeigh notes that it was not 'proactive in addressing responsibility for racist violence. It wasn't until 2014 that it finally named the issue in terms of loyalist paramilitarism.'[44] Even after the issue had been publicly admitted, it was quickly submerged again. McVeigh concludes that in the Northern Ireland context, 'politicians and criminal justice institutions and racist gangs – [are] colluding in racism in ways that remain unthinkable in, say, London'.[45] What is exceptional about Northern Ireland is not the existence of racism, but the level of collusion between state and quasi-state actors and loyalist organisations that carry out racist and sectarian attacks.

Hate and harassment in social context

The motivation of the offender is a crucial element of hate crime law. A racist motivation can be seen in the case of Ryan McBride, who was accused of a racially aggravated arson attack on a neighbour's house in east Belfast in 2006. McBride, who had been drinking heavily, had shouted at the Polish occupants of the house as they returned from a nightclub at about 1.30 a.m. He then had an argument with one of the Polish men at the front door of the Polish man's house. McBride then walked to a nearby petrol station and purchased a container and petrol and returned to the house and poured the petrol on the brick porch and steps, and then ignited it. The porch went up in flames and the house filled with smoke. McBride fled the scene. The seven Polish occupants of the house managed to escape from the back of the house and none of them were seriously hurt. When the police arrived at the scene, they found McBride nearby, smelling strongly of petrol. When they spoke to him under caution, he is alleged to have said 'fucking Poles shouldn't be here'.[46] This attack is a fairly typical example of the kind of case that is prosecuted as a 'race hate' crime. It involved an attack on a racialised minority 'group' and the assailant indicated his hate motivation when he made a negative comment about this racialised 'group'. McBride's attack seems a clear-cut example of racial harassment that could easily have had fatal consequences.

McBride confessed to, and was convicted of, the crime of arson. He denied, however, any racial motivation. He claimed that during the argument with one of his Polish neighbours the man had made a veiled threat against McBride and his mother (McBride lived in the same house as his mother). McBride said that he had poured the petrol and lit it 'just to try and put the frighteners up him'.[47] He denied that he was racially motivated and his employers at Belfast Docks provided a reference to support this claim, stating that they were not aware of any friction between McBride and the Polish workers who he worked alongside. A psychiatrist who examined McBride found 'no ideas of psychiatric significance, such as paranoid ideas, in relation to members of the immigrant community or other racial groups' that would account for the attack.[48] The defence argued that McBride's actions were out of character and that he had no previous convictions, and, as mitigation, they pointed out that he was heavily intoxicated at the time of the attack. The judge ruled that 'whilst there is a strong suspicion that the defendant was racially motivated when he made this attack', he was 'not satisfied beyond reasonable doubt'.[49] The judge argued that McBride 'was plainly motivated by resentment and what he wrongly perceived to be the attitude towards himself and his mother … [but] this was not a racist attack as such'.[50]

This attack was typical of the kinds of incidents that are prosecuted as a 'race hate' crimes, but it is also typical for the accused in such cases to contest the 'racial' element of the charge. Motivation is crucial to hate crime law, but it is something that has been disputed in many of the cases that have come to court. In England and Wales, as the NIO note, this 'has led to racially aggravated offences having less than half the conviction rate' of the same offences that are prosecuted without the aggravation charge (e.g. assault or criminal damage).[51] We might assume that McBride and other offenders were lying about their racist intent because they knew that an admission could result in a stiffer penalty. The reality, however, is likely to be much more complex.

The evidence from a number of studies with offenders who have been prosecuted for racist offences suggests that many of these 'racist' attacks are not racist as such. There appear to be a range of motivations involved in cases which are recorded as 'hate crime' incidents. Offender studies suggest that offenders who are ideologically driven by 'race hate' account for only a small proportion of all cases. Larry Ray, David Smith and Liz Wastell, for example, in a study of offenders convicted of 'race hate' crimes in England, found that 'interviewees usually talked quite openly and unapologetically about their violence, while, in most cases, denying or minimizing the element of racist motivation'.[52] These offenders were unlikely to be making this claim in the hope of gaining a reduced sentence, as they had already been convicted. Defenders of Race Relations policy, such as Banton, might claim that this denial is evidence of the success of the policy in stigmatising racism. Virtually no one wants to be considered a racist in the UK these days. The evidence from offender studies, however, suggests that it is too simplistic to explain these denials as demonstrations of the success of the stigmatising of racism. One study in the USA, for example, identified three different forms of motivation in 'hate crime' offences, which they characterised as thrill-seeking, defending their turf and 'a small group of offenders whose life's mission had become to rid the world of groups they considered evil or inferior'.[53] Other authors who have studied offenders note a complex and often ambiguous mix of motivations among those accused of hate crimes.[54] Studies that have examined offenders tend to point to social context, rather than individual psychology, to explain 'racist' behaviour. Activity that can be prosecuted as low-level hate crime – such as racist name-calling, 'pranks' such as letting the air out of the tyres of cars belonging to ethnic minorities and racist graffiti – are often carried out by youths with lots of time on their hands and little meaningful activity to fill it. More serious violent activities – such as assault or arson – can sometimes be better understood in the context of cultures of everyday violence, or excessive alcohol consumption, than as activities driven by racial hatred. In these cases, it is the criminal justice system, not the perpetrators, who are racialising the crimes.

There is evidence from Northern Ireland which supports the idea that factors other than 'hate' can help to explain 'racial' and sectarian hate crime. A number of studies of 'sectarian' rioting at the interface of Catholic and Protestant working-class residential areas in Belfast suggest that thrill-seeking and boredom are significant factors behind the riots.[55] Madeline Leonard, for example, found that the fun aspect of 'sectarian' rioting was a recurring theme in interviews she conducted with young people from a working-class interface area in north Belfast. In the words of two of her interviewees:

> All my mates and me get a chase of the peelers [police]. I like it when there are riots with the peelers. (Protestant boy)

> The only good thing about living here is the rioting. It's a terrible thing to say I suppose but rioting is the only thing to do at times. There's nothing else. It's really boring and it breaks the boredom. (Catholic boy)[56]

This thrill-seeking dimension existed alongside concerns about the dangers. As two young people put it, 'I don't like ... all the riots between taigs [Catholics] and prods [Protestants]. Sometimes they are good but when someone gets hurt they are not so good. (Protestant girl)' and 'It's very sectarian. There's always riots which leaves someone dead or injured. (Catholic girl)'.[57] In part, the difference in emphasis reflected gender differences, with girls more likely to draw attention to dangers, and boys more like to highlight excitement. Nevertheless, gender was not a decisive factor – some boys emphasised the dangers, some girls the excitement.

There was also a sectarian 'hate' dimension. As two of the young people put it, 'We riot because we hate each other. (Protestant boy)' and 'We riot with them because they're scum. (Catholic boy)'.[58] Leonard notes that in this regard riots served to define territory in sectarian terms. The riots also reinforced sectarianism in the way that they enhanced 'group unity and identity, and prioritised relationships based on "us" and "them"'.[59] The research on 'recreational rioting' points to the complexity of the phenomenon.

Some of the themes in Leonard's work recur in research conducted by Paul Connolly and Michaela Keenan on racism against immigrants and ethnic minorities in Northern Ireland. They found that racist harassment was most likely to occur in contexts where there was a strong sense of 'territory and belonging', were often justified in terms of 'messing about and having a laugh' and were associated with male cultures of aggression.[60] Their research suggests that racist motivation was not the key factor that helped to explain the behaviour of the young men that they interviewed. Instead, racial harassment appeared to be 'a logical extension of their existing sub-culture that seems to be predicated on the masculine values of territory, fighting and aggressiveness'.[61]

In its submission to the hate crime consultation, NICEM argued that 'harm caused by a racist incident goes deeper and wider than other crimes or anti-social acts. The individual victim is not chosen because of historic enmity, jealousy, gangs fighting over territory, but simply because she or he is Chinese, Pakistani, black, Traveller or asylum seeker.'[62] In other words, 'race hate' crimes cannot be understood in the same terms as other crimes of a similar nature; because they are targeted at racialised minorities, we need to understand them in that context. The evidence that we have highlighted in this section suggests otherwise. The targeting of victims 'simply because' they can be fitted into a racial category is, at most, only true of a small proportion of 'race hate' crimes. In most cases of 'hate crime' there are a variety of factors involved and the 'racial' or 'sectarian' element is only one of them. The claim, made by NICEM and other advocates of hate crime laws, that victims are targeted simply because they are 'racial' minorities (or a sectarian 'other') racialises the crimes by treating 'race' as the key explanatory factor.

Multicultural crime fighting

Our argument, that motivation is not crucial to 'hate crime', is accepted by a number of advocates of hate crime policy. Paul Iganski, one of the leading experts on hate crime in the UK, notes that the concept of 'hate crime' is problematic and that crimes which are labelled as hate crimes often have little to do with the emotion of hate. He argues that,

> contrary to media depictions of the problem, many incidents of 'hate crime' are not committed by extremist bigots, do not involve premeditated attacks by thugs who are predisposed to violence, often do not involve any physical violence at all, and in many instances do not involve 'hate'. Instead, many incidents are committed by 'ordinary' people in the context of their 'everyday' lives.[63]

We might expect that the unremarkable, everyday nature of so-called 'hate crimes' would lead Iganski to argue against hate crime laws, but he does not. He argues in favour of them, but with a different rationale. Instead of 'hate' being the central focus of the crime, he argues 'for the victim to be placed at the centre of the conceptualisation of "hate crimes" … [because] "hate crimes" hurt more than parallel crimes: this is borne out by the experience of victims'.[64] In other words, the focus should not be on the motivation of the offender, but on the experience of the victim.

Valerie Jenness, one of the leading scholars of hate crime in the USA, notes that pressure groups that campaigned for hate crime laws emphasised the motivation of the perpetrators and urged policy to target bigotry. As the policy was implemented in the criminal justice system, however, the emphasis shifted.[65] This appears to have happened in the UK too. Bill Dixon and David Gadd note that the prosecution of racially aggravated offences in England and Wales has often weakened the motivation criterion. In one important ruling, for example, the Crown Prosecutor stated that the law was 'not intended to apply only to those cases in which the offender is motivated solely, or even mainly, by racial malevolence'.[66] In other words, someone can be convicted of 'hate' crime without there being evidence of hate. They note that 'the courts have tended to treat language such as "bloody foreigners" ... as sufficient evidence of racial hostility ... without pausing to consider the particular social context in which it was used'.[67] In other words, in practice hate crime laws have racialised encounters by taking the 'racial' categorisation of victim and perpetrator, rather than the motivation, as the key criterion. The hate crimes approach continues the tendency of Race Relations policy to racialise society in the name of tackling racisms.

The Northern Ireland Hate Crimes Inquiry indicated that something other than tackling racist perpetrators lies behind the development of hate crime policy. In relation to the PSNI's claim that the law is sending out a clear message that prejudice-based crime is particularly unacceptable, the inquiry argued that 'the authorities have considerable ground to make up in persuading vulnerable groups that their concerns are being addressed seriously. This legislation is an opportunity to demonstrate that such legitimate concerns will be addressed.'[68] This rationale shifts the emphasis from the relationship between the victim and perpetrator, in which the crime is central, to the relationship between the victim 'group' and the state, in which being seen to respond to crime is central. In this regard, hate crime policy is at least as much about overcoming the crisis of authority of the state through building relationships with *particular* sections of society, as it is about sending a message out to the *whole* of society that hate will not be tolerated. Hate crime policy is not just about projecting the values of a multicultural society, but also about establishing a multicultural infrastructure through which society is governed.

The rise of hate crime policy marks a shift from the emancipatory anti-racisms of the 1960s to the overriding concern with social cohesion and social control in the twenty-first century. As Erich Bleich has noted of hate crime laws,

> it has become much riskier to express or to act upon provocatively racist thoughts in contemporary multi-racial, multi-ethnic and multi-faith democracies. Values such as community cohesion, public order, human dignity and psychological harm have been invoked as counterweights to freedom in order to justify restrictions on racism.[69]

Hate crime policy is an expression of the decline of anti-racism as a movement and the rise of anti-racism as a form of social control.

The Race Relations underpinning of hate crime policy can be seen in the assumption of racial, ethnic and faith 'group' difference as a given feature of contemporary society. Hate crime policy is multicultural in the sense that it views humanity as divided into different 'races'. It is multicultural in the sense that the notion of human dignity is based on the idea, articulated in the 1978 UNESCO Declaration, that individuals and groups have the right to be different, to consider themselves as different and to have this difference recognised by society. It is multicultural in the sense that psychological harm is considered to be done when this 'right' to difference is not acknowledged. Eugene McLaughlin articulates this idea when he says that hate crime is an anathema to a multicultural society because it 'strikes at the diversity upon which multicultural societies thrive, denying the right to self-identity and self-determination and imposing a subordinate, inferior or less-than-human status on the victim and her or his community or group'.[70]

In this section, we explore hate crime policy as an expression of the decline of anti-racism as a movement and the rise of anti-racism as a form of social control in a number of different ways. In the first part, we examine the decline of the movement and the rise of advocacy. This shift to advocacy politics is the product of an increasingly detached relationship between racialised minorities and those who claim to be the leaders of racialised 'groups'. In the second part, we examine hate crime policy from the point of view of the role that it plays in attempting to overcome the crisis of authority of the state through developing a relationship between the state and racialised minorities in society. In the third part, we examine the rise of the 'victim' and 'victimhood' as central to official anti-racism, including hate crime policy. The 'victim' is an expression of both the elitist nature of advocacy politics and the passive role that is allocated to racialised minorities. In the fourth part we locate the rise of hate crime policy within the wider growth of state authoritarianism.

From emancipation to identity politics

Advocates of hate crime laws often present themselves as descendants of the 1960s egalitarian movements that struggled for the rights of women, ethnic minorities, gays and, in the case of Northern Ireland, Catholics who were discriminated against by the state.[71] There is some justification for this view. In some cases, organisations that fought against discrimination in the 1960s and 1970s have advocated hate crime legislation in the 1980s, the 1990s and the twenty-first century. Examples of such organisations include the National Association for the Advancement of Colored People in the USA, Stonewall, the gay rights group in the UK, and the SDLP in Northern Ireland. The view that hate crime legislation represents an extension of the struggle against discrimination is, however, misleading. It ignores the other influences on hate crime legislation and the very different social contexts of the 1960s and the 1990s.

The term 'race hate' emerged in the USA in the 1970s and 1980s as part of the development of what has been referred to as 'the anti-hate crime movement'.[72] This movement is a curious beast. It developed out of the confluence of what are generally considered to be 'liberal, progressive movements' (the civil rights, women's, disabilities, and gay and lesbian rights campaigns) with the generally 'conservative crime victim movement'.[73] It involved, in other words, a convergence between the 'left' and the 'right'. This convergence was made possible by the decline of a radical grassroots movement and the incorporation of some of the reformist sections of the former movement into the running of American society. In the case of anti-racism, this incorporation involved driving a wedge between radical and reformist sections of the movement. Organisations like the Black Panther Party in the USA, which was organised in Black working-class districts and which had links with 'White' left groups, were at the brunt of state repression.[74] The reformists moved into mainstream politics. Manning Marable notes, for example, that there were 100 Black elected officials in the USA in 1964 and that this had risen to '1,400 in 1970'.[75] By the mid-1970s, Marable points out, in the face of state repression of Black radicals, most of them 'had returned to their original neighourhoods, far from the national stage, leaving their reformist counterparts firmly in place to dictate the national minority agenda'.[76]

Instead of challenging the War on Crime agenda, which the 'liberal' Lyndon B. Johnson (who had passed the Civil Rights Act) initiated and the 'conservative' Richard Nixon consolidated, reformists accommodated to it.[77] The idea that racism was a psychological problem located in the minds of racists, rather than a product of the organisation of society, was facilitated by the post-Second World War rise of the psychology industry in universities, in human resource management, in counterculture awareness-raising and self-actualisation programmes, and in crime fighting.[78] The resort to the law as a means of redress was an indication of the receding of the emancipatory dynamic of the Civil Rights era and the rise of a reformist belief in the state as an instrument for tackling racisms.

In the UK, a similar process happened when the emancipatory dynamic of the radical, grassroots anti-racist movement of the 1970s and 1980s became dissipated as the 1980s progressed, and many activists became incorporated into official Race Relations policy and practice.[79] By the end of the 1980s a number of people were talking about the crisis of radical anti-racism in the UK. Paul Gilroy's assessment of three tendencies in municipal anti-racism at the end of the 1980s provides a good summary of the success of official Race Relations policy in depoliticising the issue of racism. The dominant, equal opportunities strand identified anti-racism 'with efficiency and good management practice' and its advocates were more interested in 'practical' policy matters than grassroots campaigns.[80] The radical sectionalist tendency had embraced the multicultural politics of difference and was 'fragmented into multiple varieties each with its own claim to ethnic particularity' and this tendency was 'now emphatically culturalist rather than political'.[81] The third tendency espoused Black and White working-class unity and was the most explicitly political. It was also, however, increasingly superficial in its analysis and politically marginal.

By the 1990s the anti-racist movement had fragmented and receded. Identity politics had become the dominant form of grassroots anti-racism. The 'black struggle', as Ambalavaner Sivanandan put it, had been returned 'to its constituent parts of African Caribbean, Asian, African, Irish'.[82] The Black working class receded from the national stage 'when government moneys were used to fund community projects, destroying thereby the self-reliance and community cohesion that we built up'.[83] This government funding helped to develop a multicultural Race Relations industry. In Northern Ireland, this industry played a key role in the development of hate crime policy.[84]

Civil society and the state

In the UK, hate crime laws were introduced as part of the New Labour government's Third Way reform agenda. These reforms were designed to reorganise the relationship between the state and society in ways that were considered to be more appropriate to the context of the twenty-first century.[85] As Anthony Giddens, the academic, media commentator and advisor to Tony Blair, put it,

> The overall aim of third way politics should be to help citizens pilot their way through the major revolutions in our time: *globalization*, [and the] *transformations in personal life* ... Freedom to social democrats should mean autonomy of action, which in turn demands the involvement of the wider community. Having abandoned collectivism, third way politics looks for a new relationship between the individual and the community, a redefinition of rights and obligations ... [we need to] go beyond those on the right 'who say government is the enemy' and those on the left 'who say government is the answer' ... The crisis of democracy comes from it not being democratic enough.[86]

The 'anti-hate crime movement', with its confluence of 'progressive' and 'conservative' (escaping the left/right divide), is a paradigm example of a Third Way approach to social problems. The freedom that Giddens refers to is conceived in terms of self-actualisation, the person who feels esteemed and valued by others. The role of the state in this is viewed as enabling, providing a hand up, not a handout.

Hate crime policy is part of this broader reorganisation of the relationship between the state and society. 'Hate crime legislation', as McLaughlin puts it, is required 'as an important part of the ongoing process of identifying and articulating the values, sensibilities and ground rules of vibrant, multicultural societies, including the public recognition and affirmation of the right to be different'.[87] Hate crime policy tells us what 'we' as a society stand for, the celebration of difference through 'group' recognition in the public domain.

McGhee notes that in the UK, hate crime policy has involved a process of state and non-state 'institutions and organizations reflecting on the part they have played in perpetuating' racism, Islamophobia, homophobia and asylophobia (fear and hatred of asylum seekers).[88] A wide range of state, semi-state and non-state organisations and institutions have subsequently responded by expanding 'consultative mechanism with the communities they serve'.[89] These consultations have involved policy-makers pursuing a range of initiatives designed 'to increase trust and confidence in marginalized or antagonized communities through promoting participation and dialogue between communities or between communities and key organizations (e.g. the police)'.[90] This approach can be seen in not just hate crime policy in Northern Ireland, but in good relations policy in general. One way in which this is articulated is through the language of partnership. The Northern Ireland government's consultation on its proposed Programme for Cohesion, Sharing and Integration, for example, talks about the consultation process being 'done in close consultation with minority ethnic groups and the wider community. We are committed to the partnership process ... and of course we remain open to proposals as to how we might strengthen these.'[91] It also suggests that the 'Programme will provide a platform for the development of more innovative and creative ways of working which encourage communities to effectively and efficiently work together in partnership with each other, with Government, and with the private sector'.[92]

Hate crime policy is thus a form of politics of recognition, which aims to draw civil society 'partners' into the regulation of society. This approach encourages 'minority' entrepreneurs to use the criminal justice system as a means to gain recognition as representatives of a 'group' deserving protected status. We can see this dynamic in the way that the number of 'groups' considered to be subject to hate crime has expanded over time. In Northern Ireland, for example, the PSNI began gathering data on racist crime in 1997 and this expanded to include homophobic crime. By 2006–07 the PSNI was recording six categories of hate crime; racist, homophobic, sectarian, faith/religion, disability and transphobic.[93] In the rest of the UK there have been various attempts to extend the groups covered by hate crime laws even further. In 2013 the Greater Manchester Police started to record attacks on Goths, a youth subculture, following the murder of 20-year-old Sophie Lancaster in 2007. The GMP said that its move meant that it could now recognise 'the impact that alternative subculture hate crime has on its victims and the wider community. Any crime motivated by hate is an insidious and evil crime ... in memory of Sophie, protecting the victims of hate crime should [be] extended beyond those the law already safeguards.'[94] In the English city of Plymouth activists have lobbied for attacks on red-haired people to be treated as a hate crime, and have organised a 'Ginger Pride' event modelled on Gay Pride.[95]

The examples of Goths and the ginger-haired might seem to trivialise the issue of hate crime. Lord Macdonald, former director of public prosecutions, expressed reservations about changing the legal definition of a hate crime. He argued that

> People's racial origins, their religion, their sexual orientation, people's dignity in the face of disability – these have been lines in the sand with the law saying, look, these are crimes that threaten social cohesion as a whole and therefore national life. I'm a little cautious about watering down this concept.[96]

His defence of the existing law relies on social order as the principal criterion. If the purpose of hate crime policy, however, is broadened towards giving public recognition and affirmation of the right to be different, and towards protecting people from having a diminished identity imposed on them, then the GMP's move is entirely consistent with the tenor of hate crime policy.

Using the criminal justice system as a means to connect with society has had some unintended consequences. It has, in some regards, further undermined rather than increased trust and confidence in the PSNI and the criminal justice system more broadly. The 'sending out a message' intent of the policy has raised unrealistic expectations of what the law can achieve. One estimate suggests that of 13,655 hate-motivated incidents that were reported to the police between 2007 and 2012, only 12 cases – less than one in a thousand – were successfully prosecuted under the 2004 hate crime legislation.[97] The very low rate of prosecution led NICEM to complain that 'the successful prosecution of generic "hate crime" in Northern Ireland is infinitesimal – the proportion of this involving racist hate crime is even closer to zero … In reality the opportunity for increased tariff in Northern Ireland has done nothing to signal the seriousness of racist violence.'[98] This complaint is embarrassing for the government, but it is not a challenge to hate crime policy. NICEM is not a social movement or even the product of a social movement. It acts as an advocate for ethnic 'groups' in society, but its ability to do so relies on state recognition of it as a 'representative' of ethnic minority 'groups', not on any meaningful relationship that the organisation might actually have with racialised minorities. Its complaint about the low number of prosecutions is a mechanism through which the organisation has attempted to maintain its relationship to the state. NICEM's principal antagonism is not with the state but with other organisations that claim that NICEM's broad remit as an umbrella organisation does not adequately represent their particular ethnic 'group'. It is this organisational rivalry, not popular demands from below, that drives bodies like NICEM to complain that government policy does not provide adequate recognition to its 'group'.

Victimhood

The infinitesimal emancipatory content of hate crime policy can be seen in the prominent symbolic role it affords to victims and victimhood. The Macpherson Inquiry and hate crime legislation have institutionalised a victim focus at the heart of Race Relations policy. This can be seen, for example, in the fact that the police are now required to record all racist incidents, not just those that are criminal offences. The Macpherson-derived definition of a racist incident – any incident that is perceived to be racist by the victim, or any other person – provides the victim with a central role in deciding whether an incident is racist or not.[99] The victim-focused rationale appeals to our empathy for the plight of people who are subjected to a constant litany of petty jibes, degrading insults, aggressive harassment and the ever-present threat – and sometimes actual experience – of violence. It relies on an emotional plea. In the actual operation of the criminal justice system, however, a victim focus does not necessarily help those that it is claimed to be designed to help.

This victim focus in the criminal justice system is not confined to ethnic minorities, or even to minorities alone. James Dignan notes that, in the Anglo-American criminal justice system, there was 'a growing sensitization during the 1960s and 1970s towards the existence and needs of particular groups of "vulnerable" victims'.[100] Dignan also points out that women played a major role in drawing attention to the needs of victims in the criminal justice system. These women, 'often radicalized by feminist ideals', set up 'support networks such as the Women's Refuge Movement and "Rape Crisis Centres"', and also drew 'attention to the manifest inadequacies of the criminal justice system in dealing with' offences such as rape or incest.[101] Initially, radicals were focused on the way that the state failed minorities. As Terry A. Maroney puts it, 'women's rights advocates highlighted the problem of "secondary victimization" – abuse suffered by victims at the hands of police, prosecutors, social and medical service providers, and judges'.[102] In the early 1960s these feminist criticisms were paralleled by conservative criticisms of the criminal justice system.

These conservative criticisms were directed at a range of Supreme Court decisions made in response to the Civil Rights movement. 'Concern with civil rights', as A. Kenneth Pye put it,

> almost inevitably required attention to the rights of defendants in criminal cases ... If the Court's espousal of equality before the law was to be credible, it required not only that the poor Negro be permitted to vote and to attend a school with whites, but also that he and other disadvantaged individuals be able to exercise, as well as possess, the same rights as the affluent white when suspected of crime.[103]

Conservatives argued that these rulings recognised the rights of defendants at the expense of victims. At the end of the 1960s conservatives like Richard Nixon and George Wallace latched on to criticisms of defendants' rights and wider concerns about growing crime figures (these figures may have been due to improved recording rather than an increase in actual crime) to argue for more crime control and for a greater focus on victims of crime.[104] Maroney points out that the focus on rape and domestic violence 'and conservatives' reaction against the "due process revolution" coincided in … [their] outrage against both perpetrators of violence and a system that failed adequately to serve and protect victims'.[105] These criticisms were to merge in the 'hate crimes movement'. The focus on victims does not benefit all victims of crime equally. It favours those who are articulate, those who have access to the media to promote their case or those whose cases advocacy groups find useful as a means to advance their own interests.

The elevation of victimhood as an important status in the criminal justice system also, ironically, tends to present minorities as, by their nature, subordinate or inferior. Initially it was people in particularly vulnerable *circumstances* – such as women victims of domestic violence or child victims of incest – who were the focus of feminist criticisms of the criminal justice system. During the 1990s, however, 'vulnerability' increasingly came to be viewed as an *inherent characteristic* of children, women and minorities in general.[106] Frank Furedi notes that in contemporary Anglo-American culture there is a preoccupation with risk, and in this context, 'someone defined as being at risk is seen to exist in a permanent condition of vulnerability. It objectifies the vulnerability of the self.'[107] We can see this idea of groups being defined by their vulnerability in the PSNI submission to the Westminster-based Northern Ireland Hate Crimes Inquiry. The PSNI reported that it was currently developing a 'Cultural Awareness Guide … to provide practical advice and information in relation to the main minority and *vulnerable groups*, cultures, faiths within Northern Ireland' that would be used by 'all operational police officers and civilian support officers'.[108] The elevation of victimhood presents a demeaning picture of humanity, because victims 'are, by definition, passive objects who have been acted upon by other forces, not active agents. They are defined by the mark that has been made on them rather than the mark that they have made on the wider world.'[109]

This focus on the victim and victimhood downplays the agency of racialised minorities. The literature on racism in Northern Ireland almost exclusively portrays the racists as active people asserting their authority over racialised minorities, and their 'victims' as fearful, isolated and vulnerable. Racialised minorities, however, are not passive victims. McBride resorted to his arson attack after one of the Polish men stood up to him. When immigration officials detained Frank Kakopa he resisted. When they attempted to handcuff him he resolutely refused. Although the immigration officials arrested and detained Kakopa, he drew a line at being escorted past his wife and children in handcuffs. He was successful in this minor act of resistance. Studies of everyday anti-racism find that racialised people have a whole range of strategies for dealing with low-level and intense racial harassment.[110] Crystal Fleming, Michèle Lamont and Jessica Welburn, for example, have interviewed African Americans about their strategies for dealing with racism. They found a range of approaches adopted in response to harassment, which they characterised as confronting, deflecting conflict, educating the ignorant and 'managing the self'.[111]

In the literature on racial harassment in Northern Ireland, the agency of racialised minorities sometimes peeps through. Robbie McVeigh, for example, gives an example of a family who were subjected to a reign of harassment and intimidation by a group of teenage boys over several months. The father caught one of the boys and went to his family home and told the boy's mother what her son had been doing. The boy's mother responded by threatening the father and calling the police. When the police arrived they took the side of the boy's mother and cautioned the father. Undeterred, the father then starting photographing incidents so that he would have evidence to show the police. This led to an accusation that he was taking indecent photographs of children. The police were called again and the father was cautioned once again.[112] This case is a good example of secondary victimisation at the hands of the authorities, but it does not support the idea of racialised minorities as helpless victims.

Connolly and Keenan provide an example of a Chinese woman who faced constant harassment from a particular customer when she was working in a takeaway restaurant. As the woman herself put it,

> Every single night [he] come over give me hassle, hassle … every time I phone the police come over, sometime they never come … I just sort out myself. So first thing I argue … he tried beat me up so I just get a cup oil, pour over [him] and he still come over beat me.[113]

Connolly and Keenan, however, make no comment about the inadequacy of the police response, or about the woman's refusal to cower in the face of intimidation and assault. Instead they use this example to suggest the inherent vulnerability of racialised minorities when they go on to say that 'it would appear that minority ethnic people are vulnerable to attack at any time'.[114]

Authoritarian multiculturalism

Multicultural crime fighting is authoritarian in inclination. The infinitesimal number of prosecutions under hate crime laws in Northern Ireland led NICEM to argue that 'the current "increased sentencing" approach to racist violence is not working effectively. The Northern Ireland Assembly should introduce a specific offence of racially aggravated crime similar to that in England and Wales.'[115] NICEM, in other words, believes that the law in Northern Ireland is not punitive enough, and it wants a tougher approach. The experience of the implementation of the law in England and Wales shows that NICEM's recommendation would be likely to lead to a lowering of the standard of proof required to successfully take a case to court. The evidence from Northern Ireland, however, suggests that the problem is not a lack of effective law, but a lack of effective implementation of existing laws. As the examples from McVeigh and from Connolly and Keenan, cited in the previous subsection, indicate, the PSNI is often half-hearted in its response to racist crime or, worse, takes the side of the racist attackers, not the victims of racist harassment.

Criminal law considers motivation when sentencing someone for a crime. In that regard there is nothing novel about hate crime laws. The law makes a distinction between *mens rea* – the legal concept of intent or knowledge of wrongdoing – and *actus rea*, the act itself. Criminal law allows for variation in sentencing on grounds of *mens rea*. If, for example, someone kills impulsively rather than as a result of premeditation, this can mean the difference between a charge of murder or manslaughter. Hate crime laws, however, mark a significant change in the application of *mens rea*. As Heidi Hurd notes, traditionally 'good, or at least exculpatory, motivations' were accepted by the court as mitigating factors which could 'fully or partially exonerate persons for well-motivated or understandably ill-motivated conduct'.[116] Hate crime laws reverse the consideration of good motivations or extenuating circumstances as a basis for leniency or exoneration and make bad intentions grounds for harsher punishment. Hate crime laws deliberately make the law more punitive, and they target the motivation of the offender for punishment. The criminalisation of intent has led some commentators to characterise hate crime laws as Orwellian 'thought crime' laws.[117]

Hate crime laws are also authoritarian in the sense that elites drove the policy change, and did so by disregarding the views of ordinary people on the issue. In 2005 the Northern Ireland Life and Times annual attitudes survey asked a number of questions on the hate crime law, specifically in relation to race hate. The survey indicated that a majority (60 per cent) of people in Northern Ireland were not aware that anyone who commits a racist assault could get a more severe sentence because of the racial element. Slightly more people (44 per cent) disagreed with harsher punishment in cases of racist assault than agreed (40 per cent). The vast majority of those who opposed harsher sentencing thought that the punishment should be for the assault, not the motivation of the assailant. They justified their opposition to harsher sentencing based on ideas of equality: 'punishment should be equal for all assailants' (53 per cent; 24 per cent of all responses); 'an assault is an assault no matter who it is carried out on' (36 per cent; 16 per cent of all responses). The multicultural differentialist logic of support for hate crime policy can be seen in the fact that the largest proportion of those who supported harsher penalties on grounds of racist motivation (38 per cent; 14 per cent of total responses) did so in order to emphasise that racist attacks are different to other forms of assault.[118] A survey of the attitudes of elected representatives in Northern Ireland found that they were much more likely than the general public to support hate crime laws (61 per cent compared to 40 per cent). The same survey found that only a minority of Unionist politicians, and their supporters, were in favour of harsher penalties.[119] This could be interpreted as evidence that Protestants are more prejudiced against ethnic minorities, or it could be evidence that Protestants are more likely to value freedom of conscience. Or, then again, it could be part of the broader Unionist hostility to the human rights and equality agendas, which they view as favouring Catholics.[120]

A crucial problem with hate crime laws is that in order to tackle racist crime they undermine a key principle – equality – that has been fundamental to challenging racism. It is true that equality in the eyes of the law is a limited, formal equality. Undermining this formal equality, however, will not benefit the poor, the marginalised and the disadvantaged. The lessons from the USA should give us pause for thought. The Supreme Court reforms of the 1960s introduced many reforms designed to uphold formal equality in the practice of criminal proceedings. Pye outlines some of the ways in which the principle of equality in the eyes of the law was upheld when he says that, because of these reforms, defendants were protected by the

> prohibition against a [police] lineup in the absence of counsel … violation of the defendant's right to counsel at this stage would render the in-court identification of the defendant inadmissible if the identification was tainted by the lineup … The confession obtained without informing the witness of his rights or permitting him an opportunity to exercise them would be inadmissible … The evidence obtained from the person of the accused following his unlawful arrest would be inadmissible.[121]

It was reforms such as these, which protected defendants from the capricious exercise of state power, that provoked the conservative crime victim 'movement' to complain that the hands of the police were being tied. Under the presidency of Ronald Reagan, the War on Crime mutated into the War on Drugs, and the poorest, most marginalised and most disadvantaged sections of American society have borne the brunt of these wars. The proportion of the population of the USA who were imprisoned rose rapidly in the 1970s, 1980s and 1990s. According to the US government's own figures, in 1974 1.8 million people had been imprisoned in the USA at some point in their life; by 2001 that figure was 5.6 million.[122] Racialised minorities have been the biggest casualties of this government-promoted crime fighting.[123] In 2014 the incarceration rate for White men was 465 in every 100,000; for Black men it was 2,724, six times the rate for White men.[124]

The consequences of incarceration endure long past release from prison. As Michelle Alexander points out,

> Once you're labelled a felon, the old forms of [racial] discrimination – employment discrimination, housing discrimination, denial of the right to vote, and exclusion from jury service – are suddenly legal. As a criminal, you have scarcely more rights, and arguably less respect, than a black man living in Alabama at the height of Jim Crow. We have not ended racial caste in America; we have merely redesigned it.[125]

Okay, so this is the USA, which was founded on slave labour, has a long history of racial discrimination and which has the highest rate of incarceration in the world. We couldn't have anything like this is a multicultural, post-colonial UK. Or could we?

The introduction of hate crime laws into the UK has been part of a broader trend towards a more punitive criminal justice system. A report by the UK government's Ministry of Justice found that the UK's prison population increased after 1993 due to sentences being increased for certain crimes and an increased likelihood of offenders being imprisoned for breach of non-custodial sentences. The report also notes that the population would have increased further if it had not been for the introduction of other measures, such as the Home Detention Curfew (electronic tagging), which involved non-custodial incarceration.[126] In the UK, Black people are proportionately more likely than White people to become victims of crime. They are also, however, more likely to be stopped and searched by the police, arrested, cautioned, brought to court and imprisoned. The average custodial sentence for a Black convict, for the same category of crime, is also longer than that for a White convict.[127] A 2010 report by the UK's Equality and Human Rights Commission noted that in England and Wales, Black people were five times more likely than Whites to be imprisoned, and that the prison population of England and Wales is among the highest in western Europe.[128] Northern Ireland has a lower per capita prison population than the rest of the UK, but in the twenty-first century (after the signing of the Peace Agreement), this prison population has also grown.[129]

These frightening figures on incarceration underestimate the increasing encroachment of the criminal justice system into our everyday lives. The regulation of the population of the UK expanded significantly, and in new directions, during the 1990s.[130] Often this expansion was not presented as punitive, but as preventative, restorative or enabling.[131] The increase of CCTV surveillance, for example, is commonly presented as a deterrent, rather than as a tool for detecting crime.[132] Giddens argued for an 'emphasis upon crime prevention rather than law enforcement', and noted that for this emphasis 'to work, partnerships between government agencies, the criminal justice system, local associations and community organizations have to be inclusive – all economic and ethnic groups must be involved'.[133] In Northern Ireland, this approach to policing is evident in the area of crime prevention and community safety.[134]

This preventative policing has gone hand-in-hand with hate crime policy. The 1998 Crime and Disorder Act, which introduced hate crime laws into England, Scotland and Wales, also introduced a raft of other punitive laws. The centre-piece of the Act was the introduction of Anti-Social Behaviour Orders (ASBOs). These are used to place restrictions on individuals. An ASBO can, for example, prohibit someone from entering specific public spaces because they are deemed to have acted 'in a manner that caused or was likely to cause harassment, alarm or distress to one or more persons'.[135] In Northern Ireland, ASBOs have been used against young people as a means to regulate behaviour that is considered low-level 'race hate crime', but which is not serious enough to be considered a criminal offence.[136] The Crown Prosecution Service in England and Wales states that ASBOs 'are not criminal sanctions and are not intended to punish the individual. They are designed to be preventative, not punitive.'[137] In their operation, however, they are punitive. ASBOs have been used to prohibit named individuals from begging, from wearing a 'hoodie', from making prank calls to the emergency services and from using 'pay as you go' mobile phones. ASBOs have also been used to impose curfews, exclude people from specified areas, prevent them from congregating in groups and associating with other named individuals, and forbid them to become drunk.[138] None of these activities are criminal offences. If, however, the named individual is found to be in breach of the activity prohibited by the ASBO, then they can be prosecuted as a criminal.[139]

John Muncie notes that the 1998 Crime and Disorder Act 'represents a marked expansion of the legal means through which young people's behaviour can be circumscribed'.[140] In addition to ASBOs the Act also introduced parenting orders and child safety orders, and it abolished the legal principle of *doli incapax* (the 'presumption of criminal law that a child aged 10 or under is incapable of committing an offence').[141] Andrew Millie notes that these punitive measures were based on the assumption that 'good behaviour (and good parenting) can be enforced'.[142] Muncie warns that 'experience shows that drawing children into the justice system at a forever earlier age also holds some unintended and potentially damaging consequences'.[143] Siobhán McAlister, Phil Scraton and Deena Haydon, based on research in the Northern Ireland context, illustrate some of these dangers when they argue that new policing measures 'disproportionate[ly] focus on children, young people and families living in economically deprived areas' and they 'increased pressure on "vulnerable families" ... the likely outcome is increased exclusion, marginalisation and alienation within targeted communities'.[144]

The increasing encroachment of the criminal justice system into the everyday lives of citizens has gone hand-in-hand with the criminalisation of aspects of immigration and the development of a shadow criminal justice system with little judicial oversight. In most of the avowedly liberal democratic countries in the world today there has been an increasing criminalisation of immigration and immigrants.[145] This is also evident in Northern Ireland.[146] The criminalisation of immigration has developed a separate sphere in which the civil rights of non-citizens are severely limited. The detention of immigrants suspected of violating immigration law, as Stephanie Silverman and Evelyne Massa note, is commonly treated as an administrative matter rather than a legal one. Consequently, because 'detention is thought to facilitate the realisation of immigration goals – such as naturalisation or deportation ... it does not need further legal justification. On the basis of this logic, immigration detainees are simply waiting for the government to resolve a perceived irregularity in their immigration proceedings.'[147] Liz Fekete likens the treatment of asylum seekers to that of terrorist suspects in the global War on Terror. She argues that detention centres in which 'migrants and failed asylum seekers are warehoused … while the EU member states search for a third country willing to accept them' are similar to the Guantanamo Bay detention camp.[148] She likens deportation flights to rendition flights when she points to evidence that some of the asylum seekers, when deported, 'have been systematically handed over to the security services and subjected to harsh interrogations and torture'.[149] She notes that 'the use of administrative expulsion instead of public order legislation' to deport Muslim clerics accused of 'speech crimes' means that they 'are being excluded from the ordinary rule of law'.[150] We know about the case of Frank Kakopa, who was wrongfully detained by UK immigration officials, because his family was able to draw attention to his case and he was able to take the BIA to court. However, the fate of the other Black people who were carted off in the van with him is unknown. Even in cases where lawyers have been alerted to the detention of immigrants, it has not always been possible to find out what has happened to them. Every year an unknown number of people are 'disappeared' from the UK through this largely unaccountable shadow 'justice' system.[151]

Rather than helping racialised minorities, the overall impact of more state regulation of behaviour is likely to disadvantage them. ASBOs have not just been used to restrict suspected criminals and 'nuisance' teenagers, they have also been used to restrict political protest.[152] The Institute for Race Relations draw attention to a wide attack on civil liberties in the UK that involves 'a presumption of guilt, punishment without a fair trial, and pre-emptive restraints on liberty. These principles lie behind not only the "war on terror" but measures against asylum seekers, demonstrators and those subject to ASBOs because they are accused of "anti-social behaviour".'[153] Tony Bunyan notes that the majority of people in the European Union are unaware of the full extent of the use of state powers. They assume, he says, that it 'only affects "illegal immigrants", criminals and terrorists, not them. Those who do understand, [however], through their everyday experiences, are those directly affected, migrants, migrant communities (especially Muslim ones), the unemployed, the poor and the marginalised.'[154] The increasingly elite nature of political life, however, means that these sections of society 'have no voice and no power' in the multicultural politics of 'group' advocacy.[155]

Conclusion

Racial (and sectarian) harassment and intimidation is demeaning. It is demeaning for the target of harassment, who is treated as a threatening presence in society.

It is demeaning for the offenders, who diminish themselves by not recognising the common humanity that they share with those they vilify and threaten. Hate crime laws, however, cannot eradicate racial, sectarian or any other kind of 'hate'. Hate crime laws disavow our common humanity. They are based on assumptions of superiority (of the enlightened cosmopolitanism of elites), inferiority (of the 'irrational' holding on to 'tradition' of the rabble) and patronage towards minorities who are treated as helpless victims. Hate crime laws cannot eradicate racisms, they can only punish them. Even then, this punishment depends on the political will of elites and the willing participation of actors in the criminal justice system. Hate crime policy is an extension of Race Relations policy in a social context in which the emancipatory dynamic of the civil rights era has been eroded. We should not view hate crime policy as an extension of the fight against racisms, but as part of the broader regulation of everyday life by the state. It is punitive and inegalitarian, rather than emancipatory.

Racial (and sectarian) harassment are an everyday reality for many racialised minorities. They should be tackled where they are manifested. Our disagreement with advocates of hate crime law is not over whether racist crimes should be tackled in the here-and-now, but about *how* they should be tackled. In many cases, racialised minorities are quite capable of developing strategies for tackling harassment that fit with their own specific circumstances. In some cases, victims of harassment require the intervention of the criminal justice system. Hate crimes can be brutal, frightening, demeaning, and occasionally they can be fatal. But are they really something that should be treated differently by the criminal justice system? In many cases the problem that racialised minorities have experienced is that their harassment has not even been treated as a crime. In some cases, the attempt of racialised minorities to tackle their harassment has been criminalised (as we have seen in the case highlighted by McVeigh). In other cases, racialised minorities would have been better served by more diligent pursuit of pre-existing powers of the police and courts to investigate and prosecute the crimes that they have been victims of.

Hate crime policy focuses attention on the actions of some of the most marginal sections of society and treats the marginalised as part of the problem. The policy attempts to legitimise the role of the forces of law and order in society. These same forces of law and order are responsible for the legally sanctioned eviction of racialised minorities from their homes and the internment and forcible removal of others from the UK. If we are to develop an emancipatory anti-racism, we need to expose the ways in which the social structural contradictions of a capitalist society create racisms. We also need to expose the ways in which official anti-racisms attempt to harness our disgust at racism and direct our ire against some of the most marginalised in society, rather than against the social conditions that give rise to racisms.

Notes

1 Chrisafis, 'Racist war of the Loyalist street gangs'.

2 Eoghan Williams, 'Barred GAA stars believed to be from the British Army', *Irish Independent*, 11 January 2004.

3 'Race hate on rise in NI', *BBC News Online*, 13 January 2004.

4 Lentin and McVeigh, *After optimism?*, 145.

5 Morrow, 'Hate crime, policing and human rights'.

6 Connolly and Keenan, *The hidden truth*.

7 Banton, 'The race relations problematic'.

8 The law was introduced via the Criminal Justice (No. 2) (Northern Ireland) Order 2004, which received royal assent in July 2004.

9 The Criminal Justice (No . 2) (Northern Ireland) Order 2004.

10 Derek McGhee, *Intolerant Britain? Hate, citizenship and difference* (Maidenhead: Open University Press, 2005), 7.

11 Northern Ireland Council for Ethnic Minorities, *Response to consultation on race crime and sectarian crime legislation in Northern Ireland* (Belfast: NICEM, 2003), 2.

12 NIAC, *The challenge of diversity: volume 2*, 111.

13 NIAC, *The challenge of diversity: volume 1*, 37.

14 PPSNI, *Hate crime policy*.

15 NIAC, *The challenge of diversity: volume 1*, 63.

16 Criminal justice policy was not devolved to the NIA until 2010. For more on the sensitivity of policing and its devolution, see Henry McDonald and Nicholas Watt, 'Stormont votes to take over Northern Ireland policing powers', *The Guardian*, 9 March 2010; Robert Perry, 'The devolution of policing in Northern Ireland: politics and reform', *Politics* 31.3 (2011): 167–178; Graham Ellison and Mary O'Rawe, 'Security governance in transition: the compartmentalizing, crowding out and cor-ralling of policing and security in Northern Ireland', *Theoretical Criminology* 14.1 (2010): 31–57; Graham Ellison, Peter Shirlow and Aogán Mulcahy, 'Responsible participation, community engagement and policing in transitional societies: lessons from a local crime survey in Northern Ireland', *The Howard Journal of Criminal Justice* 51.5 (2012): 488–502.

17 'Agenda 2001: MLA calls for race-hate laws', *Belfast News Letter*, 30 May 2001.

18 'MLAs urged to back race hate laws', *Belfast News Letter*, 14 May 2002.

19 Paul Iganski, *'Hate crime' and the city* (Bristol: Policy Press, 2008), 127–129; Crime and Disorder Act 1998.

20 Northern Ireland Office, *Race crime and sectarian crime legislation in Northern Ireland: a consultation paper* (Belfast: NIO, 2002), 8.

21 Ibid., 7.

22 NIAC, *The challenge of diversity: volume 1*, 9.

23 NIO, *Race crime and sectarian crime legislation*.

24 Ibid., 20.

25 Northern Ireland Office, *Race crime and sectarian crime legislation in Northern Ireland: a summary of responses to consultation* (Belfast: NIO, 2003), 5.

26 See, for example, Committee for the Administration of Justice, *CAJ's response to*

'Race crime and sectarian crime legislation in Northern Ireland' (Belfast: CAJ, 2003); NICEM, *Response to the consultation on race crime*.

27 CAJ, *CAJ's response*, 5.

28 Chrisafis, 'Racist war of the Loyalist street gangs'.

29 See, for example, Pamela M. Clayton, *Enemies and passing friends: settler ideologies in twentieth-century Ulster* (London: Pluto Press, 1996); Adrian Guelke, 'Northern Ireland's flags crisis and the enduring legacy of the settler-native divide', *Nationalism and Ethnic Politics* 20.1 (2014): 133–151.

30 See, for example, E. Rosemary Mckeever et al., 'How racist violence becomes a virtue: an application of discourse analysis', *International Journal of Conflict and Violence* 7.1 (2013): 108–120; Samuel Pehrson, Mirona A. Gheorghiu and Tomas Ireland, 'Cultural threat and anti-immigrant prejudice: the case of Protestants in Northern Ireland', *Journal of Community and Applied Social Psychology* 22.1 (2012): 111–124; Clare Bowden, 'The connection between Loyalism and hate crimes in Northern Ireland', *The News Hub.com*, 2015.

31 See, for example, Chrisafis, 'Racist war of the Loyalist street gangs'; Rolston, 'Legacy of intolerance'; Trademark, *Racism and racist attitudes in Northern Ireland* (Belfast: TUC, 2015); Robbie McVeigh, 'Living the peace process in reverse: racist violence and British nationalism in Northern Ireland', *Race & Class* 56.4 (2015): 3–25; Henry McDonald, 'Northern Ireland at risk of a "race war", anti-fascist campaigner warns police', *The Observer*, 6 September 2009.

32 See, for example, Chris Gilligan, 'Migration and migrant workers in Northern Ireland', *ARK Update* (Belfast: ARK, 2008); Chris Gilligan and Katrina Lloyd, 'Racial prejudice in Northern Ireland', *ARK Update* (Belfast: ARK, 2005); Pehrson, Gheorghiu and Ireland, 'Cultural threat and anti-immigrant prejudice'; Rebecca McKee, 'Love thy neighbour? Exploring prejudice against ethnic minority groups in a divided society: the case of Northern Ireland', *Journal of Ethnic and Migration Studies* 42.5 (2016): 777–796.

33 See, for example, Christina Steenkamp, 'Loyalist paramilitary violence after the Belfast Agreement', *Ethnopolitics* 7.1 (2008): 159–176; Chris Kilpatrick, 'PSNI "in war of attrition" with racist thugs of UVF', *Belfast Telegraph*, 20 May 2014; Chris Kilpatrick, 'More Polish homes targeted by racist thugs in fresh bout of "ethnic cleansing" by UVF', *Belfast Telegraph*, 6 May 2014; Neil Jarman and Rachel Monaghan, *Racist harassment in Northern Ireland* (Belfast: OFMDFM, 2003); Mckeever et al., 'How racist violence becomes a virtue'.

34 Fionnuala Meredith, 'It's prejudiced to dismiss every loyalist as racist', *Belfast Telegraph*, 20 June 2014.

35 Ibid.

36 Fionnuala Meredith, '"It's good to know only a small number of people would do such a thing"; Polish-born Sydenham resident Anna Bloch won't wallow in self-pity after racist thugs targeted her home', *Belfast Telegraph*, 25 January 2014.

37 Rolston, 'Legacy of intolerance'.

38 Henry McDonald, 'Loyalists make Catholic Poles welcome', *The Observer*, 18 February 2007.

39 'Family "fears death" if deported', *BBC News Online*, 20 December 2007;

'Church cash helps deported Nigerian family in hiding', *Belfast Telegraph*, 23 April 2008.

40 Carey Doyle and Ruth McAreavey, 'Possibilities for change? Diversity in post-conflict Belfast', *City* 18.4–5 (2014): 466–475; Trademark, *Racism and racist attitudes in Northern Ireland*; Neil Jarman, *Overview analysis of racist incidents recorded in Northern Ireland by the RUC 1996–1999* (Belfast: OFMDFM, 2002).

41 Independent Monitoring Commission, *Third report of the Independent Monitoring Commission* (London: IMC, 2004), 15.

42 Independent Monitoring Commission, *Eighth report of the Independent Monitoring Commission, October* (London: IMC, 2006), 24.

43 McVeigh, 'Living the peace process in reverse', 10.

44 Ibid., 11.

45 Ibid., 20.

46 Northern Ireland Crown Court, 'The Queen versus Ryan Kenneth McBride' (Belfast: NICC, 2007).

47 Ibid.

48 Ibid.

49 Ibid.

50 Ibid.

51 NIO, *Race crime and sectarian crime*, 16.

52 Larry Ray, David Smith and Liz Wastell, 'Shame, rage and racist violence', *British Journal of Criminology* 44.3 (2004): 351.

53 Jack McDevitt, Jack Levin and Susan Bennett, 'Hate crime offenders: an expanded typology', *Journal of Social Issues* 58.2 (2002): 303–317.

54 Sarah Isal, *Preventing racist violence: work with actual and potential perpetrators – learning from practice to policy change* (London: Runnymede Trust, 2005); Gail Mason, 'Hate crime and the image of the stranger', *British Journal of Criminology* 45.6 (2005): 837–859; David Gadd, 'Aggravating racism and elusive motivation', *British Journal of Criminology* 49.6 (2009): 755–771; Elizabeth A. Stanko, 'Re-conceptualising the policing of hatred: confessions and worrying dilemmas of a consultant', *Law & Critique* 12 (2001): 309–329.

55 See, for example, Neil Jarman and Chris O'Halloran, 'Recreational rioting: young people, interface areas and violence', *Child Care in Practice* 7.1 (2001): 2–16; Marie Smyth and Patricia Campbell, *Young people and armed violence in Northern Ireland* (Belfast: Children in Organised Armed Violence, 2004); Paul Reilly, '"Anti-social" networking in Northern Ireland: policy responses to young people's use of social media for organizing anti-social behavior', *Policy & Internet* 3.1 (2011): 1–23; Madeleine Leonard, 'What's recreational about "recreational rioting"? Children on the streets in Belfast', *Children & Society* 24.1 (2010): 38–49; Madeleine Leonard, 'Building, bolstering and bridging boundaries: teenagers' negotiations of interface areas in Belfast', *Journal of Ethnic and Migration Studies* 34.3 (2008): 471–489; Leonard, 'Teens and territory in contested spaces'.

56 Leonard, 'What's recreational about "recreational rioting"?', 41.

57 Ibid., 42.

58 Ibid., 43.

59 Ibid.

60 Connolly and Keenan, *The hidden truth*, 48–53.

61 Ibid., 53.

62 NICEM, *Response to the consultation on race crime*, 2.

63 Iganski, 'Hate crime' and the city, 20.

64 Ibid.

65 Valerie Jenness, 'The hate crime canon and beyond: a critical assessment', *Law & Critique* 12 (2001): 279–308.

66 Bill Dixon and David Gadd, 'Getting the message? "New" Labour and the criminalization of "hate"', *Criminology and Criminal Justice* 6.3 (2006): 312, doi:10.1177/1748895806065532.

67 Ibid., 313.

68 NIAC, *The challenge of diversity: volume 1*, 137.

69 Erik Bleich, 'The rise of hate speech and hate crime laws in liberal democracies', *Journal of Ethnic and Migration Studies* 37.6 (2011): 918.

70 Eugene Mclaughlin, 'Rocks and hard places: the politics of hate crime', *Theoretical Criminology* 6.4 (2002): 497.

71 Terry A. Maroney, 'The struggle against hate crime: movement at a crossroads', *NYU Law Review* 73.2 (1998): 564–620; Mclaughlin, 'Rocks and hard places'; NIHRC and Nazia Latif, *Hate crime in Northern Ireland* (Belfast: Northern Ireland Human Rights Commission, 2005).

72 See, for example, Maroney, 'The struggle against hate crime'; Jenness, 'The hate crime canon and beyond'; Gail Mason, 'Not our kind of hate crime', *Law & Critique* 12 (2001): 253–278.

73 Jenness, 'The hate crime canon and beyond', 285.

74 Marable, *Race, reform and rebellion*; Elizabeth Hinton, '"A war within our own boundaries": Lyndon Johnson's Great Society and the rise of the carceral state', *Journal of American History* 102.1 (2015): 100–112.

75 Marable, *Race, reform and rebellion*, 113.

76 Ibid., 146.

77 Hinton, '"A war within our own boundaries"'; Elizabeth Hinton, 'Creating crime: the rise and impact of national juvenile delinquency programs in black urban neighborhoods', *Journal of Urban History* 41.5 (2015): 808–824; Jonathan Simon, 'Governing through crime', *Brooklyn Law Review* 67.4 (2002): 1035–1070; Leslie J. Moran, 'Affairs of the heart: hate crime and the politics of crime control', *Law & Critique* 12 (2001): 331–344.

78 Gordon, 'The individual and "the general situation"'; Christopher Kyriakides and Rodolfo D. Torres, *Race defaced: paradigms of pessimism, politics of possibility* (Stanford, CA: Stanford University Press, 2012); Elisabeth Lasch-Quinn, *Race experts: how racial etiquette, sensitivity training, and New Age therapy hijacked the civil rights revolution* (New York: Norton, 2001); Emily Gray, Jonathan Jackson and Stephen Farrall, 'In search of the fear of crime: using interdisciplinary insights to improve the conceptualisation and measurement of everyday insecurities', in *Sage Handbook of Criminological Research Methods*, ed. David Gadd, Suzanne Karstedt and Steven F. Messner (London: Sage, 2011), 268–281.

79 Robin Ward, 'Where race didn't divide: some reflections on slum clearance in Moss Side', in *Racism and political action in Britain*, ed. Robert Miles and Annie Phizacklea (London: Routledge and Kegan Paul, 1979), 204–222; Sivanandan, 'From resistance to rebellion'; Virdee, *Racism, class and the racialised outsider*.

80 Gilroy, 'The end of anti-racism', 207.

81 Ibid.

82 Sivanandan, *Communities of resistance*, 67.

83 Ibid.

84 See, for example, the contributions of anti-racism quangos and 'community' organisations to the consultations on hate crimes: NIO, *Race crime: a summary of responses*; NIAC, *The challenge of diversity: volume 1*; NIAC, *The challenge of diversity: volume 2*.

85 Anthony Giddens, *The third way: the renewal of social democracy* (Cambridge: Polity Press, 1998); Sarah Hale, Will Leggett and Luke Martell (eds), *Third way and beyond: criticisms, futures, alternatives* (Manchester: Manchester University Press, 2004); Christopher Kyriakides, 'Third way anti-racism: a contextual constructionist approach', *Ethnic and Racial Studies* 31.3 (2008): 592–610; McGhee, *Intolerant Britain?*.

86 Giddens, *The third way*, 64–71.

87 Mclaughlin, 'Rocks and hard places', 497.

88 McGhee, *Intolerant Britain?*, 6.

89 Ibid.

90 Ibid., 7.

91 OFMDFM, *Programme for cohesion, sharing and integration: consultation document*, 5.

92 Ibid., 70.

93 PSNI, *Trends in hate motivated incidents, 2004/05 to 2011/12*.

94 'Hate crime: police record attacks on punks, emos and goths', *BBC News Online*, 4 April 2013. See also Simon Price, 'Violence against goths is a hate crime', *The Guardian*, 4 April 2013.

95 See, for example, Steve Doohan, '"Ginger Pride" festival to be held in city hit by anti-redhead hate crime', *The Daily Mirror*, 14 August 2015; Nelson Jones, 'Should ginger-bashing be considered a hate crime?', *New Statesman*, January 2013.

96 BBC News, 'Hate crime: police record attacks on punks, emos and goths'.

97 Tara Mills, 'Hate crime: how effective is Northern Ireland legislation?', *BBC News Online*, 15 October 2012.

98 NICEM, *Race and criminal justice in Northern Ireland: towards a blueprint for the eradication of racism from the CJSNI* (Belfast, 2013), 52.

99 Macpherson, *The Stephen Lawrence Inquiry*.

100 James Dignan, *Understanding victims and restorative justice* (Maidenhead: McGraw-Hill International, 2005), 15.

101 Ibid.

102 Maroney, 'The struggle against hate crime', 574.

103 A. Kenneth Pye, 'The Warren Court and criminal procedure', *Michigan Law Review* 67 (1968): 256.

104 See, for example, Simon, 'Governing through crime'; Heather Ann Thompson, 'Why mass incarceration matters: rethinking crisis, decline, and transformation in postwar American history', *Journal of American History* 97.3 (2010): 705–736; Hinton, 'Creating crime'.

105 Maroney, 'The struggle against hate crime', 574–575.

106 Ronald Frankenberg, Ian Robinson and Amber Delahooke, 'Countering essentialism in behavioural social science: the example of "the vulnerable child" ethnographically examined', *Sociological Review* 48.4 (2000): 586–611; Frank Furedi, *Therapy culture: cultivating vulnerability in an uncertain age* (London: Routledge, 2003); Joel Best, 'Victimization and the victim industry', *Society* 34.4 (1994): 9–17.

107 Furedi, *Therapy culture*, 130.

108 NIAC, *The challenge of diversity: volume 2*, 46; emphasis added.

109 Chris Gilligan, 'Constant crisis/permanent process: diminished agency and weak structures in the Northern Ireland peace process', *Ethnopolitics* 3.1 (2003): 30.

110 The majority of these studies are on the experiences of the middle classes. See, for example, Kristine Aquino, 'Anti-racism "from below": exploring repertoires of everyday anti-racism', *Ethnic and Racial Studies* 39.1 (2015): 105–122; Michèle Lamont and Nissim Mizrachi, 'Ordinary people doing extraordinary things: responses to stigmatization in comparative perspective', *Ethnic and Racial Studies* 35.3 (2012): 365–381.

111 Crystal M. Fleming, Michèle Lamont and Jessica S. Welburn, 'African Americans respond to stigmatization: the meanings and salience of confronting, deflecting conflict, educating the ignorant and "managing the self"', *Ethnic and Racial Studies* 35.3 (2012): 400–417.

112 McVeigh, *The next Stephen Lawrence*, 40–41.

113 Connolly and Keenan, *The hidden truth*, 15.

114 Ibid.

115 NICEM, *Race and criminal justice*, 56.

116 Heidi M. Hurd, 'Why liberals should hate "hate crime legislation"', *Law and Philosophy* 20.2 (2001): 217.

117 See, for example, Brendan O'Neill, 'Time for a backlash against the hate-obsessed state?', *Spiked-Online*, 11 December 2006; Melanie Phillips, 'I think, therefore I'm guilty', *The Spectator*, 18 September 2010; Susan Gellman, 'Hate crime laws are thought crime laws', *Annual Survey of American Law* 1992/93 (1993): 509–531.

118 Chris Gilligan, 'Two wrongs don't make a right: (in)tolerance and hate crimes in Northern Ireland', in *Tolerance and diversity in Ireland, north and south*, ed. Iseult Honohan and Nathalie Rougier (Manchester: Manchester University Press, 2015), 171–188.

119 Chris Gilligan, Paul Hainsworth and Aidan Mcgarry, 'Questions and answers: comparing the attitudes of elected representatives, political party supporters and the general public towards minority ethnic communities in Northern Ireland', *Shared Space* 6 (2008): 85–100.

120 Peter Munce, 'Unionists as "court sceptics": exploring elite-level Unionist discourses about a Northern Ireland Bill of Rights', *British Journal of Politics and International Relations* 15 (2013): 647–667; Peter Munce, 'Unionism and the Northern Ireland

Human Rights Commission 1999–2005: hostility, hubris and hesitancy', *Irish Political Studies* 29.2 (2012): 194–214.

121 Pye, 'The Warren Court and criminal procedure', 251.

122 Thomas Bonczar, *Prevalence of imprisonment in the U.S. population, 1974–2001* (Washington, DC: Bureau of Justice, 2003).

123 See, for example, Hinton, '"A war within our own boundaries"'; Hinton, 'Creating crime'; Simon, 'Governing through crime'; Vesla M. Weaver, 'Frontlash: race and the development of punitive crime policy', *Studies in American Political Development* 21 (2007): 230–265; Thompson, 'Why mass incarceration matters'; Devah Pager and Hana Shepherd, 'The sociology of discrimination: racial discrimination in employment, housing, credit, and consumer markets', *Annual Review of Sociology* 34.1 (2008): 181–209; Alexander, 'The war on drugs and the new Jim Crow'.

124 The Sentencing Project, *Fact sheet: trends in U.S. corrections* (Washington, DC: The Sentencing Project, 2015).

125 Michelle Alexander, *The new Jim Crow: mass incarceration in the age of colorblindness* (New York: The New Press, 2012), 2.

126 Ministry of Justice, *Story of the prison population 1993–2012: England and Wales* (London: Ministry of Justice, 2013).

127 NICEM, *Race and criminal justice*.

128 Equality and Human Rights Commission, *How fair is Britain? Equality, human rights and good relations in 2010. The first triennial review* (London: Equality and Human Rights Commission, 2010), 162–163.

129 International Centre for Prison Studies, 'United Kingdom: Northern Ireland', *World Prison Brief*, www.prisonstudies.org/country/united-kingdom-northern-ireland (accessed 10 January 2017).

130 See, for example, the development of 'choice architecture', 'nudge' and other approaches designed to get citizens to behave in ways that the government wants to promote: David Halpern et al., *Personal responsibility and changing behaviour: the state of knowledge and its implications for public policy* (London: The Cabinet Office, 2004); Rhys Jones, Jessica Pykett and Mark Whitehead, 'Psychological governance and behaviour change', *Policy & Politics* 41.2 (2013): 159–182; Dan Bulley and Bal Sokhi-Bulley, 'Big society as big government: Cameron's governmentality agenda', *The British Journal of Politics & International Relations* 16.13 (2014), 452–470; Bal Sokhi-Bulley, 'Government(ality) by experts: human rights as governance', *Law and Critique* 22.3 (2011): 251–271; Will Leggett, 'The politics of behaviour change: nudge, neoliberalism and the state', *Policy & Politics* 42.1 (2014): 3–19; Adam Crawford, 'Networked governance and the post-regulatory state? Steering, rowing and anchoring the provision of policing and security', *Theoretical Criminology* 10.4 (2006): 449–479.

131 See, for example, John Muncie, 'Institutionalized intolerance: youth justice and the 1998 Crime and Disorder Act', *Critical Social Policy* 19.2 (1999): 147–175; Sara Todd, *Anti-Social Behaviour (ASB), Crime Policing Act 2014 and review of restorative justice approach* (Manchester: Manchester City Council, 2014).

132 Tony Bunyan, 'Just over the horizon: the surveillance society and the state in the EU', *Race & Class* 51.3 (2010): 1–12.

133 Giddens, *The third way*, 88.

134 Department of Justice Northern Ireland, *Building safer, shared and confident communities: a community safety strategy for Northern Ireland 2012–2017* (Belfast: DOJNI, 2012); Mark Brunger, 'Dispatches from the field: developing community safety in Northern Ireland.', *Crime Prevention and Community Safety* 14.2 (2012): 140–164; Jonny Byrne and John Topping, *Community safety: a decade of development, delivery, challenge and change in Northern Ireland* (Belfast: Belfast Conflict Resolution Consortium, 2012).

135 Crime and Disorder Act 1998, 2.

136 NIHRC, *Racist hate crime: human rights and the criminal justice system in Northern Ireland* (Belfast: NIHRC, 2013).

137 Crown Prosecution Service, 'Anti-Social Behaviour Orders on conviction (ASBOs)', *Prosecution Policy and Guidance* (London: CPS, 2016).

138 Yvette Levy and Edmund Hall, *A guide to ASBO prohibitions in reported cases* (London: Crown Prosecution Service, 2014).

139 Stuart Waiton, 'ASBOs as assurance in the post-liberal era', *International Journal of Law in Context* 9.3 (2013): 429–436; Muncie, 'Institutionalized intolerance'.

140 Muncie, 'Institutionalized intolerance', 169.

141 Crime and Disorder Act 1998, 43.

142 Andrew Millie, 'Moral politics, moral decline and anti-social behaviour', *People, Place & Policy Online* 4.1 (2010): 7.

143 Muncie, 'Institutionalized intolerance', 169.

144 Siobhán McAlister, Phil Scraton and Deena Haydon, *Childhood in transition: experiencing marginalisation and conflict in Northern Ireland* (Belfast: Save the Children, 2009), 31.

145 See, for example, Salvatore Palidda (ed.), *Criminalisation and victimization of migrants in Europe* (Genoa: Universita degli Studi di Genova, 2008); Ayse Ceyhan and Anastassia Tsoukala, 'The securitization of migration in Western societies: ambivalent discourses and policies', *Alternatives* 27 (2002): 21–39; Michael C. Ewers and Joseph M. Lewis, 'Risk and the securitisation of student migration to the United States', *Tijdschrift voor Economische en Sociale Geografie* 99.4 (2008): 470–482; Nicholas P. De Genova, 'Migrant "illegality" and deportability in everyday life', *Annual Review of Anthropology* 31.1 (2002): 419–447; Mary Bosworth, 'Border control and the limits of the sovereign state', *Social & Legal Studies* 17.2 (2008): 199–215; Richard Black et al., 'Routes to illegal residence: a case study of immigration detainees in the United Kingdom', *Geoforum* 37.4 (2006): 552–564; Home Office, *Secure borders, safe haven: integration with diversity* (London: Home Office, 2002).

146 See, for example, Latif and Martynowicz, *Our hidden borders*; Cornelius Wiesener and Patrick Corrigan, *Measuring misery: detention of asylum seekers in Northern Ireland: a statistical analysis 2002–04* (Belfast: Refugee Action Group, 2004); Robin Wilson, 'Immigration detention in Northern Ireland', *Criminal Justice Matters* 83.1 (2011): 8–9.

147 Stephanie J. Silverman and Evelyne Massa, 'Why immigration detention is unique', *Population, Space and Place* 18 (2012): 677.

148 Liz Fekete, *A suitable enemy: racism, migration and Islamophobia in Europe* (London: Pluto Press, 2009), 136.
149 Ibid., 147.
150 Ibid., 164.
151 Chris Gilligan, 'The disappeared', *Indymedia.ie*, 2009.
152 Statewatch, 'ASBOwatch', *www.statewatch.org*.
153 Institute of Race Relations, *Community responses to the War on Terror* (London: IRR, 2007).
154 Bunyan, 'Just over the horizon', 3.
155 Ibid.

8

Conclusion

Racisms, including sectarianism, prevent human beings from being fully human. The crisis of anti-racism is a crisis for humanity. It is a manifestation of humanity's estrangement from itself. As long as we aspire to human freedom, but accept the denial of freedom to sections of humanity because of their 'race', their nationality or their creed, then we will continue to be estranged, not just from other human beings, but from our own human nature. At the heart of the crisis of anti-racism lies the core belief that anti-racism is the opposite of racism. But it is not. Human emancipation is the opposite of racisms. Anti-racism is only the opposite of racisms in as far as it promotes human emancipation.

Human emancipation is possible because the vast majority of people experience capitalism as unsatisfactory and desire a better society. The working class have the numerical size and the interest in transcending capitalism. They cannot do so, however, as long as they tie themselves to the nation. They cannot do so as long as they view other people, rather than the social system, as the source of their alienation, lack of freedom and their relative inequality. The traditional left argument that racism is a ruling-class tool used to divide the working class is obviously inadequate in an age when anti-racism is one of the issues that divides the working class. Many forms of official anti-racism involve making distinctions between cosmopolitan and racist working-class people. Derek McGhee points to the example of the Inter-Community Peer Support Project that was established in the English city of Oldham following the 'race' riots there in 2001. The project worked with young people, mainly boys aged 12–14, who were considered to be potential, or were actual, perpetrators of 'race hate' crimes. The project worked to challenge the prejudices and racial stereotypes held by the young people and attempted to turn the youngsters into 'race harmony ambassadors'.[1] In effect the Project aimed to train these young people to police the attitudes and behaviours of other young people in their local communities. This type of anti-racist initiative is, as McGhee puts it, about 'changing mind-sets and habitual prejudices through personal development and exposure to the other'.[2] Like official anti-racism in general, this Project does not expose the contradictions inherent in capitalist society; instead it projects these contradictions as inherent to humanity. The anti-human nature of official anti-racism should not, however, lead us to reject anti-racism per se. It means that we should oppose racisms in ways that highlight the contradictions of capitalist society and its inhuman consequences. Or, in other words, we need to oppose racisms *and* official anti-racism. Both are dehumanising.

A changing world

We live at a portentous moment in human history. The world is undergoing immense, and as yet uncertain, changes. The fraying of the British Empire has gone so far that the UK itself shows signs of becoming disunited. The USA, the nation-state that eclipsed the UK in the first half of the twentieth century, is now facing its own demise. The weakness of the USA as a global economic power was exposed in 2008, when the credit-fuelled bubble collapsed. It was in the heart of the capitalist world, not at its extremities, that the collapse started. The shockwaves reverberated out from the centre and devastated huge swathes of the world. Some places withstood the impact. The Chinese economy slowed, but it did not receive a shock. Despite the slow-down in the growth of China, it still outpaces the sluggish USA. In the twenty-first century, nation-states in the former colonial world are developing into some of the largest economies in the world. China, India and Brazil are already, according to some ratings, in the top ten economies in the world. These 'newly emerging economies' are growing at a faster rate than the old capitalist economies. The changes are not just taking place on the economic front. The triumph of the USA in the Cold War was a hollow victory. The mighty US military, with the most extensive armoury of sophisticated weapons the world has ever known, was deployed to assert US power through bullying its way around the world. In Operation Desert Storm, the US military demonstrated its awesome firepower when it annihilated Iraq, a former colony of the UK that had been crippled by a decade of US-government sponsored war against Iran. The limits of this use of military might to maintain US dominance was exposed on 11 September 2001, when a few dozen terrorists struck fear and panic into the most powerful global superpower the world has ever known. The attack succeeded in provoking an overreaction. The US government has maintained its military supremacy, but its grip on global politics is much weaker. In the wake of 9/11, the US government enjoyed the support of nation-states all over the world for its War on Terror and intervention in Afghanistan. A few years later, it struggled to gain support for another war in Iraq.

The threat from jihadi terrorism to people living in the West is overstated. 9/11 was a fluke. The attacks on Paris in 2015, London in 2005 and Madrid in 2004 were horrific, but the French, UK and Spanish states have faced much greater violent challenges in the past – the Algerian War of Independence, the

Irish Republican campaign for national self-determination and the Basque independence movement – and survived. In the past, these struggles against Western states had the capacity to inspire broader support, because they were part of a wider desire for freedom. Jihadi terrorism is an expression of despair, rather than of hope. Jihadi terrorism is the mirror image of the USA government's War on Terror. Both have proven capable of wreaking destruction around the world, but neither is capable of building something better on the ruins they have created. Both know what they are against, but both have only vacuous ideas about what they stand for.

The much bigger threat comes from *within* the West. In the name of defending the free world, Western governments have undermined basic freedoms. It is worth remembering that the growth of mass incarceration in the USA, the growth of the surveillance state in the USA and Europe, the erosion of civil liberties and the promotion of a culture of fear were already well underway before 9/11. Jihadi terrorism provided a convenient pretext for the further erosion of civil liberties. The anti-human nature of Western governments can be clearly seen in their attitudes towards immigrants. They are happy to accept workers who can fill gaps in the labour market, but not happy to afford them full rights as human beings. They are happy to send aid to less developed countries around the world to set up refugee camps, but not happy when people from these countries draw on their own resources to make often perilous journeys to the West. They are happy to intervene militarily and politically in war zones all over the world, but treat with contempt those who become refugees as a result. They talk about freedom and equality of opportunity and they erect walls and barbed wire fences on land, and deploy patrol boats and battleships at sea, to restrict freedoms and opportunities. So-called liberal democracies all over the world are increasingly less liberal and less democratic.

There are reasons to feel fearful, but there are also reasons to feel hope. The desire for freedom smoulders all over the world, and it continues to flare up in moments of courage. It is worth remembering that the war in Syria had its origins in the Arab Spring. The thousands of refugees making their way across Europe in 2015 and 2016 are not helpless victims. Many of them have been active opponents of oppression. Many of them, unable to realise freedom within the borders of Syria, are now striving towards Europe in their quest for a better life. The repercussions of the financial crisis of 2008 are being felt all over the world. These repercussions are not only negative – housing evictions, wage restraint and state budget cuts – but also positive. The capitalist crisis is provoking resistance. Millions all over the world are asking if a better world is possible. When hope lights the way, freedom can follow.

The decay of the old

The old world, the world built by the Western industrial powers in the nineteenth and twentieth centuries, is in decay. The capitalist dynamic of economic growth for growth's sake, rather than for humanity's sake, is laying waste to the world. The words of Marx and Engels, from the *Communist Manifesto* of 1848, still speak to us today:

> The bourgeoisie has through its exploitation of the world market given a cosmopolitan character to production and consumption in every country … it has drawn from under the feet of industry the national ground on which it stood. All old-established national industries have been destroyed or are daily being destroyed … In place of the old wants, satisfied by the production of the country, we find new wants, requiring for their satisfaction the products of distant lands and climes. In place of the old local and national seclusion and self-sufficiency, we have intercourse in every direction, universal inter-dependence of nations.[3]

Their words seem to be an even more fitting description of our globalised world than when they were written, more than 150 years ago. Alongside the continuity of the onward march of global capitalism, however, there are changes from 150 years ago. Marx and Engels go on to say:

> The bourgeoisie, by the rapid improvement of all instruments of production, by the immensely facilitated means of communication, draws all, even the most barbarian, nations into civilisation. The cheap prices of commodities are the heavy artillery with which it batters down all Chinese walls, with which it forces the barbarians' intensely obstinate hatred of foreigners to capitulate. It compels all nations, on pain of extinction, to adopt the bourgeois mode of production; it compels them to introduce what it calls civilisation into their midst, i.e., to become bourgeois themselves. In one word, it creates a world after its own image.[4]

This self-image of capitalism, as driven by a mission to raise the whole world out of the Dark Ages, was the dominant one in the middle of the nineteenth century. The capitalist outlook on the world was an optimistic and confident one. In its revolutionary phase the expansion of capitalism broke down the parochial barriers of feudal Europe and put science in the place of superstition. As the century wore on, however, this optimism and confidence waned. As the industrialising powers came into conflict with each other, new barriers were erected. Nationalist movements retreated from their revolutionary role of breaking down the barriers of feudalism and capitalist nation-states erected their own walls – trade barriers and immigration controls. During the Age of Empire in the closing decades of the nineteenth century, nationalism lost its cosmopolitan character and became joined to 'race'. European powers projected an intensely obstinate hatred of foreigners, especially those in the colonial world.

The emancipatory dynamic that capitalism had released did not die. It was picked up by the working class and the oppressed around the world. The working class fought against the domination of capital. Women fought for freedom from the stifling confines of the domestic sphere and they fought for equality with men. Colonial peoples fought against the domination of empire. Black people in the USA, and in the colonial world, were treated in barbaric ways by 'civilised' Whites. The oppressed refused these attempts at dehumanisation. Black Americans did not gain civil rights as part of an attempt to draw them into civilisation. They gained them through Black Power. Colonial peoples gained national self-determination, not because 'civilised' Western powers granted it, but because colonial peoples wrenched it from them. These struggles for emancipation have forced Western powers to mount new defences. Race Relations policy, as we have seen, was a defensive response to the challenge to White supremacy in the early decades of the twentieth century. At the end of the Second World War, Race Relations policy became internationalised in response to the rise of anti-colonial independence movements and the growth of domestic anti-racist movements. In the 1960s Race Relations became domestic policy in the Anglo-American world.

Multiculturalism is the form of racialised anti-racism that best fits the conditions of the early twenty-first century. In a situation where parts of the former colonial world are centres of global capitalist production, where many small and medium enterprises (especially in the catering sector) are 'ethnic', where 'ethnic' has become a marketing tool and where diversity management has become a major subdivision of capitalist human resource management, capitalism appears to have a multicultural character. The capitalist world has changed utterly over the course of the twentieth century. Today the 'barbarians' are breaking through the trade barriers of the 'civilised' countries. They are pushing 'home-produced' commodities off the shelves, they are emptying the factory floors and relocating production to 'barbarian' lands. But this is not a 'race' war between barbarian and civilised. It is not revenge of the oppressed. Look who is profiting from this production in the Global South. The commodities that carry the 'Made in China', 'Made in Pakistan' or 'Made in Vietnam' mark on their labels include goods branded Nike, Apple, Prada, Samsung …[5] In virtually every country in the world, consumers can find McDonald's, Starbucks, iPhones and Adidas trainers. Capitalist production and consumption is global. Throughout the twentieth century, capitalism shed its White skin. It is now multicultural. That does not mean that people of all 'races' are equal. Multiculturalism tips the hierarchical racial ladder of Victorian racial science on its side. The class hierarchy, however, has not been toppled. Class is, and remains, an inherent feature of capitalism as a social system. This class hierarchy, however, is a multicultural one, and a multicultural one that gets Whiter the closer you get to the top. The British Empire has been pushed out of the colonial world, and it has been replaced by the Empire of Capital. This capitalist world is replete with contradictions.

Capitalists, as we saw when the banks were on the brink of collapse following the financial crisis, need nation-states to secure the conditions for profit-making. Capitalists also, however, as we saw over the 'creative' tax strategies of the likes of Amazon and Google, will put their own interests ahead of those of nation-states when it is in the interest of profit-making.

The decay of the old world is perhaps most clearly evident in the sphere of formal politics. The right to vote, which every section of society (the middle classes, the working classes, women and racialised minorities) has had to fight to gain, has become degraded. Traditional political parties, which at one time had been mass membership organisations with connections throughout society, have become the playthings of elites. Parliamentary democracy is increasingly hollowed out by a technocratic approach that is increasingly remote from the concerns of the mass of society. In Northern Ireland, the Ulster Unionist Party (UUP), the party that ran the state for five decades and remained the largest party throughout the conflict, has been reduced to a shadow of its former self. The Democratic Unionist Party (DUP) has trounced the UUP as the electoral favourite for Protestants in Northern Ireland, but in the process the DUP has become a professional machine that tightly controls internal debate and carefully cultivates its media image. The electoral dominance of the DUP obscures the seismic shifts that are taking place beneath the surface. The annual Northern Ireland Life and Times opinion survey indicates that the proportion of the population who identify themselves as Unionist has declined from 40 per cent in 1998 (when the Peace Agreement was signed) to 29 per cent in 2013.[6] The same survey also finds that about a third of those who identify as Unionist claim to not have a very strong identification with Unionism. The political disillusionment of Unionist voters can be seen in the fact that the four constituencies with the lowest turnout in the 2011 Assembly election (North Down, East Antrim, South Antrim, Belfast North) were all traditional Unionist constituencies.[7]

The nationalist parties are also out of touch with those who they claim to represent. The Social Democratic and Labour Party was always an elitist organisation run by a cabal of middle-class professionals and a sprinkling of trade unionists. Its position as the only non-Unionist party, however, meant that it was able to enjoy considerable electoral success among Northern Irish Catholics. With the rise of Sinn Féin as an electoral force, the position of the SDLP was challenged. Sinn Féin emerged out of the protests in support of Republican prisoners in the late 1970s and early 1980s. Initially it grew as a community-based advocacy organisation. The military campaign of the IRA, however, placed limits on the electoral rise of Sinn Féin as the political wing of the IRA. After the IRA ceasefire in 1994, however, Sinn Féin's electoral support grew and it has decisively displaced the SDLP as the largest nationalist party. The grassroots origin of the party has meant that it has have the most extensive connections with its social base. These connections, however, have been worn thin through the increasing distance of the party from its base in the Catholic working class. The obfuscations and double-speak of the leadership during the peace negotiations have sown confusion and encouraged political disengagement among the party's electoral base. The links have been further diluted by Sinn Féin's promotion of a pan-Nationalist alliance, which has seen it put more faith in other elites than in its working-class supporters as agents for change.

The old form of political representation in Northern Ireland is in decay, but new forms of representation, and the issues through which these will develop, have yet to become clear. The imposition of austerity measures on Northern Ireland by the Conservative government at Westminster, in response to the global capitalist crisis of 2008, has shaken but not stirred the Northern Irish working class. In the 2016 elections to the Northern Ireland Assembly there were signs that Sinn Féin's connection to its Catholic working-class supporters is waning. In West Belfast and in Foyle (Derry/Londonderry), the urban heartlands of support for Sinn Féin, a new anti-austerity party, People Before Profit, broke through electorally and gained two seats in the Legislative Assembly. In West Belfast the PBP candidate got the greatest number of first-preference votes of any of the candidates. In Foyle, Eamonn McCann, the veteran civil rights campaigner, frustrated Sinn Féin's efforts to gain an extra seat in the constituency.[8] The Catholic working class, who have been largely quiescent in the twenty-first century, are unhappy but are not yet an organised force for change.

A sense of disaffection from the 'new' Northern Ireland is most palpable among Protestants. This disaffection, however, is currently expressed in ways that stress the dependence of the Protestant working class, rather than its independence. There is widespread discussion about Protestant alienation.[9] This alienation has been expressed as a sense of victimhood, sectarian hostility towards Catholic advances and a defence of symbolic vestiges of Protestant supremacy. All of these have led commentators to express a mix of pity and contempt for the Protestant working class as the most sectarian and racist section of society. It is true that some of the most vociferous expressions of racism and sectarianism are found in the Protestant working class, but their content suggests that there are other, more progressive tendencies lurking within these expressions of 'hate'. In recent years, Catholic working-class mobilisation has tended to be in support of political objectives articulated by those who claim leadership of the Catholic working class. Protestant working-class mobilisation, by contrast, has tended to be against their 'leaders', who they fear will sell them out. The protests in favour of Orange Order parades, and the protests against the decision to restrict the flying of the Union flag over City Hall in Belfast, were both anti-Catholic in form, but they also expressed Protestant working-class disaffection from the traditional institutions of Unionism: the UUP, the DUP and the police.

In the late 1960s, the Protestant supremacist Stormont government imposed restrictions on civil rights demonstrations, and the forces of the state bore down heavily on those who defied these bans. Since the peace process, the Westminster government, and then the multicultural Stormont government, have imposed restrictions on the right to protest. This time, however, the target was a symbol of Protestant supremacy, the Orange Order parades. Irish Republicans and grass-roots community activists in Catholic working-class areas were often at the forefront of demands for these restrictions. The parades protests and the flag protests show that the idea of Protestant supremacy still has some appeal among the Protestant working class, but they also show something else. The Protestant working class is currently at the forefront of pushing against the militarised state response to protest and the increasing restrictions on the freedom to express dissent. Anyone interested in human emancipation should support these confrontations with state restrictions. The working class in Northern Ireland will not be able to take a truly independent stand until it transcends the sectarian divide. This requires challenging the multicultural framework of governance and transcending the division of Catholic, Protestant and other in the name of our common humanity.

Theory and practice

Throughout this book, we have examined the relationship between theory and practice, between ideas and action. In the introduction, we noted that the idea that Northern Ireland was a 'place apart' was both a product of state practices and an idea that framed many academic analyses of Northern Ireland. In the second chapter, we examined different ideas about 'race' and racism and sectarianism. We noted that the attempt to conceptually distinguish between racism and sectarianism, which had some purchase prior to significant immigration to Northern Ireland from Eastern Europe, was not very effective in practice afterwards. In the third chapter, we examined the close relationship between academic theory and policy practice in the realm of Race Relations. In Chapter 5, we introduced the Hegelian-inspired approach of Marx to the relationship between theory and practice. We noted that Marx fused idealism and materialism by pointing to the key role of active human practice as mediating between objective reality and subjective perception. 'The question whether objective truth can be attributed to human thinking is not a question of theory,' Marx said, 'but is a practical question. Man must prove the truth – i.e. the reality and power, the this-sidedness of his thinking in practice. The dispute over the reality or non-reality of thinking that is isolated from practice is a purely *scholastic* question.'[10]

We argued that intersubjective understandings of racisms, which underpin the Race Relations approach, are limited. The social constructionism of these intersubjective understandings highlights the power of ideas, but they artificially separate subjective ideas from objective reality and give ideas a life of their own. We argued that it is the nation-state as an institution, with its distinction between 'us' (citizens) and 'them' (non-citizens), rather than the subjective outlook of immigration officers, that explains why Black people are disproportionately detained and deported. In the fifth chapter, we noted that there are many different anti-racisms, and many of these incorporate rather than repudiate 'racial' ideas. Consequently, the implementation of these ideas in practice can lead to the racialisation of 'groups' of people. In Chapter 6, we used the example of the civil rights movement to examine the power of ideas when they grip a mass of people in society. We also noted that in a class-based society, ideas are not morally or politically neutral. They express the interests of sections of society. The meaning of equality, for example, is different depending on whether it is viewed from a middle-class perspective or a working-class perspective. In the previous chapter we looked at the way in which a focus on ideas, on the subjective mindset of individuals, found in 'hate' crime policy leads to repressive policy in practice. In looking at all of these different aspects, we have sought to draw attention to the *unity* of thought and practice, or in other words the ongoing and dynamic interrelationship between thought and practice.

We have also sought to draw attention to the changing nature of sectarianism as both idea and practice. We noted that structural discrimination against Catholics has significantly eroded, and consequently the basis for conflicting interests between Catholics and Protestants has been undermined. Today it is the multicultural framework of government, established by the Agreement, which maintains this sectarian antagonism. It does so, however, on weak grounds. The crisis of state authority, which was both a provocation to and a product of the civil rights movement, has been radically altered. Today it is not a demand for civil rights that constitutes the crisis of authority; in fact, it is not any demands at all. It is, if anything, the lack of ideas. The lack of anything that inspires the imagination and moves people to organise is at the root of the contemporary crisis of authority. This crisis is manifested in, for example, the periodic institutional crises of the Assembly. The fact that the Assembly can stumble on is an indication that there is significant discontent, but not yet any significant opposition to the framework of the 'new' Northern Ireland. The political disengagement of the majority of the population is both a source of strength for the state in Northern Ireland and a source of weakness. It is a source of strength because it allows the institutions to stumble on, despite the recurring crises. It is a source of weakness because there is no popular attachment to these institutions.

Northern Ireland, like the wider world of which it is part, is living through the decay of the old. The new multicultural framework does not provide a solution to the region's problems, it accommodates to them. The new framework can only survive as long as the mass of people play their part and accommodate to it. We need a different approach, one that challenges the racialised anti-racism of the Northern Ireland government. This approach will have to come from a movement in society, but ideas will be crucial to this movement. In this book, we have sought to help this task in various ways. We have sought to prepare the ground by cutting through the tangle of confused ideas surrounding racism and sectarianism. We have sought to fan the smouldering embers of the emancipatory dynamic of the civil rights era by drawing in the wider winds of change that are sweeping the world. All of these, however, are only ideas. These ideas need to be joined to a movement in order to come alive in practice. Capitalism as a social system is torn by contradictions. The leaders of the capitalist world promise freedom, but they mean the free market; goods and services are more free to move around the world than people are. The leaders of the capitalist world promise equality, but they mean equal opportunities. Through these 'opportunities' they have amassed untold wealth and they have created a world of ever-growing inequality in the process. The leaders of the capitalist world talk about humanity and human rights. And while they talk, they erect walls and border controls, they racialise humanity, they bomb, imprison and in other ways brutalise humans all over the world. These contradictions are felt most forcefully by the working class and oppressed of the world. It is they who are being driven like machines to generate profit for capitalists. It is they who are pushed back from the borders of the 'civilised' world. It is they who say 'there must be a better world than this'. We need to fuse that discontent into a movement that eradicates the distinction between Catholic, Protestant, Traveller, 'ethnic' minority and immigrant and joins us together into the wider universal humanity. We need to create a world that puts humanity – not profit, not nation, not 'race', not denomination – first. Break down the 'peace' walls. Open up the borders. A better world is possible. A human-centred world.

Notes

1 McGhee, *Intolerant Britain?*, 178.
2 Ibid.
3 Marx and Engels, *Manifesto of the Communist Party*, 16.
4 Ibid.
5 Marc Bain, '"Made in China" really doesn't mean what it used to', *Quartz*, 3 June 2015; Christina Passariello, 'Prada is making fashion in China', *Wall Street Journal*, 24 June 2011; Amanullah Bashar, 'Made in Pakistan label needs services of international designers', *Pakistan and Gulf Economist*, 9 August 1999; Kathy Chu, 'Why you may soon see more goods labeled "Made in Vietnam"', *Wall Street Journal*, 18 October 2015.
6 See NILT Survey online at www.ark.ac.uk/nilt (accessed 10 January 2017).
7 Raymond Russell, *Electoral registration statistics and voting patterns* (Belfast: OFMDFM, 2014).
8 Anna Mercer, 'Overview of NI Assembly Election 2016', *Strategem*, 9 May 2016. Available online at www.stratagem-ni.com/latest/2016/may/overview-of-ni-assem bly-election-2016/ (accessed 10 January 2017).

9   See, for example, Seamus Dunn and Valerie Morgan, *Protestant alienation in Northern Ireland: a preliminary survey* (Coleraine: Centre for the Study of Conflict, University of Ulster, 1994); Neil Southern, 'Protestant alienation in Northern Ireland: a political, cultural and geographical examination', *Journal of Ethnic and Migration Studies* 33.1 (2007): 159–180; Gareth Mulvenna, 'The Protestant working class in Belfast: education and civic erosion – an alternative analysis', *Irish Studies Review* 20.4 (2012): 427–446; Andrew Finlay, 'Defeatism and Northern Protestant "identity"', *Ethnopolitics* 1.2 (2001): 3–20; Goretti Horgan, 'The state of Loyalism', *Irish Marxist Review* 2.5 (2013): 46–52.

10 Marx, 'Theses on Feuerbach', II; emphasis in the original.

Select bibliography and notes on sources

A comment on sources

In the age of the Internet it has become much easier and cheaper for the activist and academic to access sources of information. In writing this book we have tried, where possible, to use sources that are freely available online. Many of the sources cited in the notes and select bibliography sections are available online. All of these online sources were available during August and September 2016. Two factors, however, mean that there is little value in providing the web address for every source.

First, the Internet is not free. It costs to host sites, and people have to be employed to produce the content for sites. In some cases, this work is a labour of love. (The many thousands of hours of work involved in translating, checking and uploading the content for the Marxists.org site, for example, were offered voluntarily because the people involved believe that it is important to make the writings of Marx, Engels and other Marxists readily available to readers around the world.) In most cases, however, the creation of content and its maintenance online is undertaken as wage-labour for an employer. Consequently, the material that was freely available in 2016 may be behind a paywall at the time you are reading this book. Or it may no longer be available on the Internet. If it is not available because the site has gone out of business, you may still be able to access it at the *Wayback machine* (http://archive.org/web/).

Secondly, websites are continually evolving. For various reasons many websites change as they develop. This can be because their ownership changes hands and the new owner has a different idea of purpose or layout for the site. Or it can be because the volume of content necessitates a reorganisation of the allocation of URLs for the materials, or for a variety of other reasons. Consequently, the web addresses of individual articles often date quickly. Hence, there is little value in providing the full web address because the use of an Internet search engine can often lead to the article more quickly than typing the full URL into the address bar of an Internet browser.

In the rest of this section we provide some brief information on useful sources on sectarianism and other racisms in Northern Ireland that are available online.

Research on Northern Ireland archive (ARK)

Anyone wanting to read and learn more about Northern Ireland is fortunate to have ARK as a repository of information and knowledge. The site, which is co-hosted by Northern Ireland's two universities (Queen's University Belfast and Ulster University), contains a huge and ever-growing number of materials. During the writing of this book one particular resource – the Conflict Archive on the Internet (CAIN) –www.ark.ac.uk/cain – proved particularly useful.

Accounts of the Conflict archive

The Accounts of the Conflict archive is hosted by Ulster University. It contains information about a range of personal accounts of the conflict – many of which were gathered by community-based organisations across Northern Ireland. The site also contains some audio and audio-visual accounts that have been made publicly available. At the time of writing it was available at accounts.ulster.ac.uk/repo24

News sources

There are a number of useful news sources on Northern Ireland, all of which have a web presence, but not all of which are free to access. Of the local news outlets, I found the following most useful: the *Belfast Telegraph*, *BBC Northern Ireland*, the *Irish News*, the *Belfast News Letter* and the *Derry Journal*. The two main newspapers in the Republic of Ireland – the *Irish Times* and the *Irish Independent* – are also often useful sources. Of all the London-based newspapers I have always found the *Guardian* (and its Sunday version, the *Observer*) most consistently to have extensive and informative coverage of Northern Ireland. *The Times* and the *Independent* have had good coverage, but in the case of these newspapers, since the early 1990s, it was often due to the work of a single journalist – Liam Clarke and David McKittrick, respectively.

Official sources on Northern Ireland

The UK government, at a national and regional level, gathers a lot of data. Much of this is now publicly available on the web. A lot of this is particularly useful for anyone who wants to examine the issue of racisms in Northern Ireland. Since the signing of the Agreement in 1998 both the Westminster-based Northern Ireland Office and the Northern Ireland Executive have commissioned or conducted research and gathered official statistics.

The Northern Ireland Statistics and Research Agency (NISRA) is the main source of official statistics on Northern Ireland. NISRA holds and provides reports on a range of relevant data including demography, spatial deprivation and equality. At the time of writing the website was at /www.nisra.gov.uk/

The main departments of the Northern Ireland Executive that have useful resources are the Executive Office (formerly the Office of the First Minister and Deputy First Minister) and the Department of Justice.

- The Executive Office has a wide remit and at the time of writing was accessible at www.executiveoffice-ni.gov.uk The Executive Office has main responsibility for the policy area of good relations. It also works with, and has web links to, a number of relevant quasi-autonomous government bodies including the Equality Commission Northern Ireland, the Community Relations Council and the Commission for Victims and Survivors for Northern Ireland. At the time of writing the good relations policy area was primarily being pursued through the programme *Together: Building a United Community*, which was accessible at www.executiveoffice-ni.gov.uk/articles/together-building-united-community
- The Department of Justice oversees the criminal justice system and at the time of writing was accessible at www.justice-ni.gov.uk/ The Department of Justice works with, and has web links to, a range of official criminal justice bodies including the Police Service of Northern Ireland, Victim Support Northern Ireland and the Public Prosecution Service for Northern Ireland.

The Northern Ireland Office supports the Secretary of State for Northern Ireland, the Cabinet minister who mediates between the interests of Westminster and the government of Northern Ireland. It also works with, and has web links to, the Northern Ireland Human Rights Commission and the Parades Commission. At the time of writing its website was at www.gov.uk/government/organisations/northern-ireland-office

Advocacy, activism and other non-profit organisations

There are a wide range of non-profit organisations working in areas related to racisms in Northern Ireland. Some of these are small outfits that are dependent on a few dedicated individuals, and all are dependent on the vagaries of funding for what is known locally as the voluntary and community sector. Only a few of them have the resources and remit to gather data and/or conduct research. The following organisations are the main ones that have resources that are publicly available on the web.

The Institute for Conflict Research has built up a significant body of research on aspects of 'post-conflict' peacebuilding and conflict in Northern Ireland, on migration, and on 'hate crime'. At the time of writing its website was at http://conflictresearch.org.uk/

The Northern Ireland Council for Ethnic Minorities is the longest-running organisation dedicated to improving 'race relations' and eliminating racisms in Northern Ireland. The organisation has played a role in maintaining a clear distinction between sectarianism and other racisms. It has also avoided, many would say for good reason, engaging in issues around sectarianism. NICEM has built up a body of research and position papers over the years and they can be accessed on the organisation's website, which at the time of writing was at http://nicem.org.uk/

The PSNI collects and publishes data on 'hate crime', but at the time of writing there was no organisation that attempted to flesh this data out in any systematic way. The London-based Institute of Race Relations attempts to collate newspaper reports of racist incidents across the UK, including Northern Ireland. At the time of writing its coverage of Northern Ireland could be accessed at www.irr.org.uk/search/?q=%22Northern+ireland%22

Marxists Internet Archive
The Marxists Internet Archive is a huge archive of original works by Karl Marx and post-Marx Marxists (primarily in English, but with many works also available in other languages). It also includes an encyclopaedia and a history of Marx and Marxism. All of the material is freely available under a Creative Commons licence. This publishing arrangement makes a vast array of works available to a wide audience, but it also means that the archive has gaps and the freely available versions are not always the most authoritative. The page/section references in the notes section of this book are to the .pdf versions of the relevant book cited that were available on the MIA at the time of writing.

Select bibliography

Alexander, Michelle. *The new Jim Crow: mass incarceration in the age of colorblindness.* New York: The New Press, 2012.

Allen, Theodore W. *The invention of the white race, volume 1: racial oppression and social control.* London: Verso, 1994.

Arthur, Paul. *The People's Democracy, 1968–1973.* Belfast: Blackstaff Press, 1974.

Banton, Michael. 'Progress in ethnic and racial studies'. *Ethnic and Racial Studies* 24.2 (2010): 173–194.

Banton, Michael. *The international politics of race.* Cambridge: Polity Press, 2002.

Banton, Michael. *International action against racial discrimination.* Oxford: Clarendon Press, 1996.

Banton, Michael. 'Modelling ethnic and national relations'. *Ethnic and Racial Studies* 17.1 (1994): 1–19.

Banton, Michael. 'The race relations problematic'. *British Journal of Sociology* 42.1 (1991): 115–130.

Barkan, Elazar. *The retreat of scientific racism: changing conceptions of race in Britain and the United States between the world wars.* Cambridge: Cambridge University Press, 1992.

Bean, Kevin. *The new politics of Sinn Féin.* Liverpool: Liverpool University Press, 2007.

Bonnett, Alastair. 'From the crises of whiteness to Western supremacism'. *ACRAWSA* 1 (2005): 8–20.

Bonnett, Alastair. 'From white to Western: "racial decline" and the idea of the West in Britain, 1890–1930'. *Journal of Historical Sociology* 16.3 (2003): 320–348.

Bonnett, Alastair. *Anti-racism.* London: Routledge, 2000.

Bonnett, Alastair. 'How the British working class became white: the symbolic (re) formation of racialized capitalism'. *Journal of Historical Sociology* 11.3 (1998): 316–340.

Bourne, Jenny. 'The life and times of institutional racism'. *Race & Class* 43.2 (2001): 7–22.

Boyce, David George. *The Irish Question and British politics, 1868–1996*. Basingstoke: Macmillan, 2nd edn, 1996.

Brewer, John D. 'Sectarianism and racism, their parallels and differences'. *Ethnic and Racial Studies* 15.3 (1992): 352–364.

Brewer, John D., and Gareth I. Higgins. *Anti-Catholicism in Northern Ireland: the mote and the beam*. London: Palgrave Macmillan, 1998.

Brubaker, Rogers. 'Ethnicity without groups'. *Archives Europeennes de Sociologie* 43.2 (2002): 163–189.

Bunyan, Tony. 'Just over the horizon: the surveillance society and the state in the EU'. *Race & Class* 51.3 (2010): 1–12.

Burgess, Thomas Paul, and Gareth Mulvenna (eds). *The contested identities of Ulster Protestants*. London: Palgrave Macmillan, 2015.

Burleigh, Michael, and Wolfgang Wippermann. *The racial state: Germany 1939–1945*. Cambridge: Cambridge University Press, 1991.

Cannadine, David. *Ornamentalism: how the British saw their empire*. London: Penguin, 2001.

Cantle, Ted. *Community cohesion: a report of the Independent Review Team*. London: Home Office, 2001.

CCCS. *Policing the crisis: mugging, the state, and law and order*. London: Macmillan, 1978.

Chicago Commission on Race Relations. *The negro in Chicago: a study of race relations and a race riot*. Chicago: University of Chicago Press, 1922.

Clarke, Liam. *Broadening the battlefield: the H-Blocks and the rise of Sinn Féin*. Dublin: Gill and Macmillan, 1987.

Commission on Integration and Cohesion. *Our shared future*. Wetherby: Commission on Integration and Cohesion, 2007.

Connolly, Paul. *'Race' and racism in Northern Ireland: a review of the research evidence*. Belfast: OFMDFM, 2002.

Connolly, Paul, and Michaela Keenan. *Racial attitudes and prejudice in Northern Ireland*, vol. 1. Belfast: NISRA, 2000.

Connolly, Paul, and Michaela Keenan. *The hidden truth: racist harassment in Northern Ireland*. Belfast: NISRA, 2001.

Cunningham, Michael J. *British Government policy in Northern Ireland, 1969–2000*. Manchester: Manchester University Press, 2001.

Curtis, L. Perry. *Apes and angels: the Irishman in Victorian caricature*. Newton Abbot: David & Charles, 1971.

Curtis, Liz. *Nothing but the same old story: the roots of anti-Irish racism*. London: Information on Ireland, 1985.

Dickey, Anthony. 'Anti-incitement legislation in Britain and Northern Ireland'. *New Community* 1.2 (1972): 133–138.

Dixon, Bill, and David Gadd. 'Getting the message? "New" Labour and the criminalization of "hate"'. *Criminology and Criminal Justice* 6.3 (2006): 309–328.

Dixon, Paul. 'Political skills or lying and manipulation? The choreography of the Northern Ireland peace process'. *Political Studies* 50.4 (2002): 725–741.

Donohue, Laura K. 'Regulating Northern Ireland: the Special Powers Acts, 1922–1972'. *The Historical Journal* 41.4 (1998): 1089–1120.

Dooley, Brian. *Black and green: the fight for civil rights in Northern Ireland and black America*. London: Pluto Press, 1998.

Du Bois, W. E. B. *The souls of black folk*. Philadelphia, PA: Pennsylvania State University, 1902.

Dunayevskaya, Raya. *Marxism and freedom*. Amherst, NY: Humanity Books, 3rd edn, 2000.

Dunayevskaya, Raya. *Rosa Luxemburg, women's liberation and Marx's philosophy of revolution*. Chicago: University of Illinois Press, 2nd edn, 1991.

Farrell, Michael. *Northern Ireland: the Orange state*. London: Pluto Press, 2nd edn, 1980.

Fekete, Liz. *A suitable enemy: racism, migration and Islamophobia in Europe*. London: Pluto Press, 2009.

Fenton, Steve. *Ethnicity*. Cambridge: Polity, 2nd edn, 2010.

Finney, Nissa, and Ludi Simpson. *'Sleepwalking to segregation'? Challenging myths about race and migration*. Bristol: Policy Press, 2009.

Furedi, Frank. *The silent war: imperialism and the changing perception of race*. London: Pluto Press, 1998.

Gadd, David. 'Aggravating racism and elusive motivation'. *British Journal of Criminology* 49.6 (2009): 755–771.

Garner, Steve. 'A moral economy of whiteness: behaviours, belonging and Britishness'. *Ethnicities* 12.4 (2012): 445–464.

Garner, Steve. *Racisms*. London: Sage, 2010.

Garner, Steve. *Racism in the Irish experience*. London: Pluto Press, 2004.

Geoghegan, Peter. *A difficult difference: race, religion and the new Northern Ireland*. Dublin: Irish Academic Press, 2010.

Gilligan, Chris. 'Race and ethnicity'. In *Routledge Handbook of Ethnic Conflict*, ed. Karl Cordell and Stefan Wolff, 79–88. London: Routledge, 2011.

Gilligan, Chris. 'The Irish Question and the concept "identity" in the 1980s'. *Nations and Nationalism* 13.4 (2007): 599–617.

Gilroy, Paul. 'The end of anti-racism'. In *Race and local politics*, ed. Wendy Ball and John Solomos, 191–209. Basingstoke: Macmillan, 1990.

Gilroy, Paul. *There ain't no black in the Union Jack*. Abingdon: Routledge, 2002.

Gordon, Leah N. 'The individual and "the general situation": the tension barometer and the race problem at the University of Chicago, 1947–1954'. *Journal of Historical Sociology* 46.1 (2010): 27–51. doi:10.1002/jhbs.

Guterl, Matthew Pratt. 'The new race consciousness: race, nation, and empire in American culture, 1910–1925'. *Journal of World History* 10.2 (1999): 307–352.

Hainsworth, Paul (ed). *Divided society: ethnic minorities and racism in Northern Ireland*. London: Pluto Press, 1998.

Hazard Jr, Anthony Q. *Postwar anti-racism: the United States, UNESCO, and 'race',* *1945–1968*. New York: Palgrave Macmillan, 2012.

Hinton, Elizabeth. '"A war within our own boundaries": Lyndon Johnson's Great Society and the rise of the carceral state'. *Journal of American History* 102.1 (2015): 100–112.

Hinton, Elizabeth. 'Creating crime: the rise and impact of national juvenile delinquency programs in black urban neighborhoods'. *Journal of Urban History* 41.5 (2015): 808–824.

Holloway, John, and Sol Picciotto (eds). *State and capital: a Marxist debate*. London: Edward Arnold, 1978.

Honohan, Iseult, and Nathalie Rougier (eds). *Tolerance and diversity in Ireland, north and south*. Manchester: Manchester University Press, 2015.

Horne, Gerald. *Race war! White supremacy and the Japanese attack on the British Empire*. New York: New York University Press, 2004.

Hurd, Heidi M. 'Why liberals should hate "hate crime legislation"'. *Law and Philosophy* 20.2 (2001): 215.

Iganski, Paul. *'Hate crime' and the city*. Bristol: Policy Press, 2008.

Ignatiev, Noel. *How the Irish became white*. London: Routledge, 1995.

IRR. *Community responses to the War on Terror*. London: Institute of Race Relations, 2007.

Jarman, Neil. *Overview analysis of racist incidents recorded in Northern Ireland by the RUC* *1996–1999*. Belfast: OFMDFM, 2002.

Jenness, Valerie. 'The hate crime canon and beyond: a critical assessment'. *Law & Critique* 12 (2001): 279–308.

Kaufmann, Eric. *The Orange Order: a contemporary Northern Irish history*. Oxford: Oxford University Press, 2007.

Kelley, Kevin. *The longest war: Northern Ireland and the IRA*. Dingle/London: Brandon/Zed Books, 1982.

King Jr, Martin Luther. 'Letter from Birmingham Jail.' 1963. www.uscrossier.org/pullias/wp-content/uploads/2012/06/king.pdf (accessed 1 September 2016).

Knox, Colin. 'Tackling racism in Northern Ireland: "the race hate capital of Europe"'. *Journal of Social Policy* 40.2 (2010): 387–412.

Kundnani, Arun. *The end of tolerance: racism in 21st century Britain*. London: Pluto Press, 2007.

Kyriakides, Christopher. 'Third way anti-racism: a contextual constructionist approach'. *Ethnic and Racial Studies* 31.3 (2008): 592–610.

Latif, Nazia, and Agnieszka Martynowicz. *Our hidden borders: the UK Border Agency's powers of detention*. Belfast: NIHRC, 2009.

Lauren, Paul Gordon. *Power and prejudice: politics and diplomacy of racial discrimination*. Boulder, CO: Westview Press, 1988.

Lentin, Alana. *Racism and anti-racism in Europe*. London: Pluto Press, 2004.

Lentin, Ronit, and Robbie McVeigh. *After optimism? Ireland, racism and globalisation*. Dublin: Metro Eireann, 2006.

Leonard, Madeleine. 'What's recreational about "recreational rioting"? Children on the streets in Belfast'. *Children & Society* 24.1 (2010): 38–49.

Leonard, Madeleine. 'Teens and territory in contested spaces: negotiating sectarian interfaces in Northern Ireland'. *Children's Geographies* 4.2 (2006): 225–238.

Liechty, Joseph, and Cecelia Clegg. *Moving beyond sectarianism: religion, conflict and reconciliation in Northern Ireland*. Dublin: Columba Press, 2001.

Macpherson, Sir William. *The Stephen Lawrence Inquiry*. London, 1999.

Malik, Kenan. *From fatwa to jihad: the Rushdie affair and its legacy*. London: Atlantic Books, 2009.

Malik, Kenan. *Strange fruit: why both sides are wrong in the race debate*. Oxford: Oneworld, 2008.

Malik, Kenan. 'Making a difference: culture, race and social policy'. *Patterns of Prejudice* 39.4 (2005): 361–378.

Malik, Kenan. *The meaning of race: race, history and culture in Western society*. Basingstoke: Macmillan, 1996.

Maroney, Terry A. 'The struggle against hate crime: movement at a crossroads'. *NYU Law Review* 73.2 (1998): 564–620.

McCann, Eamonn. *War and an Irish town*. London: Pluto Press, 2nd edn, 1980.

McGarry, John (ed). *Northern Ireland and the divided world: post-Agreement Northern Ireland in comparative perspective*. Oxford: Oxford University Press, 2001.

McGarry, John, and Brendan O'Leary. *Explaining Northern Ireland: broken images*. Oxford: Blackwell, 1995.

McGhee, Derek. *Intolerant Britain? Hate, citizenship and difference*. Maidenhead: Open University Press, 2005.

McKearney, Tommy. *The Provisional IRA: from insurrection to parliament*. London: Pluto Press, 2011.

McVeigh, Robbie. *Sectarianism in Northern Ireland: towards a definition in law*. Belfast: Equality Coalition, 2014.

McVeigh, Robbie. *The next Stephen Lawrence: racist violence and criminal justice in Northern Ireland*. Belfast: NICEM, 2006.

McVeigh, Robbie. 'Is sectarianism racism? Theorising the racism/sectarianism interface'. In *Rethinking Northern Ireland*, ed. David Miller, 179–198. Harlow: Longman, 1998.

McVeigh, Robbie. 'The undertheorisation of sectarianism'. *Canadian Journal of Irish Studies* 16.2 (1990): 119–122.

Miles, Robert. *Racism after 'race relations'*. London: Routledge, 1993.

Miles, Robert, and Malcolm Brown. *Racism*. London: Routledge, 2nd edn, 2003.

Mitchell, Paul, Geoffrey Evans and Brendan O'Leary. 'Extremist outbidding in ethnic party systems is not inevitable: tribune parties in Northern Ireland'. *Political Studies* 57.2 (2009): 397–421.

Moloney, Ed. *A secret history of the IRA*. London: Allen Lane, 2002.

Moore, Robert. 'Race relations in the Six Counties: colonialism, industrialization, and stratification in Ireland'. *Race* (now *Race & Class*) 14.1 (1972): 21–42.

Moran, Leslie J. 'Affairs of the heart: hate crime and the politics of crime control'. *Law & Critique* 12 (2001): 331–344.

Muncie, John. 'Institutionalized intolerance: youth justice and the 1998 Crime and Disorder Act'. *Critical Social Policy* 19.2 (1999): 147–175.

Murji, Karim, and John Solomos (eds). *Racialization: studies in theory and practice*. Oxford: Oxford University Press, 2005.

Nelson, Sarah. *Ulster's uncertain defenders: Protestant political, paramilitary and community groups and the Northern Ireland conflict*. Belfast: Appletree, 1984.

Nic Craith, Máiréad. *Culture and identity politics in Northern Ireland*. Basingstoke: Palgrave Macmillan, 2003.

O'Dochartaigh, Niall. *From civil rights to Armalites: Derry and the birth of the Irish Troubles*. Cork: Cork University Press, 1997.

O'Dowd, Liam, Bill Rolston and Mike Tomlinson. *Northern Ireland: between civil rights and civil war*. London: CSE Books, 1980.

O'Leary, Brendan. 'Nature of the British-Irish Agreement'. *New Left Review* 233 (1999): 66–96.

Osborne, Robert D., and R. J. Cormack. 'Fair employment: towards reform in Northern Ireland'. *Policy & Politics* 17.4 (1989): 287–294.

Paradies, Yin (ed.). *Ethnic and Racial Studies*, 39.1 (2016), special issue, *Whither anti-racism?*

Pitcher, Ben. *The politics of multiculturalism: race and racism in contemporary Britain*. Basingstoke: Palgrave Macmillan, 2009.

Prince, Simon. *Northern Ireland's 68: civil rights, global revolt and the origins of the Troubles*. Dublin: Irish Academic Press, 2007

Purdie, Bob. *Politics in the streets: the origins of the civil rights movement in Northern Ireland*. Belfast: Blackstaff, 1990.

Rex, John. *Race and ethnicity*. Milton Keynes: Open University Press, 1986.

Rex, John, and David Mason (eds). *Theories of race and ethnic relations*. Cambridge: Cambridge University Press, 1986.

Rolston, Bill. 'Legacy of intolerance: racism and Unionism in South Belfast'. *Institute of Race Relations*, 2004. www.irr.org.uk/news/legacy-of-intolerance-racism-and-union ism-in-south-belfast/ (accessed 10 January 2017).

Rolston, Bill. 'What's wrong with multiculturalism? Liberalism and the Irish conflict'. In *Rethinking Northern Ireland: culture, ideology and colonialism*, ed. David Miller, 253–274. Harlow: Longman, 1998.

Rose, Richard. *Governing without consensus: an Irish perspective*. London: Faber and Faber, 1971.

Ross, F. Stuart. 'Between party and movement: Sinn Féin and the popular movement against criminalisation, 1976–1982'. *Irish Political Studies* 21.3 (2006): 337–354.

Ryan, Mark. *War and peace in Ireland: Britain and the IRA in the new world order*. London: Pluto Press, 1994.

Shirlow, Peter, and Brendan Murtagh. *Belfast: segregation, violence and the city*. London: Pluto Press, 2006.

Simpson, Ludi. '"Race" statistics: theirs and ours'. *Radical Statistics* 79/80 (2002). www.radstats.org.uk/no079/simpson.htm (accessed 10 January 2017).

Sivanandan, Ambalavaner. 'Race and resistance: the IRR story'. *Race & Class* 50.2 (2008): 1–30.

Sivanandan, Ambalavaner. *Communities of resistance: writings on black struggles for socialism*. London: Verso, 1990.

Sivanandan, Ambalavaner. 'RAT and the degradation of black struggle'. *Race & Class* 26.4 (1985): 1–33.

Sivanandan, Ambalavaner. 'From resistance to rebellion: Asian and Afro-Caribbean struggles in Britain'. *Race & Class* 23.2–3 (1981): 111–152.

Small, Stephen, and John Solomos. 'Race, immigration and politics in Britain: changing policy agendas and conceptual paradigms 1940s–2000s'. *International Journal of Comparative Sociology* 47.3–4 (2006): 235–257.

Smith, M. L. R. 'The intellectual internment of a conflict: the forgotten war in Northern Ireland'. *International Affairs* 75.1 (1999): 77–97.

Smyth, Jim. *The men of no property: Irish radicals and popular politics in the late eighteenth century*. Basingstoke: Macmillan, 1998.

Stanko, Elizabeth A. 'Re-conceptualising the policing of hatred: confessions and worrying dilemmas of a consultant'. *Law & Critique* 12 (2001): 309–329.

Sunday Times Insight Team. *Ulster*. Harmondsworth: Penguin, 1972.

Taylor, Charles. 'The politics of recognition'. In *Multiculturalism*, ed. Amy Gutmann, 25–73. Princeton, NJ: Princeton University Press, 1994.

Tinker, Hugh. *Race, conflict and the international order: from empire to United Nations*. London: Macmillan, 1977.

Todd, Jennifer, and Joseph Ruane. *From 'A shared future' to 'Cohesion, sharing and integration': an analysis of Northern Ireland's policy framework documents*. York: Joseph Rowntree Foundation, 2010.

Virdee, Satnam. *Racism, class and the racialised outsider*. Basingstoke: Palgrave Macmillan, 2014.

White, Robert W. 'Don't confuse me with the facts: more on the Irish Republican Army and sectarianism'. *Terrorism and Political Violence* 10.4 (1998): 164–189.

White, Robert W. 'The Irish Republican Army and sectarianism: moving beyond the anecdote'. *Terrorism and Political Violence* 9.2 (1997): 120–131.

Whyte, John. *Interpreting Northern Ireland*. Oxford: Clarendon Press, 1990.

Whyte, John. 'How much discrimination was there under the Unionist regime, 1921–1968?' In *Contemporary Irish Studies*, ed. Tom Gallagher and James O'Connell, 1–35. Manchester: Manchester University Press, 1983.

Index